LOVE'S WHIPPING BOY

Love's Whipping Boy

Violence & Sentimentality in the American Imagination

ELIZABETH BARNES

The University of North Carolina Press
Chapel Hill

© 2011 The University of North Carolina Press
All rights reserved
Manufactured in the United States of America

Designed by Michelle Coppedge and set in Garamond Premier Pro by
Tseng Information Systems, Inc.

The paper in this book meets the guidelines for permanence and durability
of the Committee on Production Guidelines for Book Longevity of the
Council on Library Resources.

The University of North Carolina Press has been a member of the Green Press
Initiative since 2003.

Library of Congress Cataloging-in-Publication Data
Barnes, Elizabeth, 1959–
Love's whipping boy : violence and sentimentality in the American imagination /
Elizabeth Barnes.
p. cm.
Includes bibliographical references and index.
ISBN 978-0-8078-3456-5 (cloth : alk. paper)
1. American fiction—19th century—History and criticism. 2. Violence in
literature. 3. Empathy in literature. 4. Sentimentalism in literature. 5. National
characteristics, American, in literature. I. Title.
PS374.V58B37 2011
813'.309353—dc22   2010034636

15 14 13 12 11   5 4 3 2 1

Parts of this book have been reprinted in revised form from "Loving with a
Vengeance: *Wieland*, Familicide and the Crisis of Masculinity in the Early Nation,"
in *Boys Don't Cry?: Rethinking Narratives of Masculinity and Emotion in the U.S.*,
ed. Milette Shamir and Jennifer Travis (New York: Columbia University Press,
2002), 44–63, and "Fraternal Melancholies: Manhood and the Limits of Sympathy
in Douglass and Melville," in *Frederick Douglass and Herman Melville: Essays in
Relation*, ed. Robert S. Levine and Samuel Otter (Chapel Hill: University of North
Carolina Press, 2008), 233–56.

THIS BOOK WAS DIGITALLY PRINTED.

CONTENTS

Acknowledgments (vii)

Introduction (1)

CHAPTER 1
Wieland, Familicide, and the Suffering Father (25)

CHAPTER 2
Melville's Fraternal Melancholies (51)

CHAPTER 3
Fathers of Violence: Frederick Douglass, John Brown, and the Radical Reproduction of Sensibility (83)

CHAPTER 4
The Death of Boyhood and the Making of *Little Women* (123)

Afterword (167)

Notes (175)

Index (205)

ACKNOWLEDGMENTS

This book was long in the making, even as it grew shorter with each incarnation. Perhaps that is a sign of progress. In any case, I offer my thanks and gratitude to those who helped me think these ideas through—both intellectually and emotionally—along the way: Paula Blank, Bruce Burgett, Julie Ellison, Leah Fry, Tresa Grauer, Maureen Fitzgerald, Tom Heacox, Sian Hunter, Bob Levine, Leisa Meyer, Deborah Morse, Elsa Nettels, Marianne Noble, Samuel Otter, Kristen Proehl, Suzanne Raitt, Karen Sánchez-Eppler, Milette Shamir, Jennifer Travis, and Margot Weiss. I appreciated the opportunity to present some version of this argument—chapters-in-the-making, as it were—to the kind and encouraging constituencies of the College of William and Mary, American University, the University of Maryland, and the University of Pennsylvania.

To my writing group—Melanie Dawson and Jenny Putzi—I do not have the words to express my thanks (though if I did, I'm sure you would correct them). Your unflagging and unerring critical attention and acumen are valued only slightly below the loving friendship I feel for and from you. That warm and engaging camaraderie is indicative of the College of William and Mary more generally and the Departments of English and American Studies in particular. I am glad, and honored, to have come among its faculty and to have found friends there.

Because the mind seeks not only an escape from but its most vested interests in the pleasures beyond the writing desk, I thank my poker group (you know who you are) for teaching me, continually, to keep in perspective one's gains and losses in life. For this I also thank my family: Dorie Barnes, Patty Hecht, Jeff Barnes, Lorie Pellizzer-Barnes, Joshua, Danny, and Jasmin. This book is dedicated to my father, William Henry Barnes (1932–2007), a man whose loving generosity remains for me a testament to the only worthy aim of a life's work.

LOVE'S WHIPPING BOY

Introduction

For the past two decades, scholars of nineteenth-century U.S. literature have wrestled with the problems and possibilities presented by American sentimental culture. Alternately scorned as a superficial (and hypocritical) cure-all for social injustices and lauded as a radical intervention into the self-interested aims of capitalist culture, sentimentalism has evaded our attempts to pin down its particular (ab)use in U.S. society.[1] I believe this is in part because sentimental narratives tend to work both toward and against an ideal vision of democratic community. In their invocation of empathy for others, nineteenth-century sentimental texts posit the potential for breaking down hierarchical structures to acknowledge the core suffering that all human beings, regardless of rank or position, share. Yet the fullest manifestations of empathy in these texts continue to operate across a status divide, albeit an inverted one: in sentimental narratives, as Lori Merish notes, the "weak" have ethical primacy over the "strong" by virtue of the former's "intimate knowledge of suffering, a sign of Christ-like authenticity."[2] In the sentimental scenario, true personhood is attained not by social elevation but by encounters with pain, encounters to which the "strong" have access via their empathy with the "weak": through their identification with the suffering victim, even the empowered gain "authentic," "Christ-like" subjectivity.

The emphasis on shared pain as a catalyst for achieving true personhood and democratic union complicates what Merish goes on to describe as the "civilizing" process of sentimentality, a process in which the aggression of the "strong" is sublimated "into sympathetic desire."[3] As I see it, in their equation of suffering with authenticity, nineteenth-century sentimental texts implicitly (and often explicitly) authorize nonsublimated aggression as a means through

(1)

which redemptive suffering is brought about. "No pain, no gain" might be thought of as the colloquial, contemporary expression of an earlier sentimental logic that imagines violations to the body as a precursor to individual transformations. In the nineteenth-century texts I examine, such transformations do not, as one might imagine, constellate around the victims of violence, but rather the perpetrators of it. Aggressive expressions become the medium for spiritual regenerations that, somewhat paradoxically, produce their own self-lacerating effects. To put this another way: I will argue that it is precisely through their demonstrations of aggression that the strong identify themselves with the weak to become the self-proclaimed victims of the violence they employ.

One of the claims of this book is that sympathetic identifications valorized in sentimental texts reveal and encourage a bifurcation of identity—specifically, a bifurcated white masculine identity—brought on by the witness's or abuser's empathy with the sufferer. This split consciousness allows the privileged protagonist to see himself as the "true" sufferer of his demonstrable expressions of power. To understand how violence gets folded in to sentimentalism's egalitarian goals is to recognize, importantly, the deep entrenchment of aggression in the empathetic structures of liberal, Christian U.S. culture. It is also to acknowledge the ways in which the material consequences of physical power are obscured by aggression's ultimate translation into a means of achieving a more authentic life.

As Philip Fisher usefully reminds us, the "vehement passions" (for example, anger, shame, grief, fear) produce self- and social knowledge.[4] They thus constitute worthy objects of study for anyone interested in human nature and culture. But I am less concerned here with individual motivations leading to violent acts than I am with the sociopolitical structures, abetted by literary forms, that render the vehement passions a vehicle for ostensible democratic engagement and enhancement. Critics of nineteenth-century literature have tended to think about sentiment and violence as opposing strategies in the work of nation-building and in the formation of U.S. national identity. Sympathetic interventions, so the story goes, ameliorate the aggressive tendencies of the male-dominated, competitive public sphere (with more or less success) by emphasizing the kinship of all humanity. Although women have traditionally been viewed as the primary torchbearers of sympathetic, Christlike love in the early national and antebellum periods, recent work on sympathy and manhood has shown males to be key players in America's national, sentimental drama.[5] What remains to be examined is the extent to which masculine aggression itself, rather than undermining the work of sympathy, contributes to and perpetuates a sentimental ethos. As I will argue, far from being opposing strategies, sympathy — or what we today would call empathy — and violence operate in tandem to produce, problematically, a sentimental culture in which the potential dangers of aggression are marshaled in support of the salvific effects of Christian love.

In the texts I examine, empathy and aggression come together in the popularly conceived and disseminated image of the substitutionary victim or scapegoat — what I term the "whipping boy." As an innocent stand-in for the guilty party, the whipping boy's suffering on another's behalf represents a model for the personally and socially transformative work of violence. In this model, acts of aggression generate identifications that substantiate a notion of American character itself as exceptionally empathetic. At stake in the work of violence, in other words, is the production of empathy on a national scale: the perpetuation, even entrenchment, of idealizations of aggressive Americans as a people committed to personal and sociopolitical labors of love that reflect and manifest democratic, Christian values.[6] Evidence for these claims, as well as their historical contextualization, will more comprehensively unfold in this introduction and the succeeding chapters. But for now, let me offer an example: Nathaniel Hawthorne's "Roger Malvin's Burial" (1832) — a story about a bitter, callous man who finds emotional release and redemption in his "accidental" shooting of his own son.[7]

Following years of a guilt hardened into apathy, Reuben Bourne, Hawthorne's protagonist, is on the brink of a spiritual and emotional conversion. Eighteen years earlier, Reuben had left his fiancée's father, Roger Malvin, dying alone in the wilderness — a victim of the Penobscot War between colonists and Indians. Both men knew that there was no hope of Reuben returning in time to save the older man, and that Reuben himself, also wounded, would only survive by journeying on. Thus the young man departed with his assurance that, as soon as he was able, he would retrace his steps and give Roger Malvin a proper Christian burial. Reuben never returned. Now on a sojourn to begin a new life far from the memory of his disgrace, Reuben finds himself once again at the site of his betrayal. While hunting for food in the forest with his fifteen-year-old son, Cyrus, Reuben apprehends something familiar about his surroundings and comes to recognize the place where Roger Malvin last lay: "[Reuben] trusted that it was Heaven's intent to afford him an opportunity of expiating his sin," Hawthorne writes. "He hoped that he might find the bones, so long unburied; and that, having laid the earth over them, peace would throw its sunlight into the sepulchre of his heart." But no sooner has Reuben ventured this wish than he hears a rustling in some nearby undergrowth, and, "with the instinct of a hunter," he fires into the thicket. To his horror, he discovers that it is not a deer he has slain but his beloved only son. "Then Reuben's heart was stricken," the story concludes, "and the tears gushed out like water from a rock. The vow that the wounded youth had made, the blighted man had come to redeem. His sin was expiated, the curse was gone from him; and, in the hour, when he had shed blood dearer to him than his own, a prayer, the first for years, went up to Heaven from the lips of Reuben Bourne."[8]

"Roger Malvin's Burial" exemplifies what I will argue is a recurrent pattern in U.S. nineteenth-century fiction of representing acts of violence as a precondition for the perpetrator's emotional transformation into a more empathetic, more authentic human being through the identification that violence engenders. Although violence is not precisely legitimated in this pattern, it nonetheless registers as a crucial component of the sanctifying work of a particularly white, liberal, Christian sensibility. Such a sensibility gains traction through the physical and psychological beatings whereby heretofore selfish, aggressive males become identified with the victims they harm. In "Roger Malvin's Burial," Reuben's identification with his son is clearly established: having become by "secret thoughts and insulated emotions" a "selfish man," Hawthorne tells us, Reuben "could no longer love deeply, except where he saw, or imagined, some reflection or likeness of his own mind" (351). Cyrus is that beloved, mirroring back to Reuben a familiar, and as yet unscarred, image of himself: "In Cyrus, [Reuben] recognized what he had himself been in other days" (351). Cyrus's likeness to Reuben's former self suggests the son's substitutionary value—it is not Cyrus, per se, but Reuben's younger, innocent self who is sacrificed, implicitly staging the father's shooting of the son as an act of *self*-sacrifice, one that results in a renewed subjectivity: that is, his ability to weep and to pray. Nor are the Christian overtones in the story incidental. Nineteenth-century narratives of substitution and sacrifice locate the sentimental work of violence within a theological framework that posits the victimization of an innocent as, like Christ's crucifixion, a necessary vehicle through which the guilty may not only be saved but restored to innocence.

Reuben's role as both father and son in the story exemplifies the transformational work of violence and identification, where the blurring of boundaries between "self" and "other" produces potentially redemptive effects. Reuben's original sin regarding Malvin is not his failure to bury him (an omission for which Hawthorne makes numerous allowances), but his lie about doing so: he lets his wife, Dorcas, believe that he remained with her father until he died and then buried him. The psychological damage of this omission ramifies to dictate Reuben's unhappy fate. What remains "unburied" in this story is thus ultimately less important than what *doesn't*: a secret—an estranging and alienating falsehood that turns Reuben's heart into a "sepulchre," opened only through violence. To remain locked up with only one's self and one's sins is a kind of psychological death, Hawthorne implies, a death from which his protagonist is resurrected through identification with his son's goodness: "The boy was loved by his father, with a deep and silent strength, as if whatever was good and happy in his own nature had been transferred to his child, and all his affections with it" (351). Through identification with the other, recast into an image of himself, Reuben may regain what innocence he has lost and "be revived with a fresh and happy life" (351).

Of course, if Cyrus represents the beloved in relation to whom Reuben can access his more authentic self, it is also true that Reuben's love for Cyrus—abetted by the displacement of his own former innocence onto the son—marks Cyrus for his own, literal death. Cyrus's substitutionary sacrifice points up the potential for identification, and the projections and displacements that animate it, to initiate violence. And not only literal violence but psychological violence—a dynamic through which the other is remade into a version of the self. In psychoanalytic theory, such violence is at the heart of identification. Born of love and loss, identification symbolically murders the other and takes its place.[9] It does so, as the works of Eve Sedgwick, René Girard, and Diana Fuss stress, via the triangular nature of subjectification—the object or other's function in representing, simultaneously, the "me" and the "not-me" in response to which the self is formed.[10] As Fuss puts it, "Identification sets into motion the complicated dynamic of recognition and misrecognition that brings a sense of identity into being, [yet] also immediately calls that identity into question. The astonishing capacity of identifications to reverse and disguise themselves, to multiply and contravene one another . . . renders identity profoundly unstable and perpetually open to change." It is not only the other or object that is dismantled through identification, in other words, but the self. Yet it is the work of identification to obscure such knowledge and to make possible "the formation of an *illusion* of identity as immediate, secure, and totalizable."[11] In the case of "Roger Malvin's Burial," Reuben identifies with Cyrus not only as an innocent but as a substitute for his own guilty self (in consequence of which Reuben, "with the instinct of a hunter," slays him). Cyrus thus represents a projective object of both innocence *and* guilt; he reflects Reuben's own fractured identity as "wounded son" and "blighted man" and serves as a vehicle through which Reuben can feel himself re-Bourne.[12]

By opening his story with a brief summary of "one of the few incidents of Indian warfare" in early American history ("Lovell's

Fight," of 1752), Hawthorne not only provides an explanation for Reuben and Roger's presence in the wilderness but also locates his story of guilt and redemption in a specifically *American* (though prerevolutionary) context (337). He thus invites readers to contemplate the far-reaching, even national, implications of identification and violence. Read in this vein, the death of young Cyrus, who is spoken of by his community as "a future leader of the land," signifies not only the cutting off of a family line (he is Reuben and his wife's only child) but the potentially truncated dreams of a vulnerable, emerging republic (351). Reuben is similarly invested with symbolic significance: made childless by his own hand, the dispossessed patriarch attains salvation, but only through what Hawthorne implies is an unconscious desire, driven by guilt, to kill his son and thus atone for his sin. The Christian thematics of Hawthorne's story, where Reuben, like God, sheds "blood dearer to him than his own," frames American history, both past and future, within a father-son dynamic. Yet the implications of this dynamic are problematic at best. After all, the father's murder of innocence in order to regain it renders (American) innocence itself suspect. Since it is achieved through violence, innocence (including "innocent" American sons) appears inseparable from the guilty act and/or person that (re)creates it.

Hawthorne's closed circuit of morality, one in which a victim's innocence is appropriated by a guilty party who identifies it as his own, illuminates a paradigm I will be tracing from Charles Brockden Brown's *Wieland* (1798) to Louisa May Alcott's *Little Women* trilogy (1868–86). It is a paradigm that situates protagonists and their victims within an ever-shifting dynamic of self and other, father and son, abuser and abused, to show the emotionally transformative work of violence. Rarely does this paradigm concern itself with the effects of violence on the true objects of it, however; rather, these objects, or others, become vehicles through which the narratives' protagonists are made, in a fictional sense, new men. They are recast, that is, as the *sufferers* of the violence they deploy, thereby potentially redeeming violence itself from its scandalous ends. In this American paradigm, fathers and father figures ultimately return through identification to their position as suffering sons, a pattern made evident in Hawthorne's story by the reference made to Reuben as "wounded son" at the end of the tale. The reference, in fact, alludes to Reuben's former relation to his *own* father figure, Roger Malvin, the image of whose "unburied corpse" so haunts Reuben that he at times "almost imagined himself a murderer" (349). Both alive and dead, suggests Hawthorne, fathers (Roger and Reuben) represent a curse whose inheritance American sons (Cyrus and Reuben) can only avoid by dying and/or being born again through empathetic identification: that is, by becoming, or identifying as, the abused whipping boy.

In the following chapters, I look at the particular role that physical and psychological violence plays in nineteenth-century U.S. fictions, primarily as it relates to the bonds forged and the identifications produced between white fathers and sons. By limiting the scope (though, I trust, not the significance) of my findings to white male and white male-identified figures, I aim to center our attention on a particular paradox: the perpetuation of sentimental values through one of America's more radically entrenched, but ethically and emotionally indigestible, expressions of power: masculine aggression. Though women, like men, are susceptible to the pleasures and plights of aggression, white men are the presumptive champions, and transmitters, of American democratic values in the nineteenth century. As head of the family, the white male occupies varied, and often contradictory, positions as aggressive protector, defender, *and* lover of his charges. What I find especially noteworthy in these fictions are the ways in which manifestations of male violence — in local, communal, and national arenas — become overlaid with a patriotic sensibility that confirms, rather than denies, American empathetic character. As a generational legacy handed down from fathers to sons, expressions of violence have the potential to undermine, if not obliterate, sentimental commands to sympathy. Yet, as the example of Reuben Bourne suggests, violence may be redeemed through an identificatory dynamic that substitutes father for son, guilty for innocent. Power itself, with all of its coercive associations, is essentially disavowed in this scenario by means of the aggressive father's adoption of the victim's position: that is, his imaginative assumption of the role of the Christlike "whipping boy."

Insofar as scholars of nineteenth-century literature have investigated the relationship between sentiment and aggression, they have tended to emphasize the apparent irreconcilability of these forms of expression. Richard Brodhead, following Foucault, for example, famously posits that the cultural backlash against violations of the body in the United States (including the whipping of slaves, naval flogging, and corporal punishment in schools) aids in the development of a new model of child rearing that he labels "disciplinary intimacy, or simply discipline through love." In their perceived ability to envelop children within the parental sphere of loving influence, Brodhead goes on, mothers rather than fathers become the de facto leaders in these disciplinary methods and transactions.[13] In a similar vein, Gail Bederman emphasizes the antebellum focus on teaching sons, in particular, to practice self-restraint as a way of curbing their aggression without neutralizing its force: "Middle-class parents taught their sons to build a strong, manly 'character' as they would build a muscle, through repetitive exercises of control over impulse."[14] As these two critics depict it, aggressive impulses (on the parent's or teacher's part in the first example and on the child's in the second) are ameliorated through new disciplinary measures compatible with a nineteenth-century ethos of sympathy and care for others. I contend, by contrast, that masculine aggression serves an integral function to America's sentimental work. It is one of the means by which protagonists come to a more authentic relationship to others and a "truer" (that is, more emotional) sense of themselves.

What I see as the mutually reinforcing concepts of violence and empathy in the U.S. imagination also has its disciplinary function, of course, as the model of the whipping boy reveals. The "whipping boy" refers to a tradition of educating a young prince together with a boy who is to be flogged in the prince's place when the latter commits a fault.[15] The prince's body remains untouched, but his sensibilities are aroused and sharpened: he is chastened through his identification with the boy who stands in his place. The relatively healthful, socializing effects of empathy were widely popularized in the eighteenth century by Scottish moral philosophers like David Hume, Adam Smith, and Francis Hutcheson, who framed their theories of empathy, or "sympathy," mostly in secular terms.[16] Nineteenth-century American authors, by contrast, repeatedly articulate sympathy through a Christian iconography that magnifies the importance of suffering and violence in the production of affective bonds. For these authors, Christ represents the ultimate whipping boy.

The Christian model of vicarious suffering centers on the sacrifice of God's innocent son, Jesus Christ, whose willingness to die for the sinful is meant to effect in the latter a sense of his or her own guilt. Taking on the sins of others, Christ invokes identification on the part of believers, who recognize both his voluntary assumption of their guilt and their restoration to innocence by the shedding of his blood. Like Cyrus in Hawthorne's tale, one might assume that Christ-as-whipping-boy functions solely as the object of another's identification. Yet, as novelists like Harriet Beecher Stowe represent him, Christ is not only the object but the *agent* of empathy; he thus embodies a model for fathers as well as for sons in the transformative effects of violence. "Not one throb of anguish, not one tear of the oppressed is forgotten by the Man of Sorrows," writes Stowe in *Uncle Tom's Cabin*. "In his patient, generous bosom he bears the anguish of a world."[17] For Stowe, Christ represents not only the suffering innocent but also the empathetic attitude gained from that suffering, an attitude shared by his own Father.[18] According to the doctrine of the Holy Trinity, the Father, Son, and Holy Spirit operate as one being. What Christ suffers, God the Father suffers as well. Having assumed the sins of the Father's creation, the Son is then sacrificed by the all-powerful Father, who demands atonement. One could say then that Christ represents the "powerless" dimension of the Trinity, a powerlessness with which the Father, as one with Christ, necessarily identifies.

Christ's martyrdom provides a paradigm through which nineteenth-century writers envision and depict fathers identified with sons to become, simultaneously, objects and subjects of "fellow-feeling" or sympathy (literally translated, "sym" plus "pathos" means "suffering together"). This paradigm, moreover, represents love as the motivating force undergirding these familial identifications. The innocent son becomes a worthy sacrifice precisely *because* the father loves him, making love a precipitating cause, as well as effect, of violence. That is, love may connote the value of the object to be violated, even as it becomes, via its synonymic relation to empathy, the valued feeling produced in the witness or perpetrator of abuse. In this paradigm, love, far from standing in opposition to acts of violence, is manifested and engendered through them.

In the works I examine, the constitutive relationship between violence and love is dramatized in a number of thematically related but psychologically differentiated ways — including familicide (the murder of one's family) in chapter 1; "fraternal melancholy" (Herman Melville's term for the sorrow deriving from identifying with a brother's pain) in chapter 2; the disciplinary concept of *pater flagellans*, or the father who whips the sons he loves, in chapter 3; and a pre-Freudian disciplinary masochism in chapter 4, where children, especially boys, learn to internalize their (often pleasurable) aggressive impulses.[19] Connecting these chapters is not only an empathetic teleology but an often unarticulated yet pervasive desire on the part of mature and maturing males to maintain or regain their innocence by doing violence to those others with whom they identify. Representing "others" are a diverse array of socially disempowered and psychologically unformed objects of identification (including employees, African American slaves, Native Americans, young children, and dolls) who function as virtual receptacles for the projections, displacements, and disavowals of the protagonist. With respect to the last in this list of psychological defenses — disavowal — I submit that we must include in the dynamic of identification the *refusal* to identify, for even dis-identifications may represent, as Judith Butler argues, "an identification that one fears to make only because one has already made it."[20]

Butler's proposition that disavowed identifications often represent a half-known but suppressed fear of likeness extends and complicates what I am arguing is an American fantasy of victimization and innocence — an idealization of transformative violence predicated on white male empathetic suffering. The danger to one's sense of self elicited by identification includes, as Herman Melville repeatedly thematizes, the danger of *too fully* feeling another's pain and powerlessness, even as that empathetic stance constitutes, for him, the basis of humanity. In America's antebellum years, this emotional double bind structures the reversals and contraventions apparent in identificatory moments by centering on an issue of national guilt — slavery — and the troubling image of its transmission — the whip. In the crucible of slavery, identities merge and coalesce, as otherwise autonomous males are made to feel as (if they were) another. Thus we find Melville condemning naval flogging as an instrument that "convert[s] into slaves some of the citizens of a nation of freemen" in his novel *White-Jacket*; we find Frederick Douglass identifying whipping as "the blood-stained gate" through which he passes to enter his hellish life as a slave in *Narrative of the Life of Frederick Douglass*; and we find white radical abolitionist John Brown proclaiming his being "*whiped* [*sic*]" by pro-slavers as he goes to his execution and "mingle[s] [his] blood . . . with the blood of millions in this slave country." For these men, whipping effects an identification with suffering that is torturous in itself.[21]

Since American literature addressed a nation internally divided and haunted by the shadow of slavery, its preoccupation with the whip is hardly surprising. But if whipping marks the simultaneous conjunction (all are slaves) and disjunction (some are free) of identities made painful in either case, it also serves as a locus for disavowals and displacements of aggression that render whipping socially productive. In the case of John Brown, for example, a proponent of corporal punishment, aggressive impulses are not only obscured through the loving motivation that ostensibly channels them (the concept of *pater flagellans*) but also displaced through the sympathetic dynamic that revisits the son's pain, à la the whipping boy, back onto the father. At one point, tellingly, Brown has his son, John Jr., beat *Brown* for the boy's misdeeds. In a reversal of the Hawthorne story, John Brown Sr. substitutes his own body for his guilty son's, compelling John Jr. to an identification with his "victim" and preparing the boy for his entrance into the fight for abolition. Brown's unorthodox (but as we will see, not entirely uncommon) disciplinary method rescripts the (ab)use of power so necessary to war as an instance of *self*-flagellation, one brought about by forcing the whip into other, younger hands. In chapter 4, I examine such displacements in the context of the U.S. postwar period. In Louisa May Alcott's popular postwar children's novels, we find boys (and tomboys) represented as the sacrificial bearers of national violence and its emotionally transformative identifications. After the Civil War, I argue, sons came to represent scapegoats, not only in their function as objects of violence, as in Hawthorne's story, but as perpetrators of it.

Insofar as white males serve as the principal agents in the use of the lash, they also become the primary target of its redemptive effects in U.S. fiction. The attention to dominant culture's sentimental responses to violence is not in itself new. In *Hard Facts*, for example, Philip Fisher argues for antebellum literature's important work in creating identifications between privileged white witnesses (and, by extension, readers) and those "classes of figures from whom [compassion] has been socially withheld" — madmen, prisoners, children, slaves.[22] Although progressive in intention, the focus on what Franny Nudelman terms "the responsive anguish of the witness to trauma" in sentimental constructions has come under some important scrutiny in the last decade. Citing Laura Wexler's critique of middle-class identifications with victims, Nudelman notes that there is nothing transformative for the oppressed in having her feelings acknowledged by others. Wexler's critique, Nudelman goes on, underscores "what Fisher's analysis acknowledges more obliquely — sentimental narration, while concerned with the plight of the oppressed, remains relatively uninterested in exploring the experience of victimization."[23] Lauren Berlant goes further, arguing that sympathetic identification by the witness for the victim engenders in the former a "civic-minded but passive ideal of empathy" that ultimately allows injustice to spread.[24] Examinations of the "sentimental wounding" of the privileged, in other words, only goes so far in eradicating the structures of inequity they claim to denounce.[25]

I would like to move beyond this critique of sentimentality's failure to obviate the suffering of its (presumed) victim in order to acknowledge what lies implicit in Wexler's, Nudelman's, and Berlant's observations: that the true object of sentimentalism's sympathetic strategies is not the abused but the perpetrator of violence. The implications for this shift in focus are both crucial and multilayered. By representing violence as a generational legacy handed down from loving fathers to obedient sons, American fictions contextualize aggression within an interpersonal and sociopolitical family drama that depletes violence of its coercive associations and renders it instead part of a liberal, Christian disciplinary tradition. Moreover, insofar as protagonists make their claims to manly *submission* to empathetic feeling, empathetic identification itself — rather than the violence that engenders it — can be seen as the locus of oppression and victimization. In this narrative, the perpetrators of violence are, by virtue of their identification with their objects, the "real" victims in the story. Despite the ostensible victimization of white manhood, however, the transformational possibilities of violence made manifest through empathy work to secure as well as disavow white male privilege. Repeatedly likened to those abject others with whom they identify, white male and white-male-identified protagonists are imaginatively stripped of their sociopolitical power. Yet in their very *choice* to empathize, free white American fathers and sons represent a self-sacrificing martyrdom through which they become, both paradoxically and perversely, the cultural guarantors of fellow-feeling.[26]

The paradigm I am outlining — one in which white masculine aggression becomes its own form of punishment and salvation — is not confined to America's nineteenth century, of course. As I note in the afterword, it is a pattern appearing most recently in the years after the war on Iraq, when the discourse of an American "exceptionalism" has centered on Americans' capacity, in George W. Bush's words, to "love a neighbor in need."[27] In my examination of the particularly American sentimental structures made efficacious, even redemptive, through violent acts, this book participates in the ongoing critique of American exceptionalism. This critique remains important—for, as Donald Pease has recently observed, to ignore the "US state's power to describe the US as a permanent state of exception" is to fail to understand why we are continually thrown back upon exceptionalist rhetoric and ideology. Even the new "transnational American studies," writes Pease, "cannot effect the democratizing transformations within the global order without explaining how the US state has impeded their accomplishment."[28] In other words, to fail to grasp the historical, literary, and cultural roots of American exceptionalism is to be unequipped to move beyond it.

Ultimately, Pease supports Amy Kaplan's call for a comparative analysis of empires, an analysis that would "remove the US from its claims to uniqueness and insularity."[29] In focusing our attention on the dynamic of the whipping boy, I do not mean to suggest that the United States is unique in its self-presentation as an exceptional nation but instead to open up an investigation into the particular shape this self-presentation takes in the nineteenth century and into why it appears so powerfully persuasive in its formulation of Americans as an exceptionally empathetic people. As we will see, the intersecting discourses of empathy, violence, and American character are far-reaching, crossing boundaries of race, gender, and genre. We find it in sea tales, slave narratives, children's books, and gothic novels and in literature by and about African Americans and Anglo Americans and by and about women and men. Its manifestation appears especially acute in the years surrounding the Civil War, when sentimental ideology saturates depictions of national, institutionalized violence, including slavery, naval flogging, Indian removal, and corporal punishment in schools.[30] In these years, as in ours, representations of violence and identification dovetail in complex and sometimes contradictory ways, producing narratives of empathy that constitute a virtual battleground for the transmission of nationalized ideas about freedom, coercion, and the oftentimes punishing effects of fellow-feeling.

To lay the groundwork for this examination, I begin this book in the aftermath of a different war. Chapter 1, "*Wieland*, Familicide, and the Suffering Father," examines a postrevolutionary phenomenon in which a number of otherwise loving and mild-mannered fathers kill their entire families as a sign of their obedience to God. Charles Brockden Brown's 1798 novel, *Wieland, or The Transformation*, is based on at least one of these historical incidents. Written less than two decades after the Revolutionary War, *Wieland* confronts anxieties over the nature of a new U.S. patriarchal authority through the story of a man who, precisely *because* of his love for his family, sacrifices them to the omnipotent Father. Modeled on the biblical story of Abraham and Isaac, Brockden Brown's novel exemplifies the rhetorical "transformation" of guilty, aggressive fathers into innocent, submissive sons: that is, while explicitly assuming God's power over life and death, Wieland's identification with the Father is disavowed in the end through his figuration as "the Man of Sorrows," or the suffering, empathetic Son, Jesus Christ.[31] *Wieland, or The Transformation*, subtitled *An American Tale* by its author, sets the stage for what I argue is the translation of privilege and power into empathetic feeling through scenes of violence from whose effects the protagonists themselves suffer.

Chapter 2, "Melville's Fraternal Melancholies," extends this idea into the 1850s by considering Melville's tortured vacillation between two points: his belief, on the one hand, in American social reforms and, on the other, his sense that the emotional structures contributing to reform end up reproducing the pain men are seeking to ameliorate. For Melville, the locus of both the ideal and the experiential is fraternal attachment: in the "infinite fraternity of feeling," as Melville calls it in his now famous letter to Hawthorne, there is created the potential for democracy based on shared experiences and a corresponding emotional and spiritual understanding.[32] But, as the narrators in "Bartleby, the Scrivener" (1853) and *White-Jacket* (1850) discover, to share the "bond of a common humanity" is also to be drawn "irresistibly to gloom. A fraternal melancholy!"[33] Set on Wall Street, "Bartleby" examines the intersection of Christian empathy and capitalist self-interest through a privileged narrator whose attempts to identify with his employee prove too emotionally costly: "To a sensitive being, pity is not seldom pain," Melville's lawyer-narrator observes. "And when at last it is perceived that such pity cannot lead to effectual succor, common sense bids the soul be rid of it."[34]

In his semiautobiographical novel *White-Jacket*, Melville enlarges upon the theme of the suffering, sensitive male through racial identifications that punish the white witness. A novel detailing Melville's year as a sailor serving on a man-of-war, *White-Jacket* serves primarily as an exposé on the abuses of the American navy: in the three chapters on flogging, in particular, Melville focuses his attention on the incompatibility between democratic ideals and authorized coercions, including the sailor's forced witnessing of, and subsequent identification with, the flogging of comrades. As the eponymous narrator, White-Jacket, describes it, empathy is itself a form of the lash that scourges sensitive souls, bonding the witness with, as he puts it, men "of his own type and badge" and forcing upon him a recognition of his own powerlessness.[35] Naval flogging in general, White-Jacket declares, blurs the boundary between slave and free, rendering the white man akin to the black and reducing all sailors to the status of slaves. Yet, for freedom to be complete, men must be liberated not only from the threat of the whip but also from those forced identifications that convert the sailor, against his sensitive will, into a "slave" to his empathetic feelings.

As Melville represents it, witnessing abuse done to others forces a man into both an identification with powerlessness and complicity with powerful sociopolitical structures that reproduce inequality. The equation of privilege and power with the *choice* to identify— not only with other men but with one's own race or another's—is the subject of chapter 3, "Fathers of Violence: Frederick Douglass, John Brown, and the Radical Reproduction of Sensibility." In a sentiment that shares the "common-sense" philosophy of the narrator in "Bartleby," Frederick Douglass writes in *My Bondage and My Freedom* that "a man, without force, is without the essential dignity of humanity. Human nature is so constituted, that it cannot *honor* a helpless man, although it can *pity* him; and even this it cannot do long, if the signs of power do not arise."[36] Although Douglass, like Melville's lawyer, notes the conditions that render sympathy untenable, he does not ascribe sympathy's limits to the witness's sensitive nature but instead to something lacking in the victim himself. One cannot sympathize with what is not human, Douglass implies, and what constitutes humanity is power. For Douglass, then, unlike Melville's narrators, sympathy is not that which bonds men, white and black, in a cycle of pain, but a volitional feeling predicated on the "force" with which a victim can demonstrate his manhood and humanity. Put another way, the man who would be pitied must show himself worthy of sympathy by acting like a white man — a man with whom (other) white men would choose to identify.

Douglass's observation about human nature comes on the heels of his memorable battle with his overseer, Edward Covey, a personal triumph for Douglass that ends with his "whipping" his white foe. Arguably the climactic moment of both his first and second autobiographies, this scene focuses on the mutual aggression between master and slave, a violent expression through which the black man re-creates himself in relation to the other — in particular, the slave "other" that he once was — and discovers a more feeling self: "[The fight with Covey] recalled to life my crushed self-respect and my self-confidence. . . . I *felt* as I had never *felt* before."[37] But if Douglass is freed from the desensitizing effects of slavery through violence, included in his liberation is an escape from identifications with blackness itself. Throughout *My Bondage*, Douglass associates force with whiteness and whiteness with sensibility; in his articulation and assumption of the power to choose with whom to identify, Douglass differentiates himself from his biological family of slaves to become an authentic (white) man of feeling.

Like Douglass, John Brown's abolitionist strategies rely on an inversion of racial identifications, a realignment or reconfiguration of familial identity meant to resurrect, through violence, Americans' capacity for fellow-feeling. But whereas Douglass, a black man, rejects the popular construction of slaves as objects of sympathy, positioning black men and women in his narrative as substitutes for a slave self with which he dis-identifies, Brown, a white man, offers himself as substitute for the sins of a white nation, finding power in his own objectification. Declaring on the eve of his execution for the raid on Harper's Ferry his willingness to "mingle my blood further with the blood of my children and with the blood of millions" of tortured slaves, Brown not only expands his family to include blacks as well as sons but also prefigures his cultural transformation into a national "whipping boy" with whose sacrifice *white* Americans are meant to identify. As an inevitable civil war approaches, whites will find that the pain they inflict on others will soon become their own.[38]

Of course, John Brown, a radical abolitionist who believed that only bloodshed would wash his nation clean, was held by many to be more murderer than martyr.[39] The complex interchange between aggression and sacrifice is crystallized in the disciplinary method cited above, where Brown forces his son to beat *him* for the boy's juvenile infractions, an experiment that reduces his son to tears. A manipulative demonstration of both Brown's own power as "victim" and the responsibilities attending aggressive manhood, Brown's method offers a stunning example of the idea that white males grow to a mature sensibility through vicarious means — that is, not simply by experiencing pain themselves but by witnessing or even inflicting it on others. That Brown's son is *compelled* to this recognition — compelled, that is, to identify with the abused even as he holds the whip — returns us to questions of choice and agency in the creation of the empathetic self. It suggests as well the possible psychological inversions at play in the whipping scenario, where subjects and objects, beating and being beaten, interchange and even coalesce in the white imagination.

What I am arguing is a particularly "white" construction of the operation of violence in antebellum America is one in which inverted positions distribute pain across a broad spectrum, imaginatively putting slave owners and sailors in the position of slaves and fathers in the position of sons (and vice versa). The socially leveling potential of these identifications may be undercut, of course, in a number of ways, not least by the *pleasure* a person may take in causing another pain. Complaining that fifteen-year-old midshipmen have the authority to flog at will, for example, White-Jacket theorizes about the psychological repercussions of boys' newly acquired power: "Having so recently escaped the posterior discipline of the nursery and the infant school" (that is, some form of spanking), midshipmen "are impatient to recover from those smarting reminiscences by mincing the backs of full-grown American freemen."[40] One of the objections White-Jacket has to the practice is the satisfaction boys experience from whipping "full-grown" men. As Michael Paul Rogin notes, Melville associates the midshipmen's enjoyment of whipping with the other "iniquities" in which they participate: that is, homosexual behavior. Thus, for Melville, as for many other abolitionists of the period, argues Rogin, whipping signifies an eroticized sadism — an opportunity for young officers (and the slave masters for whom they stand in) to displace their feelings of powerlessness onto another while becoming sexually gratified in the process.[41]

Rogin's reading makes explicit the potentially eroticized desire inhering not only in whipping but in identification itself, where the fracturing and reconstituting of identity render pleasure and pain mutually constitutive. Perhaps nowhere is the complex relationship between pleasure, pain, and identification more usefully outlined than in Freud's theories of sadism and masochism, or, as Freud defines the latter, "sadism which has been turned round upon the self."[42] In "A Child Is Being Beaten" (1919), Freud identifies the condensation of two unconscious childhood wishes often at the heart of childhood beating fantasies: the wish to have another child beaten and the wish to be the beaten child. Although the first wish appears to evince a sadistic satisfaction by which the child is assured of the father's love (because *not* beaten), Freud notes that "only the form of this phantasy is sadistic; the satisfaction derived from it is masochistic." Originating in the "forbidden genital relation" to the father for which whipping acts as both punishment *and*, crucially, substitute, masochistic fantasies, observes Freud, derive their "libidinal excitation" from the regressive substitution whereby "I am beaten by my father" stands in the child's mind for "*I am loved by my father.*"[43] For the child, in other words, the father's punishment is an expression of love, a love the child vicariously achieves and atones for through his/her identification with the object of abuse.[44]

In chapter 4, "The Death of Boyhood and the Making of *Little*

Women," I examine the interlocking pleasures of beating and being beaten through a treatment of Louisa May Alcott's popular children's trilogy, *Little Women* (1868), *Little Men* (1871), and *Jo's Boys* (1886). While not explicitly sexualized or eroticized, Alcott's children, especially boys, are presented — apropos of Melville's midshipmen — as essentially sadistic in nature. As Alcott's famous tomboy, "Jo" March, confesses early on in *Little Women*, "I get so savage, I could hurt any one and *enjoy* it."[45] Likewise in *Little Men*, we find boys and tomboys gleefully engaging in the ritual torture (burning, whipping, hanging) of dolls and their real-life counterparts — other children. But if boyish pleasure initially finds an outlet in the displacement of "smarting reminiscences" onto powerless others in Alcott's novels, that pleasure is ultimately converted into a desire of a different kind: the desire to be the object under the whip. Sadistic impulses are ultimately converted into masochistic ones in Alcott's novels, a transformation that affords its own form of pleasure by the children's understanding that the one who is "beaten" is the one who is loved.[46]

Alcott's trilogy offers repeated examples of the ways in which masculine aggressive impulses are redirected back to the self by channeling them through people and objects with which the child-protagonists are made to identify. The novelistic conversion of sadism into masochism has historical as well as psychological significance. Writing in the wake of the Civil War, Alcott's boy-books reflect a broad-based cultural ambivalence about the nature of boys in America's postwar, Christian nation.[47] Whereas throughout much of the nineteenth century, fathers sought to identify themselves with and as innocent sons, after the Civil War sons take up the burden of aggression and turn it upon themselves. Fathers and father figures are again key in this process. As with Brown and his son, Alcott's fathers foster the aggression that they then employ to a higher end: the child's internalization of the pain he inflicts. But whereas Brown's ultimate goal in this dynamic is to make his son a literal soldier in the battle against social injustice, Alcott's postwar, peace-loving fathers require their boys to battle themselves. Importantly, Alcott depicts such masochistic turns as a precondition for the attainment of Christian maturity (rather than Oedipal regression, as in Freud's reading), manifested in the protagonist's de-masculinization: tears, passivity, self-renunciation. Thus one of the paradoxes in Alcott's fiction is not only the alignment of a person's emotional and psychological growth, males included, with stereotypically "feminine" qualities but also its foundation in a victimized object-identification. To attain true subjectivity, as Alcott portrays it, is to recognize oneself as a whipping boy.

In Alcott's trilogy, we find the culmination of a pattern traced from *Wieland* to John Brown, one in which the impulse toward, and enactment of, violence catalyzes identifications that transform mature male and male-identified aggressors into "whipping boys." This pattern complicates what Herbert Marcuse (following Freud) argues is the foundation of modern social life: that is, the individual's need "to submit to the exigencies of parents and 'other societal agencies'" by introjecting the parent and developing an inner sense of guilt. The "primal father," as Marcuse explains, is "the archetype of domination," initiating "the chain reaction of enslavement, rebellion, and reinforced domination which marks the history of civilization."[48] In the pages of American literature, this "chain reaction" is transactional and intergenerational—that is, it is not only sons who "introject their masters" but also fathers who find or put themselves in the place of sons to create a recurring cycle of aggression, oppression, and newfound empathetic feeling. Perhaps this is in part because, in the American myth, the "primal father" is the Judeo-Christian God, a figure whose omnipotence is manifested through the sacrifice of his beloved—specifically, the Son with whom, as part of the Holy Trinity, God is inseparably identified. That sacrifice, moreover, paradoxically defines the aggressive nature of the archetypal Father's love. From the Old Testament story of Abraham's reluctant but voluntary sacrifice of his son Isaac at God's command, to the New Testament's climactic moment this story prefigures—Christ's death on the cross—the F/father's love is represented as practically indistinguishable from his violence. As we will see, this Christian paradigm structures the cycles of violence and vicarious pain found in these chapters, cycles that appear as unending as the successive generations that reproduce them. In these generations, Oedipal relations are subsumed in Christian ones through fathers who "sacrifice" their sons as a sign not simply of omnipotence but of solidarity: an (over)identification with the pain of victims whose suffering these protagonists participate in and then make their own.

CHAPTER 1

Wieland, *Familicide,* and the *Suffering* *Father*

There was little pain. All of them were dead in less than five minutes. I hit them with a hammer in their sleep and then put them face down in the bathtub to make sure they did not wake up in pain. To make sure they were dead.
   I am so sorry. I wish I didn't. Words cannot tell the agony.
   Why did I?
—Mark Barton's letter of confession, August 1999

When Mark Barton killed his wife, his eight-year-old daughter, and his twelve-year-old son with a hammer in July 1999 and then proceeded to shoot nine people at two different brokerage houses before shooting himself, his murderous "rampage" was attributed by the press to his newfound habit of day trading. Although little was known about this man, who one fellow trader claimed was "one of the nicest guys you ever met," Barton's reasons for murdering his children on that Wednesday night, and his wife the night before, appeared self-evident to journalists. As a *Newsweek* article summed up the case, "His debts going up, his marriage going bad, an Atlanta day trader bludgeons his family to death and goes on a shooting spree — a tragedy with a twist of cybergreed."[1] Rather than "husband," "father," or even "man," Barton is characterized simply as "day trader," rendering his "shooting spree" the predictable outcome of an acquisitive, impulsive, and undisciplined nature.[2]

Such a reading has the advantage of giving what at first appears to be an inexplicable act the reassuring moral of a cautionary tale. But this moral addresses only part of the story. In a letter of confession left at the family scene, Barton represents his violence as a

(25)

legitimate expression not only of hatred but of devotion. As Barton has it, he murdered his children in an entirely different spirit, and with a different motive, than he murdered his fellow traders at the brokerage firms. The latter were those who deserved to die because they "greedily sought [his] destruction." His children, by contrast, were killed to spare them from future woe: "I killed the children to exchange for them five minutes of pain for a lifetime of pain," writes Barton. "I forced myself to do it to keep them from suffering later."[3] One murder represents an act of vengeance, but the other represents an act of intimacy and of paternal care. As counterintuitive as it seems, in Barton's case love becomes a motive for murder.

Familicide—the killing of one's spouse and children—has been increasingly documented by psychologists for the past thirty years, and as these professionals attest, it is a peculiarly male crime.[4] According to Charles Patrick Ewing, the typical familicide perpetrator is a white male in his thirties or forties, controlling yet dependent on family. He views himself as the center of the family and believes that only he can satisfy the members' needs. When some crisis occurs, such as a severe financial reversal, the man may convince himself, as Ewing puts it, "that familicide followed by suicide is not just the only way out but the honorable and right thing to do."[5] Ewing's profile accords with Barton's written narrative. By killing his children, Barton sees himself fulfilling his responsibility to save them—from disgrace (of his financial collapse), from loss (of the head of the family, when he commits suicide), and from inevitable heartache: "No mother, no father, no relatives.... The fears of the father are transferred to the son. It was from my father to me and from me to my son. He already had it. And now to be left alone. I had to take him with me." These words point not only to Barton's confused state of mind but to his sense of the double-edged nature of family bonds: that is, family attachments can destroy you equally by their absence ("No mother, no father, no relatives . . . now to be left alone") and by their presence ("The fears of the father are transferred to the son [and] it was from my father to me and from me to my son").

Such a double bind was, according to Barton, the curse his own son would inevitably inherit. His wife and daughter, by contrast, would suffer from their dependence on a man who could never truly protect them. Some years before, after his first wife's death, Barton had been suspected of sexually molesting his daughter.[6] Whether this was what Barton was attempting to spare his son (the ambiguous reference to the fact that his son "already had it" might in this case mean that the son, like Barton, had already been the victim and/or perpetrator of incest) or whether his anxiety was a more generalized, though acute, symptom of depression will never be known. What is clear is that Barton believed the curse was hereditary and male-oriented. As Barton's minister told reporters, "[Barton] feared that he had inherited some mental imbalance from his father."[7] His only hope of saving the family, and his own compromised masculinity, was in sending them to a better, or at least more effectual, father: "I know that Jehovah will take care of them all in the next life. . . . If Jehovah is willing I would like to see them all again in the resurrection. To have a second chance."

Barton's "second chance," I would suggest, hinges not only on what he sees as the fulfillment of his paternal responsibility but also on his acquiescence to a power greater than his own. Though brought about through his own actions, the deaths of his family members now place them, as well as Barton himself, in the "Father's" hands. In this submissive state, Barton's power is disavowed through his identification with, and as, a son. This psychological move is reaffirmed by Barton's insistence that his son "already had it," a pronouncement that reinscribes Barton's murderous act as loving because, at heart, empathetic: he knows what his boy feels because he has felt it too. "The fears of the father are transferred to the son. It was from my father to me and me to my son." His words speak to an endless cycle in which fathers re-experience the helplessness, and thus the blamelessness, of their filial relation: for Barton, the son's power to act is always already circumscribed by the father who has made him who he is.

In Barton's drama of identification, the son's impotence to act against his father's aggression becomes a mirror for Barton's own sense of powerlessness, rendering the twelve-year-old a vehicle through which Barton stages his own pain. Barton's narration thus highlights the irreconcilable subject positions of father and son, even as it seamlessly, and seductively, conflates these positions by imagining powerful fathers as at the mercy of their own feelings. In the end, the father's character as loving and affectionate is potentially reaffirmed, rather than categorically nullified, by his recourse to violence. It is precisely this kind of contradiction that I wish to explore with respect to early U.S. narratives of familicide, narratives that allow us insight into a peculiarly sentimentalized formulation about the work of aggression at the turn of the nineteenth century. In this formulation, violence operates in part as a manifestation of the *value* of family bonds by the men's singling out of family members as objects of sacrifice.

Although familicide has been a subject of scrutiny for mental health care professionals only recently, it was a popular topic of murder narratives, biographies, sermons, and poetry in the U.S. postrevolutionary and early national periods. And for good reason. As Daniel A. Cohen notes, an alarming seven cases of familicide were recorded in Anglo-American society between 1781 and 1836.[8] Although only one of these men, John Cowan, explicitly affirmed that, like Barton, he took the lives of his children to spare them being "left to be knocked and cuffed about by the world" as he himself had been, six out of seven expressed the opinion that their families should not be left alone on earth and would be better off "in the hands of their God."[9] In fact, in the majority of these cases, religious conviction motivated or justified the deed in the perpetrators' minds: two of the men claimed their belief that God condoned the murders, and three others maintained that God directly ordered the slaughter. Going back to a Judeo-Christian tradition of sacrificial offering, exemplified in the story of Abraham and Isaac, these latter individuals were determined to, in the words of one of the perpetrators, destroy all their "idols" — including their wives and children — as a sign of their obedience to God.[10]

The notion that family murder constitutes an imperative from above informs the literary subject of this chapter: Charles Brockden Brown's early national novel, *Wieland, or The Transformation*

(1798). Based on at least one historical case of familicide in the 1780s, *Wieland* recounts the story of a man who, having heard what he believes to be the voice of God, murders his family to prove his devotion to the Deity.[11] As one of the first American novels, *Wieland* lays the literary groundwork for a succeeding century of U.S. narratives in which acts of violence are uneasily reconciled with an ethos, socially constructed and personally internalized, of empathy and love. As in Barton's story, the relationship between father and son in Brockden Brown's novel is key to understanding the ever-shifting dynamics of power that render brutal acts an affirmative sign of familial attachment. In *Wieland*, however, as in the historical case(s) on which it is based, the primary father-son relationship is between God the father and his obedient son — the earthly father. For Theodore Wieland, Brockden Brown's protagonist, it is God himself who enacts the conflation of "father" and "son" by offering a divine imperative through which Wieland simultaneously experiences power over life and death *and* a disavowal of that power — that is, as a child of God, Wieland had no choice but to submit to God's will. That such submission leads to suffering is importantly observed by the novel's narrator, Wieland's sister, who claims that the story's tragedies can be ascribed to the "errors of the *sufferers*" — most explicitly, Wieland himself.[12] Ultimately, as I will argue, *Wieland* represents one of the ways in which nineteenth-century literary representations of patriarchal authority bury the traces of the father's coercive power through identification with suffering — specifically, the father's suffering on his loved ones' behalf.

LOVING WITH A VENGEANCE

For most readers, the actions of the fathers cited above probably repulse the very empathetic identification that Mark Barton describes himself as so powerfully, and tragically, experiencing with his son. How could a father, we ask ourselves, consider for a moment killing his child, no matter what the circumstance? What is more, what kind of vision of God's character would prompt one to imagine His participation in, and even demand for, the sacrifice of children?

The latter is a question that goes back to the foundation of Judeo-Christian thought and tradition and the story of Abraham's near-slaying of his son Isaac. "Is there a more famous story in all of history," asks Myron Tuman, "or a more perplexing one?" He goes on:

> The binding of Isaac ... even today remains at the core of Jewish sense of self-identity, its belief in a unique and transforming covenant with God. In compelling ways, it also prefigures God's sacrifice of His only son as the founding act of the Christian era. The early Church Father Tertullian writes: "Isaac when delivered up by his father for sacrifice, himself carried the wood ... and did at that early date set forth the death of Christ, who when surrendered as a victim by his Father carried the wood of his own passion.[13]

Cultural and literary critics and theorists from Søren Kierkegaard to René Girard and Susan Mizruchi have addressed the significance of ritual sacrifice, and this biblical story in particular, to modern society.[14] The question here, however, is what the Abraham-Isaac story may have meant to early American writers — what, that is, do narratives about familicide, this one included, suggest about the nature of paternal feeling and responsibility in the postrevolutionary and early national periods, and how are acts of family murder reconciled with a notion of divine Fatherhood?

Although, as Tuman notes, Christ's victimization is prefigured by Isaac's, the latter's, unlike Christ's, is curiously devoid of affective detail. Jesus' death is narratively rendered through his own eyes, and with the poignancy of foreknowledge — he has a dreaded understanding of his coming suffering. Thus, on the eve of his arrest, Jesus prays to God, "My Father, if it be possible, let this cup [of sacrifice] pass from me; nevertheless, not as I will, but as thou wilt."[15] Isaac, by contrast, is ignorant of what awaits him. Although he metaphorically (as well as literally) carries the burden of God's command, he is represented as unconscious of doing so: "Behold the fire and the wood," Isaac says to his father, "but where is the lamb for the burnt offering?" "God will provide himself the lamb ... my son," Abraham replies.[16] None of the emotions one may presume that the boy experiences are recorded. When his father binds him and lays him on the altar, and then when he is released (on command from the angel of the Lord), Isaac appears silent. In point of fact, neither the feelings of the son *nor* those of the father are offered in this third-person account. Nevertheless, this is clearly the father's story. Its dramatic effect comes from the implied pain of the father's awareness of what he must do ("Take your son ... whom you love ... and offer him there as a burnt offering," God says to Abraham), just as its conclusion focuses on Abraham's reward for his obedience ("By myself I have sworn, says the Lord, because you ... have not withheld your son, your only son, I will indeed bless you, and I will multiply your descendants as the stars of heaven").[17] The "covenant with God" from which the Jewish nation springs originates in premeditated violence against the family—specifically, the son "whom [Abraham] love[s]." That covenant is completed, so Christian theology tells us, in Christ's crucifixion, an act whose dramatic power is achieved, like Abraham's, through the victim's painful awareness of his position. This is not to say, however, that Christ's story is the son's story and not the father's; rather, the very foundation upon which Christianity stands—Christ's mythic identification as both son and father, both fully man and fully God—makes the son's and the father's suffering one. This idea is reinforced in the catechism of Christianity, where Christ's sacrifice is attributed to the work of the Father: "For God so loved the world, that He gave His only begotten Son," famously writes the apostle John.[18] All suffering, in other words, goes through the Father, who experiences Himself the pain of every "son."

Narratives of familicide, I am suggesting, focus chiefly on the father's feelings, the most "perplexing" and disturbing of which is the father's love for his child. In fact, according to this archetype, it is the father's love that catalyzes the event; it is the child "whom [he] loves" that makes the latter a meaningful object of sacrifice. Of course, not all domestic narratives of family murder contain this element of sacrificial offering. Yet the majority of them are concerned, first and foremost, with the father's emotional state at the time of the crime and how the man's feelings might account for the tragedy that ensues. Like Mark Barton, the majority of early American perpetrators were regularly described by friends and neighbors as "kind," "affectionate," "tender," and "sensitive" fathers.[19] There was no suggestion of domestic abuse in these cases. Thus one of the startling aspects of the crime is the seeming disconnect between the man's character and his deed. According to Karen Halttunen, it was exactly the mysterious, alien, and inexplicable nature of the crime that so disturbed and thrilled eighteenth-century readers of murder narratives.[20] Addressing such readers, Stephen Mix Mitchell, in *A Narrative of the Life of William Beadle*, concedes, "'Tis very natural for you to ask, whether it was possible a man could be transformed from an affectionate husband and an indulgent parent to a secret murderer, without some previous alteration, which must have been noticed by the family or acquaintance? Yet this was the case."[21] I would argue, however, that what remains most opaque in these narratives is not the mystery of a man's "alteration" but of his potential consistency—that is, the way in which Beadle's "affectionate" and "indulgent" nature might contribute to, rather than contradict, his crime.

The attempt to decode the relationship between paternal feeling and paternal violence preoccupies contemporary accounts, interpretations, and moral commentaries about familicide.[22] But even as these works aim at identifying where precisely these men went wrong, the reasons they offer are as contradictory as they are various. For example, in the 1805 poetical commentary "Lines on the Horrid Murder," published on the same page as the more objective report of Abel Clemmens's crime, the poet refers to Clemmens as an "assassin wild / Unfeeling and severe"; "The laws of nature he broke thro— / And all its tender ties." The author implies that Clemmens suffered from a *lack* of feeling, itself, the author notes, a reflection of that "deprav'd" state of man when "God withdraws his guardian hand."[23] Yet in the report above it, Clemmens is said to have "always lived with [his family] in a most affectionate manner, and they bore the character of honesty and industry." For several weeks, it goes on, Clemmens had been "in a gloomy melancholy mood, occasioned, it was supposed, by his great anxiety for the welfare of his numerous family." (Clemmens had eight children, with another one on the way.)[24] Rather than "unfeeling and severe," Clemmens is here described as a man of too *much* feeling: his affection for his family leads to a melancholy that ends in horror.

In a similar contradiction, an anonymous author titles his 1806 account of the Purrinton murders "Horrid Massacre!! Sketches of the Life of James Purrinton, Who ... Murdered His Wife, Six Children, and Himself." Yet, despite the "horrid" nature of the "massacre," the author offers an editorial comment that practically exonerates the murderer on the grounds of filial affection: "Finding himself discovered, and his intentions [of suicide] suspected by his wife and family, and seeing their distress, and anticipating how poignant it would be on his death, [Purrinton] no doubt determined to take them with himself; believing they would thus lose their sorrows, suffer but a momentary pang, and be with him eternally happy."[25] The narrative is then followed by those theological "Remarks" that conventionally attend sensational murder accounts as a moral instructive to readers. This section offers an entirely different perspective on the murders, observing that the "Unbelief in the superintending providence of God" reduces a man "to a state of brutal degradation." "With contemptuous indifference" and "cool calculation," the author goes on, "[the murderer] invades the rights of his fellowmen ... and when passion or phrenzy dictate, lifts a remorseless hand against their lives, or his own."[26] Purrinton's sensitivity toward his family's "distress," as well as his concern with their eternal happiness, here turns to his exemplification of "cool calculation" and "indifference" — the inevitable "brutal degradation" of feeling that attends "unbelief."

Finally, James Dana's sermon on William Beadle's murder of his family in 1782 attributes the crime to the perpetrator's "haughty" and "hardned [sic]" heart — a natural condition for men who are indifferent to God's grace.[27] Beadle's emotional shortcomings were moreover magnified, according to Dana, by his deist principles — his belief that men are mere "machines," predetermined in their actions by a God who creates them and then disinterestedly observes the consequences.[28] Such a "doctrine of mechanism," writes Dana, inevitably "terminate[s] in atheism" — "a violence to reason! — to all the tenderest ties in life!"[29] Beadle's apparent belief in God's insensibility toward his creations is linked by Dana to Beadle's insensitivity toward his *own* family; behaving as the "machine" he believes God made him, Beadle acts out the "hardness" of heart that ends in murder. But as with the Clemmens and the Purrinton cases, Beadle's situation suggests there is another side to the story. In a suicide note mailed to a friend before the murders, Beadle claims that he means "to close the eyes of six persons through perfect humanity and the most endearing fondness and friendship; for never mortal father felt more of those tender ties than myself."[30]

The repetition of the phrase "tender ties" in so many of these documents, signifying, on the one hand, evidence for the "violence" done to paternal feeling and, on the other, evidence of its depth, alerts us to the ideological as well as rhetorical battleground that notions of paternal tenderness and love occupy at this time. Scoffing at Beadle's assertions of devotion, Dana writes, "an [*sic*] husband and parent, appointed by providence to guard life, armed with the weapons of death against those whose preservation and happiness every obligation and motive impelled him to consult! — closing the eyes of his family, and then his own, from the greatest tenderness! Was ever crime so black in its nature, and so circumstanced! — Good God!"[31] Yet, despite Dana's incredulity, accounts of familicide, rendered by the men themselves and by others, point to a complicated and problematic intersecting of paternal feeling, rights, and responsibilities in which the bonds of affection and the father's right to express that affection in his own way create texts of overdetermined meaning.

In many of these sermons and commentaries, the need to debate whether familicide perpetrators feel too much or too little for their families is obviated by the writers' return to the criminal's overarching fatal flaw: his inability to comprehend and accept God's sovereignty. Regardless of one's predisposition toward family, the authors argue, to be haughty, proud, or indifferent *toward God* will lead one to tragedy — and everlasting torment. "Bow to the will of God," the author of "Remarks" instructs his readers, for in the final days, "the 'Lamb of God' will become the 'Lion of the Tribe of Judah'" and disobedient men will feel "God's wrath."[32] "Men *strive with God*," writes John Marsh in his sermon on the Beadle murders, "when they refuse to submit to him as their *Law giver*." But such striving is not only reckless, he continues; it is useless: "Having made them [God] has an absolute propriety in them," and "they, who strive with their Maker" will be "exposed to his vindictive pleasure, and will finally be made the monuments of his eternal vengeance, if they persist in opposing his compassionate efforts to save them from perishing."[33] What differentiates earthly fathers from the Heavenly one, it seems, is God's right to violently dispose of His children as He sees fit. For mortal men to assert such a right is thus heretical arrogance — a sign of the murderer's "hardned" and "deprav'd" state.

This theological differentiation between divine and earthly paternal rights to violence necessarily leads to some moral confusion, a confusion exacerbated, I would contend, by the biblical story of Abraham and Isaac with which this section began and upon which the delusions of these "affectionate" men may be at least partially based. In Dana's sermon, "Men's Sins Not Chargeable on God but on Themselves," for example, he warns his readers, quoting James 1:13–14, "Let no man say when he is tempted, I am tempted of God: For God cannot be tempted with evil, neither tempteth any man. But every man is tempted, when he is drawn away of his own lust, and enticed." It was Beadle's own passions, or "lust," Dana asserts, that tempted him to murder, and earthly temptations derive from "Satan," who is "described as *working in the children of disobedience*."[34] Yet what is obedience and what is disobedience, what actions count as good, or God-given, and what as evil, becomes increasingly unclear. Directly after this pronouncement about Satan, Dana acknowledges that the Bible states, "GOD *did tempt Abraham*." He then follows with, "Let us determine in what sense":

God was pleased to try or prove Abraham's faith and obedience in a singular case, the oblation of his son Isaac. May not

The Suffering Father (35)

the LORD of all resume the life he has given when he pleaseth? And by what instrument he pleaseth? Might he not then command Abraham to offer up his son? If so, was this command a temptation to moral evil? It was a peculiar trial of Abraham's faith and submission, and therefore is it said, GOD did tempt Abraham. When Abraham certainly knew that it was an order from GOD, had he refused to offer his son, he must then have been tempted in another sense; he must have been drawn away of his own lust, by confering [sic] with flesh and blood in opposition to the express and plain command of heaven.[35]

Employing the very language he used about Satan's temptation to murder, Dana here claims that Abraham's *refusal* to kill his son would evince sinful "lust" or personal desire. As Dana has it, *not* to kill one's family is also a temptation, and one prompted by "the devil, or the lust of our own heart."[36]

Despite Dana's confidence in his own circuitous logic, the case of Abraham presents us with a broader understanding of the contradictions surrounding a man's "tender ties" to family and their relation to, or competition with, his filial obedience to God. It is just such contradictions that inform Brockden Brown's pedagogically minded musings on the "moral constitution of man" in *Wieland* (3). In Brockden Brown's novel, as in Dana's sermon, God and "the devil" appear less as diametrically opposed combatants — one representing obedience and the other disobedience, respectively — than as partners in crime. Each lures men to murder, either in accordance with or opposition to a man's own desires. Though Dana asserts that it naturally follows from "this discourse that sinners are their *own destroyers*," they seem to have some help in their own and others' destruction from those supernatural agencies whose identities merge at the moment of crisis.[37] John Marsh's reference to God making men "the monuments of his eternal vengeance" should they oppose his "compassionate efforts" to save them is especially telling in this regard: it reminds us that even in the realm of divine justice, love and violence go hand in hand.

SATAN'S DISGUISE

"My Wife and children I have slain,"
He said, "and mock'd their dying pain . . .
"I saw a man exceeding bright,
"Like to an angel of the light;
"A splendid guard attend around,
"He stood in air above the ground,
"Clad with a bright celestial robe,
"I thought it was the son of God.
"'Womble,' said he, 'I'm come to you,
"'To let you know what you must do,
"'If you to heaven would e're attain,
"'Your wife and children must be slain;
"'To win that prize, no man but you,
"'The meritorious work must do.'
"Obedient to the orders giv'n,
"I kill'd them all to get to heaven."
—John Leland's rendition of Matthew Womble's confession

John Leland's poem summarizing Matthew Womble's confession of familicide in 1784 is a sketch in miniature of Charles Brockden Brown's full-length treatment of the subject in *Wieland, or The Transformation: An American Tale*.[38] Brockden Brown's novel centers on the transformation of the protagonist, Theodore Wieland, from a rational, sober, tender-hearted man to a convicted murderer and, finally, to a suicide. According to his trial testimony, Wieland was seeking "the blissful privilege of direct communication with [God], and of listening to the audible enunciation of [God's] pleasure," when he had a revelation. "What task would I not undertake," he remembers praying, "what privation would I not cheerfully endure, to testify my love of thee?" (167). For an answer, Wieland hears a voice that commands him to kill his wife, and after, his children. Much as Womble explains after his arrest that he killed his family in obedience to a supernatural emissary, "Satan in disguise," Wieland

The Suffering Father (37)

is convinced by the end of the novel that he has been duped by evil in the form of a friend—a ventriloquist named Francis Carwin.[39] Nevertheless, Wieland asserts, though "this minister is evil ... he from whom his commission is received is God" (226). As Brockden Brown portrays it, Wieland is incapable of disentangling evil from good, or a "deprav'd" and "hardned [sic]" state from a "tender" and loving one. For Wieland, "Satan in disguise" is God in disguise.

Informing the tragedy of *Wieland*, in other words, is the very dilemma we noted in the historical cases of familicide, where the rectitude of a man's desires, or the "lust of [his] own heart," is constructed in relation to a Deity who *may* or *may not* desire the destruction of His children. Moreover, the allusion to Abraham in Wieland's dilemma is made explicit in the protagonist's fictional patrilineal line: his family goes back to the eighteenth-century German poet Christoph Martin Wieland, a real-life poet whose popular work *Der Gepryfte Abraham* (*The Trial of Abraham*) (1754), as Alan Axelrod has shown, served as an important source for Brockden Brown's novel. "Like Theodore Wieland," writes Axelrod, "C. M. Wieland's Abraham consciously subdues 'natural affection' to the command of the divine will."[40] As a source text, *The Trial of Abraham* exemplifies what I am suggesting is the impossibility of discerning good from evil, loving acts from violent ones, in *Wieland*. Such a moral quandary is further complicated by the novel's psychological dynamics: given the improbability of Wieland's assertion that the voice of God audibly commanded him to murder, readers might surmise that God's will and Wieland's will are the same—that is, that God's "will" is Wieland's own unconscious wish projected onto a Father figure he dare not refuse. As I will argue, Wieland's identification with a loving but murderous God allows him both to exert his own paternal power over his family and to *disavow* that power by representing his murders as the actions of an obedient "son," a son whose desires, like Abraham's, are made subservient to the will of the Father.

Wieland opens with a biographical chapter about Wieland's father, a man whose religious delusion sets in motion the tragedy that follows. Wieland's Sr.'s lonely and aimless life is changed, we are told, when he discovers a book containing "an exposition of the doctrine of the sect of the Camissards." "His mind was in a state peculiarly fitted for the reception of devotional sentiments," explains Clara Wieland, Theodore's sister and the novel's narrator. "The craving [for happiness] which had haunted him was now supplied with an object. His mind was at no loss for a theme of meditation" (8). The book "abounded with allusions to the Bible," and her father procured one. However, Clara goes on, "his constructions of the text were hasty, and formed on a narrow scale. . . . One action and one precept were not employed to illustrate and restrict the meaning of another. Hence arose a thousand scruples to which he had hitherto been a stranger. He was alternately agitated by fear and by ecstacy [sic]" (9). As Clara sees it, her father's too-literal reading of the Bible forms the basis of a religious mania that enslaves him to certain "precepts" and "scruples" with which he is intellectually ill equipped to deal. His rigid devotion eventually ends in his mysterious death. When the Wieland children are still small, their father becomes obsessed by a conviction that there is "a command which had been laid upon him, which he had delayed to perform" (12). There had been given him a time for hesitancy, he tells his wife, but that time had passed, and now "the duty assigned to him was transferred, in consequence of his disobedience, to another." All that remains for him "[is] to endure the penalty" (13). What this penalty is, he can't say, but some days later, alone at midnight while worshiping in a temple he has built for his "Deity," Clara and Theodore's father meets his demise by suddenly and inexplicably bursting into flame.

Given later events in the novel—that is, the younger Wieland's murder of his family at what he believes is God's behest—readers may assume that "the duty assigned" to Wieland's father (now "transferred" to another) is familicide. As with Dana's interpretation of the temptation of Abraham, the elder Wieland construes his loyalty to family as a sign of "disobedience," a sin for which he pays with his life. Such an ostensible error has been read by critics as having its foundation in the external conditions of American life. For example, Axelrod contends that solitary living (the Wielands live far away from church or town) prompts the father and son to a religious fanaticism aimed at filling the void of healthy social intercourse.[41] Similarly, Jane Tompkins asserts that "the disintegration of the Wielands' miniature society is a more or less direct reflection of Federalist skepticism about the efficacy of religion and education in preparing citizens to govern themselves." Countering Jeffersonian optimism in the virtue of the U.S. populace, Tompkins argues, Brockden Brown means to show that too much "independence" would have "horrifying consequences."[42] Yet neither social estrangement nor independent reasoning can account for the elder Wieland's spontaneous combustion, nor for why the younger Wieland suffers the same delusion as his father — why, that is, the "duty assigned" to the latter is "transferred" to the former. Rather than too much independence, the Wielands seem to suffer from the curse of identification — a religious and/or psychological orientation passed between father and son.

According to Clara, a certain morbid constitution of character links the elder Wieland and the younger Wieland. Clara writes of the "thrilling melancholy" that possesses her brother, observing that "I scarcely ever knew him to laugh." She then goes on: "There was an obvious resemblance between him and my father, in their conceptions of the importance of certain topics, and in the light in which the vicissitudes of human life were accustomed to be viewed. Their characters were similar, but the mind of the son was enriched by science, and embellished with literature" (23). Despite the son's intellectual gifts and well-rounded education, however, he falls into the same religious error as his father, leaving readers to wonder about Clara's nicely packaged moral at the beginning of the novel, where she states that her narrative will "exemplify the force of early impressions, and show the immeasurable evils that flow from an erroneous or imperfect discipline" (5). Perhaps the "force" to which Clara refers is the younger Wieland's "early impressions" of his father. In this reading, Wieland, overpowered by his childhood history, falls victim to his father's "melancholy" as well as his father's construction of (dis)obedience. The fact that his "miniature society," as Tompkins terms it — his community of sister, wife, children, and best friend, Henry Pleyel — cannot save him, speaks to the inadequacy of either social intercourse or education to sunder the psychological "resemblance" between father and son.

Wieland, in other words, rejects efforts to find rational reasons for the Wielands' behavior, focusing instead on the familial identifications that reproduce the tragedy. Axelrod's and Tompkins's situating of *Wieland* in its historical, American context is apt in this regard. As Jay Fliegelman has persuasively argued, the parent-child relation symbolized political conflict for Americans in the revolutionary and postrevolutionary eras; in its bid for independence from England, America cast itself as the abused son of a tyrannical father who refused to recognize the son's maturity.[43] In Axelrod's view, the liberation from British tyranny created anxieties about the lack of paternal authority in the new nation; it left a void that religious certitude and a personal relationship to the Deity must fill. I read these anxieties oppositely, arguing that the problem of paternal *presence*, rather than absence, preoccupies Brockden Brown's novel. In a sociopolitical reading, the question that arises is, Having occupied the parent's position, what gross injustices might the Founding Fathers find themselves powerfully enacting? How does one evade the "force of early impressions"? Such questions haunt Brockden Brown's "American Tale," a story in which an overly identified son grows up to enact the brutality his father was commanded, but refused, to perform.

As a metaphor for political fatherhood, Wieland's example is chilling indeed. However, in what I would argue is true American style, *Wieland* does not follow abusive fatherhood through to its conclusion, but displaces and disavows it by locating it in an overly sentimental (even incestuous) attachment to family. Although *Wieland* confronts the problem of blind obedience to authoritarian violence, it accounts for such obedience by framing it as an indication of the protagonist's (or nation's) depth of feeling. Much as Abraham's (and God's) love for his son informs the worthiness of his sacrifice, Wieland's love for his family becomes the basis for their murders. As Clara observes late in the story, "In vain should I endeavour to stay his hand by urging the claims of a sister or a friend: these were his only reasons for pursuing my destruction. Had I been a stranger to his blood; had I been the most worthless of human kind; my safety had not been endangered" (189). The sacrificial object, in other words, is also the love object—an object with which the slayer identifies and whose suffering, as we shall see, the perpetrator makes his own.

Like many gothic novels, *Wieland* examines not only the horrors that lurk in the characters' surroundings but also the horrors within. Brockden Brown pursues these psychological dark spots through a series of contrapositions, or doubles: two different states, objects, or characters whose ostensible opposition to each other break down to reveal thematically charged affinities. This includes Brockden Brown's contrapoints of waking and sleeping states. In *Wieland*, characters move in and out of waking and sleeping states, often without a sense of which is which. Clear perception and somnambulist reverie become muddled, and it is sometimes during their cloudiest moments when the characters' true perceptions are revealed. For example, early on in the novel, Clara describes her domestic situation in idyllic terms. Living in relative seclusion with her brother, her brother's wife, Catharine, and Catharine's brother, Henry Pleyel, Clara notes that "every day added strength to the triple bonds that united us. We gradually withdrew ourselves from the society of others, and found every moment irksome that was not devoted to each other. My brother's advance in age made no change in our situation. . . . His fortune exempted him from the necessity of personal labour" (21). Yet four chapters later Clara experiences the first in a series of premonitions that her brother means to do her harm. Having fallen asleep on a bench, Clara writes that she "at length imagined myself walking, in the evening twilight, to my brother's habitation. A pit, methought, had been dug in the path I had taken, of which I was not aware. As I carelessly pursued my walk, I thought I saw my brother, standing at some distance before me, beckoning and calling me to make haste. He stood on the opposite edge of the gulph. I mended my pace, and one step more would have plunged me into this abyss, had not some one from behind caught suddenly my arm, and exclaimed, in a voice of eagerness and terror, 'Hold! Hold!'" (62). The "abyss" into which Clara almost plunges is all too real. The voice that saves her, readers later discover, belongs to Carwin, a ventriloquist whose ability to manipulate sound may (or may not) be partially responsible for Wieland's hallucinations. Of significance in this scene is both the dream state that associates Wieland, in Clara's mind, with danger *and* Carwin's presence at such a moment. In fact, Wieland and Carwin are themselves doubles in the novel — as loving brother and deceiving stranger, respectively, Wieland and Carwin come together to manifest the potential, crucially, for lovers and destroyers to mirror one another. Soon after this incident Clara is again falling asleep when she intuits that there is someone hiding in her closet: "Who was it whose suffocating grasp I was to feel, should I dare enter [the closet]?" she asks herself. "What monstrous conception is this? My brother!" (87). In reality, the person is Carwin, who has hidden in her bedroom, he tells her, in an attempt to catch her defenseless and rape her.[44]

Clara's mistaking Wieland for Carwin speaks to her unconscious sense of the danger her brother poses. As critics have noted, that danger is not only mortal but sexual in nature. Writing of Clara's sleepwalking toward the "abyss," David Brion Davis concludes that "this dream suggested that Carwin [the someone who apprehended her] had saved Clara from an incestuous relation with her brother," an idea supported by the fact that Wieland is on his way to Clara's house when he hears God's voice and, being told to kill his wife, murders Catharine in *Clara's bed*.[45] Clara herself declares that Wieland "was wont to love [me] with a passion more than fraternal" (185), while Wieland announces to Clara that "there is no human being whom I love with more tenderness" (109). Read in this light, Clara's dream of Wieland "luring her into a gulph" suggests a seduction that threatens to obliterate, or engulf, Clara's individual identity.

Clara's dream makes explicit the psychological violence inhering in Wieland's "more than fraternal" passion for his sister — an identification with the love object that always involves, as Diana Fuss puts it, "a measure of temporary mastery and possession." "Identification operates on one level as an endless process of violent negation," writes Fuss, "a process of killing off the other in fantasy in order to usurp the other's place, the place where the subject desires to be."[46] In order to possess the other completely, in other words, the subject "kills off" the beloved and internalizes him/her through identification, rendering the love object a part of the subject's internal fantasy. In *Wieland*, the desire to possess and to be the other is *externalized* through the "killing off" of familicide. Through literal murder, Wieland symbolically internalizes the father (and the father's religious delusion), as well as "mastering" and "possessing" the other members of his family, Clara included. As a nonsexual but sexualized part of Wieland's family, Clara represents (and as narrator, articulates) the psychoanalytic concept of identification as one in which possession and (symbolic) murder of the love object is always already entwined.[47] As Clara herself succinctly puts it, "I was hunted to death . . . by one . . . whose implacability was proportioned to the reverence and love he felt for me" (189).

Although Wieland's rhetoric of familial "tenderness" works to obscure the connection between violence and love, it is everywhere manifest in Brockden Brown's tale. Upon finding Catharine's dead body in her bedroom, Clara laments, "I was the object of [the murderer's] fury; but by some tremendous mistake, his fury was misplaced" (151). In fact, it is Clara who is mistaken. Objects of "fury" and desire are rendered inextricable in *Wieland*, as are the expressions of aggression and affection. This is apparent not only in Wieland's ambivalent "passion" for Clara but in his best friend Pleyel's manifestation of his "love" for her. Though Pleyel has previously worshiped Clara as the feminine ideal, the "certainty" (although he is wrong) that she has engaged in illicit acts with Carwin transforms her into the object of his rage; he verbally attacks her and she faints. His only justification for the sudden "phrenzy" of his emotion, he says, is his devotion to her: "Should I see you rushing to the verge of a dizzy precipice, and not stretch forth a hand to pull you back?" (129). His metaphor recalls the very service that Carwin, Clara's would-be ravisher, had earlier performed for Clara. As we discover in the next chapter, while Pleyel is warning Clara of God's willingness to "exterminate" her for her (alleged) promiscuity, Wieland is at Clara's house, murdering his wife (118).

As these examples illustrate, masculine aggression (including God's) occupies a central role in *Wieland*, yet that aggression is consistently represented as rooted in feelings of "love," "tenderness," and "passion." Perhaps most noteworthy in Brockden Brown's construction of familicide is the way in which it portrays familial ties as a site for possessive identifications that render aggressive acts indistinguishable from loving ones. Framing this paradox is a theological paradigm — the story of Abraham and Isaac — whose model makes legible the logic inhering in both sacrifice *and* identification: the murdered object is the love object. It is precisely the latter status, after all, that confirms the victim's worthiness to be killed. Thus, on the night of the murders, Wieland reports in his testimony, he is praying to his Heavenly Father that he might have "knowledge of [God's] will" (165) when his thoughts recur to his family — to that "parental and conjugal love" that knows no limits and for which his heart "overflows with gratification" (166). "The author of my being was likewise the dispenser of every gift with which that being was embellished," Wieland continues. "The service to which a benefactor like this was entitled, could not be circumscribed.... All passions are base, all joys feeble, all energies malignant, which are not drawn from [God]" (166). We know what Wieland hears in answer to his supplicating meditations: God demands that all of Wieland's earthly "passions," "joys," and "energies" be relinquished as a testament to his love for God. Wieland complies, and, after first murdering his wife, he goes home and slaughters all of his children.

Implicit in Wieland's acquiescence is his conception of God as fully justified in demanding back what He has given: that is, what the Father creates, the Father may destroy. In Wieland's murder of his family we see his identification, not only with his victims but with God — a consummation of the F/father's "mastery and possession" that makes manifest his loved ones' status as objects, or creations, to be disposed of as Wieland wishes. Although Wieland at first pleads with God to spare Catharine's "precious life, or commission some other than her husband to perform the bloody deed" (168), after the deed is accomplished Wieland refers to it as "a moment of triumph." "Thus had I successfully subdued the stubbornness of human passions: the victim which had been demanded was given: the deed was done past recal [sic]" (172). So successful, in fact, is Wieland in subduing "the stubbornness of human passions" that after the murder Catharine becomes virtually unrecognizable to him: "I asked myself who it was whom I saw? Methought it could not be Catharine.... Where was her bloom! These deadly and blood-suffused orbs but ill resemble the azure and exstatic [sic] tenderness of her eyes" (173). Likewise in his murder of his attractive young ward, Louisa Conway, Clara is horrified to report that "*not a lineament [of her face] remained*" (157).

Wieland's love for his family precipitates a "sacrifice" that puts him on a par with God, a transcendent moment in which his identificatory objects are revealed as exactly that: not subjects, but objects of the father-murderer's own internal fantasy, with all traces of their own identities obliterated. But in keeping with the familicide narrative as a story of the father's identification with those he kills, Wieland's delusion immediately reveals itself as a fantasy of *self*-objectification as well. It is not Wieland's will or desire that has been fulfilled, according to Wieland, but God's. Wieland himself is but an object, or vehicle, through which God does his divine work. Addressing himself directly to God during his trial, Wieland asserts, "Thou, Omnipotent and Holy! Thou knowest that my actions were conformable to thy will. I know not what is crime; what actions are evil in their ultimate and comprehensive tendency or what are good. Thy knowledge, as thy power, is unlimited. I have taken thee for my guide, and cannot err. To the arms of thy protection, I entrust my safety. In the awards of thy justice, I confide for my recompense" (176). Wieland's responsibility for his acts — his self-aggrandizing display of power over life and death — is disavowed in his claim not to know what actions are "evil" and "what are good." Absolute morality is God's domain, suggests Wieland, and all earthly beings (including Wieland himself) are simply objects for God to use as He sees fit.

Brocken Brown's protagonist, in other words, does not simply render his family members objects in his identification with them, but he identifies with them *as* object, and eventual victim, of the Father's overriding will. It is as God's chosen one that Wieland stages his final attack and completes his apotheosis into suffering victim-son. Having escaped from prison, Wieland hurries to Clara's house to complete God's plan by murdering his sister. He finds Clara there with Carwin. "Poor girl!" he tells Clara; "a dismal fate has set its mark upon thee. Thy life is demanded as a sacrifice" (218). However, Carwin has just been confessing to Clara his past trickeries, including his feigning of her voice to deceive Pleyel into thinking she was Carwin's lover. Now convinced that Carwin is responsible for the disembodied voice Wieland has been hearing, she beseeches Wieland: "O brother! spare me, spare thyself: There is thy betrayer. He counterfeited the voice and face of an angel, for the purpose of destroying thee and me" (218). When Carwin concedes that indeed he is "able to speak where he is not" (but denies imitating an angel), Wieland becomes dejected and orders Carwin to leave the premises (218). What follows is as incredible as it is perplexing. After offering a number of mute appeals to heaven, Wieland responds to Clara with the chilling announcement that "indeed [he] was deceived," but though "this minister is evil . . . he from whom his commission was received is God. Submit then with all thy wonted resignation to a decree that cannot be reversed or resisted. Mark the clock. Three minutes are allowed to thee, in which to call up thy fortitude, and prepare thee for thy doom" (225–26).

According to Wieland, there was an answer to his prayer, although unheard by Clara; God apparently spoke to Wieland and confirmed that his actions were divinely inspired (225). Though God did not speak directly to Wieland at Clara's house, he sent an emissary, a "minister of evil," to carry out His plan. "As the performer of thy behests," Wieland gratefully remarks to God, "[Carwin] is my friend" (225). In a thematic consummation of the doubling evident throughout Brockden Brown's novel, God and Satan here mirror one another: colluding with evil, God makes a mockery of men's senses, allowing humankind to hear voices that may or

The Suffering Father (47)

may not be real but whose results achieve the same disastrous end. As if to underscore this point, Brockden Brown has that ostensible "minister of evil," Carwin, return to Clara's house and—finding her in the predicament just described—use his ventriloquist skills to (un)deceive the would-be murderer. Hiding behind a door, Carwin throws his voice and commands Wieland "to *hold!*" (229). Clara narrates what happens next (230):

> Silence took place for a moment; so much as allowed the attention to recover its post. Then new sounds were uttered from above.
>
> "Man of errors! cease to cherish thy delusion: not heaven or hell, but thy senses have misled thee to commit these acts. Shake off thy phrenzy, and ascend into rational and human. Be lunatic no longer."
>
> My brother opened his lips to speak. His tone was terrific and faint. He muttered an appeal to heaven. It was not difficult to comprehend the theme of his inquiries. They implied doubt as to the nature of the impulse that hitherto had guided him, and questioned whether he had acted in consequence of insane perceptions.
>
> To these interrogatories the voice, which now seemed to hover at his shoulder, loudly answered in the affirmative. Then uninterrupted silence ensued.

Now convinced that he was deluded, Wieland falls, Clara writes, "from his lofty and heroic station" and, "weighed to earth by the recollection of his own deeds" and "consoled no longer by a consciousness of rectitude," is "transformed at once into the *man of sorrows* . . . a monument of woe" (230–31). Taking a pen knife, Wieland stabs it into his own neck and dies instantly.

Wieland's "transformation" is not, as one might imagine, his transition from man into monster, but from man into myth, and a particular one at that. Having all along represented himself as submissive to the demands of his heavenly Father, Wieland becomes in his sister's rendition the embodiment of the perfect son—the "*man of sorrows*," or Jesus Christ. Clara's comparison of Wieland to

Christ makes clear Wieland's ultimate identification with victimhood; in her eyes, Wieland stands as a "monument" not "of [God's] eternal vengeance," as Marsh describes the forsaken, but of martyred woe. It is a transformation that epitomizes the trajectory of many American familicide narratives: although Wieland is responsible for the "loss of offspring and wife" (230), which he now finds unbearable, their pain, as their sacrifice, is subsumed in his own. In an ironic (and perverse) reversal of Christ's sacrifice, Wieland suffers as one with, as well as for, those loved ones he killed.

"That virtue should become the victim of treachery is, no doubt, a mournful consideration," writes Clara in the final paragraph of the novel, "but it will not escape your notice, that the evils of which [others] were the authors, owed their existence to the errors of the sufferers" (244). Tellingly, Clara includes Wieland in the group of sufferers rather than authors of evil. Wieland's earlier declaration that "[he] know[s] not what is crime" suggests his ready-made complicity in Clara's views. Moreover, his moral confusion returns us to the spiritual and psychological dilemma informing familicide narratives in general and Brockden Brown's novel in particular. Whether Wieland's actions are prompted by "the devil, the lust of [his] own heart," in Dana's words, or whether the true crime would lie in "confering [*sic*] with flesh and blood" and not kill his family is a question left unanswered by the novel. After all, Carwin is nowhere in sight (or sound) when Wieland hears the voice commanding him to murder Clara, suggesting either a supernatural or a psychological origin for his beliefs. And in the end, it is Carwin's voice, not God's, that Wieland hears telling him to "shake off [his] phrenzy"—the voice, that is, of a "deceiver" who may or may not have revealed Wieland's actions as the result of an earthly, rather than divine, fantasy of identification.

Like Barton's reading of his own situation as a cursed familial legacy handed down from father to son, *Wieland* ultimately frames its protagonist as always already powerless to evade the dictates of paternal inheritance. Wieland's actions as a father are ultimately obscured by his suffering as a son, specifically a son of God. In contrast to God the Father's omnipotence, Wieland the son is transformed into a figure of virtual powerlessness. Mitigating anxieties about the potential for coercive fatherhood, Brockden Brown's novel represents the younger Wieland as a perpetual minor — a character whose sociopolitical privilege and power are subordinated to, and mystified by, his impotence in the face of not only paternal "melancholy" but Paternal authority as well. In this respect, Brockden Brown's novel is a particularly "American Tale": in *Wieland*, as in the works that follow, Christian mythology becomes the lens through which writers most artfully, and sometimes skeptically, investigate U.S. culture's investment in vicarious suffering as a personally, and nationally, salvific experience. As we will see, Wieland's identification with victimhood lays the sentimental groundwork for a succeeding generation of literary narratives in which empathy becomes itself a source of pain and powerlessness for the protagonist — a way in which privileged men suffer, and are saved, through their identification with the things they harm.

CHAPTER 2

Melville's Fraternal *Melancholies*

That mortal man who hath more of joy than sorrow in him, that mortal man cannot be true—not true, or undeveloped. With books the same. The truest of all men was the Man of Sorrows, and the truest of all books is Solomon's, and Ecclesiastes is the fine hammered steel of woe.
—Herman Melville, Moby-Dick

Melancholy . . . is the character of mortality.
— Thomas Burton, Anatomy of Melancholy

In his 1850 novel *White-Jacket, or The World in a Man-Of-War*, Herman Melville pursues a theme recurrent throughout his fiction: that of the suffering of politically, socially, and emotionally vulnerable white men. In *White-Jacket*, this idea is specifically located in what Melville views as the degrading effects of naval flogging on the common sailor. Although acknowledging the necessity of a code of government at sea "more stringent than the law that governs the land," Melville's eponymous narrator nevertheless contends that "that code should conform to the spirit of the political institutions of the country that ordains it. It should not convert into slaves some of the citizens of a nation of freemen."[1] The terms of "slavery" are this: that "for the most trivial alleged offences, of which [the sailor] may be entirely innocent," he must "without trial, undergo a penalty the traces whereof he carries to the grave; for to a man-of-war's-man's experienced eye the marks of a naval scourging with the 'cat' are through life discernible" (141–42). Without benefit of due process, in other words, where guilt and innocence might be fairly and objectively determined, otherwise free men are liable to beatings that forever mark them as "slaves"—they lose sense of themselves as "men." The idea that sailors in a like situation will always be able to discern such scars—"the man-of-war's-man's experienced eye"—links the condition of slavery to the identifications it produces between oppressed men. "To the sensitive seaman," writes White-Jacket, the summons to witness another man's punishment "sounds like a doom. He knows that the same law which impels it... by that very law he also is liable at anytime to be judged and condemned" (135). Even if the sailor does not himself carry "these marks on his back" with which the beaten "must rise on the Last Day," he is able to perceive the traces of them on others. He knows from his own experience what they are, and, through empathy, how they feel.

The troubling irony of Melville's eloquent and thorough critique of lawful beatings on board ship arises when one considers Melville's private history in the years that follow the writing of *White-Jacket*. As biographical material on the Melville family history has brought to light, Herman Melville himself was an abusive husband and father, "periodically violent to his wife" between 1851 and 1856, and prompting friends and family of his wife, Elizabeth, to propose a feigned kidnapping in 1867 in order to remove her from the house.[2] Described by Edwin S. Shneidman as a "rejecting father" who "battered his ... children psychologically," Melville appears in oral and documented family annals as a tortured man. His authorial desire to "strike through the mask," in the famous line from *Moby-Dick*, of epistemological uncertainty, was, as Elizabeth Renker has argued, consistently frustrated in his own mind by the women and children of the house, whose presence hindered his professional and artistic endeavors.[3]

Biographers seem to agree that in the years before Melville went to sea in 1839, years when he lived with his mother and sisters, and in the years after his marriage in 1847 the Melville household could be characterized, as Leon Howard puts it, as one "adjusted to an entirely feminine regime."[4] Although Renker notes that Melville relied on, and in some cases forced, his wife, sister, and daughters to copy his manuscripts and read out proofs, that dependence, she claims, also produced extreme resentment, the combination of which "constitutes the secret 'madness & anguish' of his writing."[5] The practical impediments to Melville's writing—the needs and noises of children, the financial and emotional claims of a life partner—produce frustrations analogous to Melville's battles with his writing, so that women and paper come to represent concrete signs of Melville's desire, but inability, to penetrate material reality by "striking through" the surface of bodies and texts and discovering a "satisfactory relation" between himself and the world.[6]

My intention here is not to rehearse the evidence of Melville's physical and psychological abuse of his family (material impressively assembled and lucidly presented by Renker), nor to label Melville a hypocrite in his call for naval reforms in *White-Jacket*. Rather, my aim is to situate Melville's battles with anger within a larger framework of his idea that sensitive men are made "true," if troubled, by their identification with sorrow (of which Christ, "the Man of Sorrows," is the quintessential representative). Melville's sorrow, in fact, informs much of the biographical work on him. In Henry A. Murray's unpublished biography of Melville, for example, Murray identifies Melville's "disastrous" marriage as "the incommunicable grief, the ever-gnawing pain that he, apostle of chivalry, could never confess to anyone."[7] Hershel Parker, the foremost Melville scholar and biographer, explains Melville's domestic violence as a possible consequence of Melville's suffering critical rejection and subsequent financial insolvency. Melville's attempts to then write himself out from under his debts resulted in a physical collapse that left him, according to Elizabeth Melville's memoir, "helpless."[8] Lewis Mumford likewise links Melville's treatment of his wife to professional disappointment—specifically, the savage responses to his work in the wake of his 1852 novel, *Pierre*: "When harassed by external circumstances, one wants to attack the universe: but, like Ahab, one finds that the universe will not get in one's way: so one takes revenge on the first creature that crosses one's path. Too likely it will be a creature one holds dear: the animus is not directed against that one, but it strikes as if it were. An explosion: a blow: a raised hand: an uncontrollable outburst of vituperation — then drink, remorse, repentance, the ugly vanity of it all."[9]

The displacement of rage onto those he "holds dear" in these theories represents Melville's wife, Elizabeth, as a substitute for the things (blank page, negative reviews, lack of money) that leave the author feeling "helpless." Yet if Elizabeth is a whipping boy of sorts for those things against which Melville would like to strike, she is also arguably a figure with which he identifies. Melville's recurrent association in his fiction of witnessing abuse as itself a source of pain (the "experienced eye" that sees and, through identification, feels) positions him in this nonfictional scenario as one punished by the abuse he inflicts. The "remorse and repentance" that Mumford attributes to Melville in the wake of his outbursts suggests his powerlessness in the face of forces (including his own rage and resentment) he cannot control. This is consistent with Melville's idea in *White-Jacket* and in "Bartleby" (1853) that "sensitive" men suffer most. Although domestic violence is often linked in the popular imagination to the perceived insensibility of working-class men, it cuts across class lines, linked as it is to the gender expectations — male control and female submissiveness — that structure middle- and upper-class as well as lower-class heterosexual relations. Melville, a man who lived an upper-middle-class life beyond his means, may have found the dual roles of provider and artist untenable, the latter calling on sensibilities that worked against him when he felt he failed at the former.

If, as critics contend, Melville struggled with the "feminine regime" of his domestic circumstances, he seems to have found some emotional release and redemption in his bonds with other men. Thus we find Melville, in the oft-quoted passage from "Hawthorne and His Mosses," declaring that reading the work of his idol and mentor "has dropped germinous seeds into my soul. [Hawthorne] expands and deeps down, the more I contemplate him; and further, and further, shoots his strong New-England roots into the hot soil of my Southern soul."[10] He expresses a similar sentiment after having received a complimentary letter from Hawthorne about *Moby-Dick*: "I can't write what I felt," Melville responds in his return letter; "your heart beat in my ribs and mine in yours, and both in God's. A sense of unspeakable security is in me this moment, on account of your having understood the book.... Whence come you, Hawthorne? By what right do you drink from my flagon of life? And when I put it to my lips—lo, they are yours and not mine. I feel that the Godhead is broken up like the bread at the Supper, and we are the pieces. Hence this infinite fraternity of feeling."[11] In contrast to the troubling dynamic of dependence and resentment, desire for control and the manifest lack of it, in his relation to women, Melville represents Hawthorne as part of a holy Trinity signifying complete sympathy: "Your heart beat in my ribs and mine in yours, and both in God's." Yet the sympathetic unity alluded to in Melville's metaphor of the "Godhead" is necessarily qualified by its earthly incarnation as fragmented identity: "Broken up like the bread at the Supper" suggests the violence both engendered by, and potentially redeemed through, identification. Because men live as separate beings, or "pieces," implies Melville, their sympathetic relation is somewhat miraculous; it points to a heavenly world in which one's own and another's "hearts" and "lips" feel the same.

The potential for man's restoration to wholeness through empathy is a theme Melville pursues throughout much of his work. Identification's joys *and* sorrows are encapsulated in what his narrator in "Bartleby" refers to as "fraternal melancholy." Poignantly complementing Melville's "infinite fraternity of feeling," fraternal melancholy represents a man's experience of common brotherhood as essentially located in, and *dependent upon*, shared suffering. Though suffering is linked to oppression in Melville's works (physical and psychological "beatings"), it is ultimately synonymous with loss—most often the loss of one's sense of oneself as a man. Ironically, what binds men in a common humanity, Melville suggests, is their mutual estrangement, from themselves and from each other. Handled with irony in "Bartleby" and pathos in *White-Jacket*, Melville offers his readers a view into the emotional cost of fraternal feeling: the painful experience of identifying with other men whose helplessness and suffering mirror and exacerbate the protagonist's own. In his analogy between sailors and slaves with which I opened this chapter, Melville provides a metaphor for the oftentimes punishing effects of identifications between men, effects that render the sensitive man — both privileged lawyer and common sailor alike — a virtual "slave" to his empathetic feelings.

THE COST OF CONNECTION

Perhaps reflecting on a literary career that had failed to find a sympathetic audience, Herman Melville concludes his short story "Bartleby" with an anecdote about literal mis-communication — a rumor the story's narrator has heard that Bartleby was previously employed in the Dead Letter Office in Washington, D.C. The story proper has followed the downward trajectory of an alienated young man, Bartleby, who, after coming to work as a law-copyist or "scrivener" for the narrator, gives up all engagement with life and starves himself to death in a debtor's prison. The narrator's final words comprise a rueful meditation on the aborted communication symbolized both by dead letters and by Bartleby himself: "Pardon for those who died despairing; hope for those who died unhoping; good tidings for those who died stifled by unrelieved calamities. On errands of life, these letters speed to death. Ah, Bartleby! Ah, humanity!"[12] By linking Bartleby's fate to the fate of humanity, Melville's narrator casts the "incurably forlorn" scrivener as a kind of Everyman figure; the alienation represented by dead letters is thus ironically juxtaposed with the narrator's implication of humanity's *shared* isolation. The paradox of mutual estrangement is echoed in the narrator's previous attempts to place himself in some relation to this man, to identify with and thereby help him. After all, "both I and Bartleby were sons of Adam," muses the narrator. But that "bond of common humanity," he confesses, "drew me irresistibly to gloom. A fraternal melancholy!" (17). Identifying with Bartleby drives home for the narrator his own "forlorn" position, with the result that he finds his "melancholy merge into fear" and his "pity into repulsion." Yet such antipathy is to be expected from a sympathetic man, claims the narrator without irony, for "to a sensitive being, pity is not seldom pain. And when at last it is perceived that such pity cannot lead to effectual succor, common sense bids the soul be rid of it" (19–20).

In the last few years, scholars of American literature, myself included, have employed the theories of the sympathetic imagination of eighteenth-century moral philosopher and economist Adam Smith to argue for the power of sympathy, or what we today would call empathy, as a culturally unifying or homogenizing force in nineteenth-century literature. In *Theory of Moral Sentiments*, Smith posits "sympathy" or "fellow-feeling" as one of the foundations for society, binding individuals together into an empathetic whole. Sentimental literature, I argued, worked to a similar purpose in young America by evoking predictable empathetic responses from reader-citizens that then unified them in their thoughts and sentiments. I would like to take a different tack in this chapter to investigate a path as yet largely unexplored with regard to "fellow-feeling" — that is, how one imagines the cost of human connection and what specifically that cost might be to men in their identifications with other men. Our notions of the sentimental have heretofore presupposed a world in which feeling is in infinite supply. As a closer reading of Smith suggests, however, feelings are exhaustible as well as provisional; it is the limit to sympathy that makes sympathy possible. Smith's *Theory* predates his better-known economic treatise *Wealth of Nations* by four years, but even in his earlier work we see an emphasis on the need for an *economy* of sympathy: "To what purpose should we trouble ourselves about the world in the moon? . . . That we should be little interested . . . in the fortune of those whom we can neither serve nor hurt, seems wisely ordered by Nature; and if it were possible to alter in this respect the original constitution of our frame, we could yet gain nothing by the change."[13] Emotional investments, in short, should pay off. Melville's narrator at first surmises that in helping Bartleby he will be making a shrewd investment, but he eventually discovers that the price of sympathy, in this case, is too high. Bartleby's "unaccountable" behavior, says the narrator, has both "disarmed" and "unmanned" him (16). Though united in melancholy, the narrator experiences his identification with Bartleby as self-alienating; it represents a sorrowful confrontation with mankind's condition as "pieces" of the Godhead, as Melville puts it in his letter to Hawthorne, "broken up like the bread at the Supper."

"Bartleby," however, is not simply a story of failed sympathy. After all, it is not the narrator's insensitivity to his employee that leads to his rejection of Bartleby, but rather the lawyer's potential for *too much* feeling. In this regard, Melville's story participates in antebellum America's view of fellow-feeling as double-edged: for a man's emotions to be productive, he must learn to invest them judiciously, lest he expend them on an object whose helplessness drives the witness to a morbid, fraternal melancholy — an identification with suffering that paradoxically alienates and/or emasculates the witness to it. Subtitled "A Story of Wall-Street," Melville's story brings together two competing emotional paradigms, one located in the giving of self that characterizes Christian charity and the other in the idea of self-interested exchange represented by capitalism. The narrator's attempts to reconcile these paradigms and thereby alleviate or ameliorate the conditions of Bartleby's ailment provide one of the central psychological tensions of the story. Ultimately, Christian charity fails to pay off when Bartleby's resistance to his ministrations leaves the narrator himself feeling "unmanned." Bartleby's recalcitrance — his refusal to play by the rules of exchange — undermines the careful management of emotion that typifies the narrator's preferred way of life and the business model that informs it.

Melville's unnamed narrator is a practical, money-minded man who confesses to his readers at the outset of the story his belief that "the easiest way of life is best" (4). "Bartleby," with its commercial setting, contributes to the lawyer-narrator's self-characterization as someone habitually and/or constitutionally prone to self-protection. "One end [of my chambers] looked upon the white wall of the interior of a spacious sky-light shaft," the narrator tells us. "In [another] direction my windows commanded an unobstructed view of a lofty brick wall, black by age and an everlasting shade" (5). That the narrator finds "lurking beauties" in the sides of buildings pressed up against him is not surprising; several paragraphs earlier he has announced that all those who know him consider him "an eminently *safe* man," a dramatically ironic confession of the narrator's equation of emotional complacency with physical enclosure and monetary holdings (4). For the lawyer, both money and emotions are to be held in reserve, kept (in a) "safe." Though the narrator finds himself in a profession "proverbially energetic and nervous, even to turbulence, at times," he manages his life in such a way as to avoid letting anything or anyone suffer "to invade [his] peace" (4). That peace is psychologically tied not only to his fortresslike surroundings, but to what the narrator describes as his "pleasantly remunerative" position as Master in Chancery, a position which keeps him "*snug* . . . among rich men's bonds and mortgages and title-deeds" (4) (emphasis mine).

Both literally and figuratively, money operates for the narrator as a protection against the vicissitudes of life, including the unfathomable and unpredictable relations between human beings. At the outset of the story, the narrator finds Bartleby a perfect complement to his own sensibilities. In the "motionless" Bartleby, "so pallidly neat, pitiably respectable, incurably forlorn" (9), the narrator seems to discover a soul kindred to his own. Bartleby evinces none of the tumultuous passions of the narrator's other employees, Nippers and Turkey. On the contrary, Bartleby at first seems to work without ceasing, "copying by sun-light and by candle-light . . . silently, paley, mechanically" (10). The narrator places Bartleby close by his own desk, behind a "high green folding screen" that "isolates" him from sight but keeps him within easy call: "And thus, in a manner, privacy and society were conjoined" (10). This "satisfactory arrangement," however, is disrupted one day when Bartleby refuses to examine a document at the narrator's request with the now-infamous line, "I would prefer not to." As time goes by, Bartleby refuses to copy documents as well as proofread them and spends his time behind his screen in a "dead-wall reverie." Even so, the narrator is reluctant to fire him. He determines instead that Bartleby's otherwise placid and predictable behavior ("his steadiness, his freedom from all dissipation, his incessant industry") makes him a "valuable acquisition" (15). The narrator's association of comfort and safety with those things that neither vary nor fluctuate seems embodied in Bartleby, whose "unalterableness of demeanor" translates, for the narrator, into a spiritual and financial value (15).

As critics have noted, in terming Bartleby a "valuable acquisition," the narrator unconsciously alludes to the reification of personhood outlined in Marx's theory of alienated labor, where workers correlate to the things they produce.[14] As I will argue, however, Melville depicts the typical nineteenth-century solution to the plight of the oppressed — empathetic identification — as itself potentially alienating. In "Bartleby," empathy's success in harmonizing socially disparate individuals is undermined in part by the capitalist model that structures it, a model in which the "other," namely Bartleby, becomes an object for the narrator's self-gain. Faced with an insubordinate employee who, little by little, withdraws from doing his job, for example, the lawyer finds himself drawing on the principles of Christian charity, or "love." At the same time, he attempts to align charity with those business principles upon which he maintained his "easy" way of life: "[Bartleby] is useful to me," rationalizes the narrator when he initially finds Bartleby unwilling to complete a task. "I can get along with him. If I turn him away, the chances are he will fall in with some less indulgent employer, and then he will be rudely treated, and perhaps driven forth miserably to starve. Yes. Here I can cheaply purchase a delicious self-approval. To befriend Bartleby; to humor him in his strange willfulness, will cost me little or nothing, while I lay up in my soul what will eventually prove a sweet morsel for my conscience" (13–14). For the narrator, indulgence toward Bartleby is like money in the bank. What one gives of oneself tangibly, in the act of charity, or emotionally, in the act of sympathy, is never truly given *away* but becomes part of a human transaction where good deeds and good feelings prove potentially profitable investments, to be drawn upon at a future time when the spiritual occasion arises.

The idea that the narrator will himself gain something from a loving disposition toward Bartleby is evidenced again later in the story, when Bartleby has increased his resistance and the narrator finds his own temper rising (25):

But when this old Adam of resentment rose in me and tempted me concerning Bartleby, I grappled him and threw him. How? Why, simply by recalling the divine injunction: 'A new commandment give I unto you, that ye love one another.' Yes, this it was that saved me. Aside from higher considerations, charity often operates as a vastly wise and prudent principle—a great safeguard to its possessor. Men have committed murder for jealousy's sake, and anger's sake, and hatred's sake . . . but no man that ever I heard of, ever committed a diabolical murder for sweet charity's sake. Mere self-interest, then, if no better motive can be enlisted, should, especially with high-tempered men, prompt all beings to charity and philanthropy.

The "new" commandment to which the narrator refers is meant to replace, historically and ideologically, an Old Law: an eye for an eye. "Resentment" about what Bartleby owes him is to be supplanted by a new duty to give "love"; but the new paradigm is obscured by the narrator's expedient translation of giving into a form of self-centered exchange. We see this not only in his equation of philanthropy with self-interest but also in his unconsciously ironic declaration, "Yes, this it was that saved me." Christ's assumed intention for the new commandment—it is one's duty to save others through love—becomes for the narrator the means of his *own* salvation.

Of course, Melville is twisting Christian ideals here for the sake of showing the perversity of wedding them to a capitalist logic, where all forms of self-interest are made to appear as a universal good: that is, the capitalist's financial gain is a vehicle to bettering *every* person's condition. In Melville's hands, "loving one's neighbor as oneself"—the Golden Rule to which the narrator's charitable thoughts allude—leads to its obverse: loving, or "saving," oneself through one's neighbor. Melville's use of Christian scripture to determine the use-value of sympathy is not simply ironic, however, but representative. It reflects U.S. culture's preoccupation with charity and benevolence as a means of personal and national prosperity and salvation. As Susan Ryan has argued, "In the mid-nineteenth century, *benevolence* was what Raymond Williams has called a 'keyword,' a term that defies brief or singular definition, engaging instead a complex field of 'ideas and values.'"[15] Ryan herself conceives of it as a "contested paradigm," producing a broad range of discourses that often opposed each other: "Contributors to antislavery newspapers mocked the benevolent claims of slaveholders; ministers, in their printed sermons, exhorted readers to accept certain definitions of benevolence over others; charity society officers used their annual reports to assert proper means of expressing benevolence and to warn against those means they deemed dangerous; and novelists created fictions in which the values of charity were realized, betrayed, or reconceived."[16] Although *who* should receive charity and under what conditions was fiercely debated, it was generally acknowledged that benevolence was a concept integral to U.S. national and cultural identity. "We know there is an eternal, indissoluble connection . . . between national virtue and national prosperity," George B. Cheever wrote in 1830, "as there is a connection, equally indissoluble, and terribly certain, between national crime and national misery."[17]

The connection between virtue and prosperity is virtually axiomatic among Christian treatises in the mid-nineteenth century. S. D. Clark's *The Faithful Steward* (1850), to cite just one example, asserts three main principles of charitable giving: that God requires that men imitate Him in a uniform and unceasing benevolence; that men are naturally selfish and so struggle with this demand; and that the demand be met by applying one's principles of getting rich to one's charitable giving. Charitable giving should "evince the same principle," writes Clark, as the principle by which "practical men" successfully "acquire property" — that is, their giving should be methodical, habitual, and disciplined. Though benevolence is a key aspect of the American Christian character, one must apply it wisely — with the habit, but also the scrutiny, with which one invests in material property. But in the end, Clark assures his readers, the giving will pay off: "What amazing consequences are depending on your present determination! It will affect your usefulness here, and your relations in eternity!"[18] In other words, what you sow (or give away) in this life, you will reap in greater rewards later on.

Publications like Clark's offer both a context for Melville's narrator and an explanation for his failure. The narrator's attempts to find common ground between himself and Bartleby—ground on which he can empathize with Bartleby and thus "save" them both—are frustrated by their apparent lack of like-mindedness. Yet in making self-love a basis for empathy, the narrator exposes his woeful misunderstanding of charity. To be Christlike, writes Clark, "the ardor of man's love may never cool; his hand of charity never weary."[19] Charity, which has come to mean the giving of money but which comes from the Latin "caritas," or love, is, according to Clark, financially and emotionally boundless and boundary-less. It exceeds on principle all personal or practical limits. Its application to an economic model in which one balances what one gives with what one gets thus presents an irreconcilable contradiction. After all, according to this model, one could argue that the best way to remain a philanthropic person in the future is to resist giving now.

And this is precisely the conclusion the narrator comes to. Although he says that his first emotions regarding Bartleby had been those "of pure melancholy and sincerest pity," those feelings, he confesses, have changed: "Just in proportion as the forlornness of Bartleby grew and grew to my imagination, did that same melancholy merge into fear, that pity into repulsion. So true it is, and so terrible, too, that up to a certain point the thought or sight of misery enlists our best affections; but, in certain special cases, beyond that point it does not. . . . To a sensitive being, pity is not seldom pain. And when at last it is perceived that such pity cannot lead to effectual succor, common sense bids the soul be rid of it." The narrator's appeal to "common sense" not only alludes to the necessity of rational judgment in matters of the heart but also to the heart's rejection of a pain that it cannot alleviate but only identify with. It is the narrator's very sensitivity, he declares, that inspires his repulsion. With characteristic irony, Melville suggests that what is common about our "common sense" is not mutual suffering nor universal benevolence but a common rejection of pain by any sensitive person when he discovers that it can do neither the giver nor the receiver any good.

Bartleby functions in the story as a vehicle through which the narrator gains a sense of himself as a charitable man. This includes, paradoxically, the point at which the narrator finds empathy too emotionally costly and attempts to rid himself of his fellow-feeling. No longer persuaded that empathizing with Bartleby will prove beneficial to himself, the narrator instead embraces "repulsion" as proof his own overly developed sensibility. Yet, as Melville represents it, this kind of psychological beating is itself evidence of the "bond of common humanity." The narrator's rhetorical assurance that it is not "selfishness" but "*hopelessness*" that actuates his refusal to pity Bartleby unconsciously signals their mutual "forlornness." Even in his declaration of the limits of compassion, that is, the lawyer makes clear his identification with Bartleby. It is an identification that *reproduces*, rather than remedies, the other's pain. Why this is so is answered in part by Melville's suggestion that identification is founded on projection. In this, he follows Adam Smith's observation that "we have no immediate experience of what other men feel . . . but by conceiving what we ourselves should feel in the like situation. . . . [Our senses] never did, and never can, carry us beyond our own person, and it is by the imagination only that we can form any conception of what are [another's] sensations."[20] Like Smith, Melville depicts empathetic identification as always already a drama of the self. Unable to carry him "beyond [his] own person," the lawyer's identification reinforces, even as it seeks to transcend, his individual, "forlorn" identity.

The potentially alienating effects of identification are underscored by Melville's representation of Bartleby as an enigma or blank slate: Bartleby consistently refuses to accept what the narrator offers or to give back to the narrator some correspondent show of feeling. The narrator himself has stated at the beginning of the story that "no materials exist for a full and satisfactory biography of this man" of whom "nothing is ascertainable, except from the original sources, and in his case those are very small" (4). In his frustrated attempts to help his employee, the lawyer is thus forced to call upon his projected imaginings about what Bartleby desires or what he suffers. Perhaps the lesson that "Bartleby" teaches, then, is that in one's sympathetic relations with others, one can rarely get past the self. This would explain the extent to which the narrator's responses to Bartleby are consistently indicative of the narrator's own interior world: "Gradually I slid into the persuasion that these troubles of mine touching [Bartleby], had been all predestined from eternity, and Bartleby was billeted upon me for some mysterious purpose of an all-wise Providence, which it was not for a mere mortal like me to fathom" (26). In this scenario, Bartleby exists to facilitate the narrator's life purpose.

What that purpose might be is never discovered, however, for the narrator has hardly had time to satisfy himself in this providential view of his condition before he decides to abandon Bartleby and move offices, leaving Bartleby in the hands of a new landlord, who commits him to the Tombs for vagrancy, where Bartleby subsequently dies. The narrator is compelled to this extreme, I suggest, by the oppressive sense, finally, of his complete identification with Bartleby and the risk to self, and manhood, that it portends. As he imagines the future, the narrator sees Bartleby "turning out a long-lived man . . . occupying [the narrator's] chambers . . . and casting a general gloom over the premises" for many years to come. And "in the end," says the narrator, he will "perhaps outlive me, and claim possession of my office by right of his perpetual occupancy: as all these dark anticipations crowded upon me . . . I resolved to gather all my faculties together, and for ever rid me of this intolerable incubus" (27). The dissolution of ego and social boundaries is signaled in the narrator's vision of his and Bartleby's roles someday reversed, with Bartleby as possessor of the narrator's office and the narrator dead. Just as telling is Bartleby's "possession" of the narrator himself as the narrator sees it: the image of Bartleby as an "incubus," a metaphor that feminizes the narrator in relation to the oppressive male spirit that figuratively lies atop him.

The narrator's initial equanimity regarding the eccentricities of his scrivener, grounded in his view that Christian charity involves an exchange of services that benefits both parties, finally gives way to a projected paranoia: the sense that his employee will someday possess *him*. Thus, when the competing claims of Christian love and self-interested exchange prove irreconcilable (in part because Bartleby will not participate in the exchange), the narrator abandons the former, and Bartleby with it. He is helped to do so by his ability to literally flee the scene of his traumatic encounters. In a telling juxtaposition, the "motionless" Bartleby is forcibly removed to the Tombs while the narrator takes to the road for a few days in his carriage, avoiding the happenings at home. His mobility bespeaks, in comparison to the imprisoned Bartleby, an ostensible social and spiritual freedom, one that corresponds to the liberation of his imagination's "dark anticipations." But though Bartleby's body dies, his spirit lives on in the "one little rumor" with which the narrator ends his tale: Bartleby's work at the Dead Letter Office.[21]

As the narrator has it, in being forced to handle aborted letters and sort them for the flames, Bartleby, already prone to a "pallid hopelessness," is overcome by depression. Of course, being based on speculation, the anecdote fails to verify Bartleby's emotions but serves only to confirm the narrator's: "When I think over this rumor," writes the narrator, "I cannot adequately express the emotions that seize me" (34). Here, as elsewhere, the narrator projects onto Bartleby an empathy with the pain of others that belongs chiefly to the narrator himself. It is an identification that returns both the narrator and Melville's readers to the idea of male melancholy, compounded rather than alleviated by fraternity. The rumor also, however, affirms for the narrator his own redeemed sensibility, one summed up in his sentimental final line: "Ah Bartleby! Ah humanity!" Returning full circle to the beginning of the tale, where the narrator boasts his ability to "relate diverse histories, at which good-natured gentlemen might smile, and sentimental souls might weep" (4), the narrator establishes his own empathetic credibility in narrativizing humanity's common plight of brotherly sorrow. What goes unmentioned in this self-construction of sensibility, of course, is the true cost to self and other in fraternal identifications—the fact, that is, that one may securely weep for one's brother only after he, and all that one imagines him to be, is safely buried.

"To read *Bartleby* well," observes H. Bruce Franklin, "we must first realize that we can never know who or what Bartleby is.... We must see that he may be anything from a mere bit of human flotsam to a conscious and forceful rejecter of the world to an incarnation of God." Yet, even as "human flotsam," argues Franklin, Bartleby is identified with the "incarnation of God," or Christ: "The possibility that Bartleby may be the very least of men," writes Franklin, "does not necessarily contradict the possibility that Bartleby may be an embodiment of God. For as Christ explains in Matthew 25, the least of men (particularly when he appears as a stranger) is the physical representative and representation of Christ: 'Then shall the righteous answer him, saying, Lord, when saw we thee ahungered, and fed thee? Or thirsty, and gave thee drink?... And the King shall answer and say unto them, Verily I say unto you, Inasmuch as ye have done it unto one of the least of these my brethren, ye have done it unto me.'"[22] Who or what Bartleby is, in other words, is a matter of perception, a perception that Melville links to a Christian ethic by which all men, even "the least," are identified with Christ. If, as Franklin declares, the narrator's salvation depends upon his recognition of this identification, he unwittingly succeeds. His failure to appreciate the full implications of his "charity" toward Bartleby, as self-serving as it is, proves not so much a failure of the imagination as an unconscious acknowledgment of its painful accomplishment: his is an identification with the "forlornnest of mankind" whose projective power ironically translates the narrator himself, like Bartleby, into "the Man of Sorrows" (20).

In "Bartleby," Melville plays out with ironic gravity mankind's condition as "pieces" of the Godhead, "sons of Adam" bonded yet alienated by the imaginative force of fraternal melancholy. The narrator's repudiation of Bartleby stems from his fear that his employee will someday "master" him, a fear ultimately disguised and disavowed by his sentimental summation of mankind's plight as innocent victims, or whipping boys, sacrificed to the vagaries of earthly mis-communication. In *White-Jacket*, Melville examines the abuse of innocence and its transformative effects through a largely unironic analogy to race. As Melville argues, the white sailor's potential to be flogged reduces his condition—both physical and emotional — to that of a slave. The identification between sailor and slave incites an anxious discourse on the un-manning of white men in their relation to blacks. However, the white sailor is ultimately redeemed from his degraded condition by the very empathy he feels for those who live their lives in bondage. Compelled to identify with a class of people whose oppression for all practical purposes negates U.S. democratic ideals, White-Jacket serves as a symbol of the otherwise privileged white man's physical and psychological enslavement. His sensitivity to the pain of others gestures toward the transcendence of racial difference, even as it importantly locates such empathetic enlightenment in America's "sons" — white men whose articulated suffering speaks for a nation.

"WHO AIN'T A SLAVE?"

In her 1831 abolitionist essay "Mental Metempsychosis," Elizabeth Chandler confidently claims that "could we but persuade those with whom we plead, in behalf of the slave, to imagine themselves for a few moments in his very circumstances, to enter into his feelings, comprehend all his wretchedness, transform themselves mentally into his very self, they would not surely long withhold their compassion."[23] Despite Chandler's assurance that sympathetic imaginings will lead to compassion (and thus abolition), the task set before Americans appears to involve more psychological obstacles than Chandler acknowledges. For example, according to William McNally's *Evils and Abuses in the Naval and Merchant Service, Exposed* (1839), white sailors have ample opportunity for imagining at least one of the physically painful and psychologically degrading experiences of the slave — that of being whipped. Yet the mental transformation "into [the slave's] very self" through naval flogging is anything but liberating. "Seamen know that they are born free," writes McNally, "and freemen will never submit to the lash of slavery."[24] At issue for McNally are both the unchallenged authority of the captain, who acts as judge and jury in offenses, and the infliction of a punishment that humiliates the victim by being applied to the body. In the claim that "freemen will never submit to the lash of slavery," McNally implicitly distinguishes between those who are whipped but, as *men*, will not stand for it, and those (slaves) who deserve the reader's sympathy because they are in no position to object.

As Samuel Otter observes, the slavery analogy "was at the center of antebellum political debate. It was made by northern labor radicals, slavery apologists, women's rights advocates, and nationalists."[25] McNally's treatise epitomizes the conflicted and conflicting cultural work performed by the analogy. Addressing northern abolitionists' hypocritical complacency with regard to flogging, McNally warns, "Never let American citizens in the Northern states rail at slavery, or the punishment inflicted on slaves, or say that it is wrong, so long as their *own sons*, their own flesh and blood, their own seamen, their own free citizens ... are daily subject to the same treatment as the slaves, whose degraded situation in the southern states calls forth, so justly, the warmest sensibilities of the heart and nature of philanthropists."[26] Although slaves deserve "the warmest sensibilities" of the philanthropist, the treatment of the implied readers' own "sons" is, suggests McNally, an even greater affront to nature. In the absence of sympathy with one's own kin there can be no true freedom. This is made explicit as McNally goes on to explain the necessity of properly placed attentions: "Oh, Americans ... those who exclaim loudest against slavery, had better turn their attention to objects of suffering and benevolence at home, before they look for them abroad, hundreds of whom will be found to stand in need of their assistance, and emancipation from the yoke of tyranny and oppression, as the swarthy sons and daughters of Africa."[27] In juxtaposing the suffering of "family" ("objects of suffering ... at home") with the suffering of "the swarthy sons and daughters of Africa," McNally simultaneously identifies sailors with slaves and signals their essential difference: white sailors are to be the first objects of American sympathies by right of their authentic relation to American fathers.

In narratives meant to marshal abolitionist sentiments on behalf of whites as well as blacks, then, a competition for resources, both emotional and financial, ensues. As Frederick Douglass points out in his autobiography of life as a slave, *My Bondage and My Freedom*, the existence of slavery in America forces even those men in like circumstances into an antagonistic relation. Explaining his attack by white laborers while working in a shipyard in Baltimore, Douglass discourses on the "*conflict of slavery with the interests of the white mechanics and laborers of the south.*"[28] Slaves like Douglass who are hired out cheaply for their labor by their masters compete for jobs with poor white men, who, says Douglass, do not even realize who their true enemy is: "The white man is robbed by the slave system, of the just results of his labor, because he is flung into competition with a class of laborers who work without wages." But "at present," Douglass goes on, "the slaveholders blind [the whites] to this competition, by keeping alive their prejudice against the slaves, *as men* — not against them *as slaves.*"[29] In other words, rather than turn southern white workers against the institution of slavery, the fear of being identified as a slave results in the worker's attempt to preserve his pitiful position as superior to somebody: "The impression is cunningly made, that slavery is the only power that can prevent the laboring white man from falling to the level of the slave's poverty and degradation. To make this enmity deep and broad . . . the [white worker] is allowed to abuse and whip the [black slave], without hindrance."[30] Douglass notes the irony of poor white laborers attempting to bolster their manhood by participating in a system that, in effect, has already turned *them* into slaves: "by encouraging the enmity . . . [the slaveholder] succeeds in making the said white man almost as much a slave as the black slave himself. The difference between the white slave, and the black slave, is this: the latter belongs to *one* slaveholder, and the former belongs to *all* the slaveholders, collectively."[31] By turning on the black slave rather than the white master, the white laborer unwittingly affirms his own position as object of abuse.

As evidenced by Douglass's example, wage slavery, or white slavery, as it was then termed, provides another analogy linking the oppression of whites to the enslavement of blacks, but with a result similar to what we saw in McNally's treatise and in "Bartleby": a man's forced identification with a person more disadvantaged than himself, rather than engendering fellow-feeling, tends to create anxieties about what such an identification means—how it might affect the identity of the person whose manhood is tenuously supported by the fragile pyramid of social differentiations. As Melville suggests, with irony in "Bartleby" and with pathos in *White-Jacket*, identification's dangers are especially evident to the "sensitive" man whose feelings "pain" him.

White-Jacket, or The World in a Man-Of-War offers a powerful discourse on the harm done to American "sons," individually and as a collective, by whipping. Partway through his novel-length narration of his year aboard the man-of-war ship, the *Neversink*, the eponymous narrator White-Jacket describes an incident of flogging, followed by three chapters outlining the impracticality, as well as immorality, of flogging based on what we might think of as its coercive manipulation of the sympathetic imagination.[32] In the chapter titled simply "A Flogging," White-Jacket describes the sensations of such men as himself upon hearing the announcement, "*All hands witness punishment, ahoy!*": "To the sensitive seaman that summons sounds like a doom. He knows that the same law which impels it ... by that very law he also is liable at any time to be judged and condemned. And the inevitableness of his own presence at the scene; the strong arm that drags him in view of the scourge, and holds him there till all is over; forcing upon his loathing eye and soul the sufferings and groans of men who have familiarly consorted with him ... —men of his own type and badge—all this conveys a terrible hint of the omnipotent authority under which he lives" (135). White-Jacket's identification with the beaten in this scene is clear. Although describing another man's flogging, White-Jacket reports it in terms of physical coercion to *himself*: the "*strong* arm that *drags* him" and "*holds* him there," "*forcing* upon his loathing eye and soul" the suffering of others. The fact that those others are men "of his own type and badge," moreover, reinforces the idea that what happens to one sailor could happen, and *is* happening, to White-Jacket "by the same law that impels it."

And what is this law? It is literally the law that allows captains, like slave masters, the legal right to beat whom they choose without accountability, a law whose basic injustice is, for White-Jacket and for Melville, attested to by its violation of the greater, more natural "law" of empathy. Not only may the captain, at his own discretion or his own whim, have a man flogged "for the most trivial alleged offences, of which [the sailor] may be entirely innocent" (141), but because officers are themselves exempt from the lash, the captain may order, and the officers inflict, a punishment that they will never suffer. Thus, although, as White-Jacket repeatedly points out, all men are made in the image of God, it is only the common sailor who is forced to occupy the position of whipping boy — forced, that is, to confront his own powerlessness, whether tangibly or vicariously, in the face of "omnipotent authority." Without identification — the intellectual and affective acknowledgment that all men are in the same boat, so to speak — there can be no equality, and thus no justice. So White-Jacket suggests when he declares his wish that "in the name of immortal manhood" every man who "upholds [flogging] were scourged at the gangway till he recanted!" (146). In an ironic reversal of Chandler's thesis, White-Jacket advises that men who can't imagine other men's suffering should be beaten until they can.

White-Jacket locates justice in the potential for an equal distribution of pain — a democracy of suffering that would ultimately end abuse through empathetic understanding. Such understanding is importantly tethered to real and imagined displays of violence, where all men confront the possibility of being beaten. At present, only noncommissioned sailors are made to confront this possibility, and of these, only the "sensitive seaman" truly suffers. There are those sailors who can witness a flogging unmoved, but, as White-Jacket remarks, "it is hard to decide whether one should be glad" that this is so — "whether it is grateful to know that so much pain is avoided, or whether it is far sadder to think that either from constitutional hard-heartedness or the multiplied searings of habit, hundreds of men-of-war's-men have been made proof against the sense of degradation, pity, and shame" (135). It seems the only thing more dangerous to a civilized society than men who are made to feel another's pain is a nation of men made immune to sympathetic identification, and who therefore tolerate, if not perpetuate, abuse.

For Melville, whipping typifies slavery because of the vulnerable position into which it forces its victims. Treated as objects whose bodies and minds are subject to another's manipulations, abused men may, at worst, be reduced to "hard-heartedness," apathy, or depressive melancholy or, at best, to a painful dislocation of identity that renders empathy another form of abuse. Of the former, the most dangerous, because unredemptive, are those men whose "hard-heartedness" stems from "the multiplied searings of habit" — those men, in other words, who have been repeatedly whipped. Although Melville does not differentiate between blacks and whites in this description, the allusion to slavery is clear. For him, as for other writers at the time, flogging exposes the white sailor to the slave's condition, thereby rendering his sensibilities either acutely painful, or worse, deadened.

The vulnerability of white sailors to the experience of black slaves is made explicit in Richard Henry Dana's popular autobiography, *Two Years before the Mast* (1840), a work that Melville knew well.[33] Dana's tale climaxes in a racially charged scene of violated identity in which Sam, a white sailor unfairly strung up by the captain, announces, "I'm no negro slave." "Then I'll make you one," replies the captain. When John, another white sailor, objects to Sam's punishment, he, too, is whipped. Sam's attempt to differentiate himself from a slave — to remind the captain of their common white skin — is negated by the captain, just as John's efforts to help Sam force him into the same psychological, as well as physical, position. "You see your condition!" cries the captain when he's finished whipping John. "Now you know what I am! . . . You've got a driver over you! Yes, a *slave-driver — a negro-driver*!" Dana, as witness and narrator, looks on "disgusted, sick, and horror-struck" but is powerless to intercede: "What is there for sailors to do?" he asks. "If they resist, it is mutiny; and if they succeed, and take the vessel, it is piracy. If they ever yield again, their punishment must come; and if they do not yield, they are pirates for life."[34]

For Dana, as for Melville, whipping and the slave condition it symbolizes forces upon white men an involuntary identification with powerlessness whose effects threaten to nullify the sailor's white heroic ancestry: "Will you say," writes Melville, "that an American-born citizen, whose grandsire may have ennobled him by pouring out his blood at Bunker Hill—will you say that, by entering the service of his country as a common seaman... [he] thereby loses his manhood at the very time he most asserts it?" (146).[35] The idea that the sailor is ennobled through the shedding of his ancestors' blood but emasculated by the shedding of his own seems somewhat paradoxical—after all, both the soldier and the flogged man are "pouring out [their] blood." But while the former case involves choice and an ultimate telos of "freedom," the former is whipped without consent. For White-Jacket, the sailor's beating is a beating without (national) purpose—a sign not of patriotic power but of coerced degradation.

The potential dissolution of powerful white manhood into "black" subjugation is made manifest many chapters after White-Jacket's theoretical discourse on naval flogging when he is forced to view the punishment of a black sailor named Rose-Water. Writing in retrospect, he remarks on his initial instinct to pity the man, before his pity is turned into a tangible identification: "Poor mulatto! thought I, one of an oppressed race, they degrade you like a hound. Thank God! I am white. Yet I had seen whites also scourged; for, black or white, all my shipmates were liable to that. Still, there is something in us, somehow, that, in the most degraded condition, we snatch at a chance to deceive ourselves into a fancied superiority to others, whom we suppose lower in the scale than ourselves" (277). As in his earlier remarks on naval flogging, White-Jacket focuses here on his own feelings of compassion for the victim. In this case, however, those feelings arise from his sense of a "fancied superiority" whereby he imagines only those of "an oppressed race" being "degrade[d]... like a hound." White-Jacket sets up the scene in order to reveal the self-deception at work in fancying others "lower in the scale than ourselves." The next day, having been found absent from a post he was never told he should occupy, White-Jacket is called before the captain and sentenced to be whipped. As he notes with the irony of retrospect, "When with five hundred others I made one of the compelled spectators at the scourging of poor Rose-Water, I little thought what Fate had ordained for myself the next day" (277). The "poor mulatto" turns out to be White-Jacket himself.

In a somewhat surprising turn, the otherwise passive White-Jacket vows to preserve his noble (white) identity, even at the risk of his life. Two officers intervene on White-Jacket's behalf and persuade the captain to relent, but not before White-Jacket mentally prepares himself to make a rush at the captain and to pitch both himself and the captain overboard: "My blood seemed clotting in my veins; I felt icy cold at the tips of my fingers, and a dimness was before my eyes. But through that dimness the boatswain's mate, scourge in hand, loomed like a giant, and Captain Claret, and the blue sea seen through the opening at the gangway, showed with an awful vividness.... I can not analyze my heart.... I but swung to an instinct in me—the instinct diffused through all animated nature, the same that prompts even a worm to turn under the heel. Locking souls with him, I meant to drag Captain Claret from this earthly tribunal of his to that of Jehovah, and let Him decide between us" (280). White-Jacket decides to take the case of justice out of the earthly master's hands and put it in God's. In doing so, he writes, he is responding to a sense of "manhood ... bottomless within [him]": "Nature has not implanted any power in man that was not meant to be exercised at times, though too often our powers have been abused. The privilege, inborn and inalienable, that every man has, of dying himself, and inflicting death upon another, was not given to us without a purpose. These are the last resources of an insulted and unendurable existence" (280). Brought to what he sees as the most degrading of circumstances, White-Jacket is ready to assert every man's "privilege." It is not only the power to die but the power to kill that White-Jacket ironically describes as man's "privilege." But in killing, of course, he is also assuring his own death. His only real form of resistance is self-destruction.

The free will that White-Jacket exercises in weighing the option to kill and be killed is important to his sense of white manhood, but in making suicide and murder his protagonist's only option, Melville reveals identification, resistance, and death as an endless cycle from which men in general are never freed. As if to put his near-flogging in this larger context, White-Jacket closely follows up his chapter "White-Jacket's Arraignment at the Mast" with a chapter on the Articles of War that are ritually read on the first Sunday of every month. "Of some twenty offences . . . a seaman may commit," White-Jacket informs the reader, "thirteen are punishable by death." "To a mere amateur reader," White-Jacket remarks, "the quiet perusal of these Articles of War would be attended to with some nervous emotions. Imagine, then, what *my* feelings must have been, when . . . I stood before my lord and master, Captain Claret, and heard these Articles read as the law and gospel, the infallible, unappealable dispensation and code, whereby I lived, and moved, and had my being on board of the United States ship Neversink" (292). Just as the reader is meant to imagine what White-Jacket feels, having come so close to being whipped, so White-Jacket finds himself imagining what other men, even white men like himself, have suffered as a result of these Articles. Trying to console himself with the idea that such "bloodthirsty laws" have no relevance during peacetime, White-Jacket then remembers the American sailors aboard the U.S.S. *Somers* who, without benefit of trial, were found guilty of mutiny and summarily hung. They, like you, he tells himself, "once were alive, but now are dead. . . . Have a care, then, have a care, lest you come to a sad end, even the end of a rope. . . . It is a hard case, truly, White-Jacket; but it cannot be helped. . . . You live under this same martial law" (294–95).[36] White-Jacket's identification with the hopeless and abused includes his identification with white men like himself, men who are made slaves to a "martial law" that puts power, even the power over life and death, in the hands of officers, or "slave-driver[s]."

White-Jacket's trials end, as Otter notes, with a fantasy: his metaphorical shedding of his white skin, whose proximity to blackness keeps threatening to prove fatal. Having fallen overboard and at risk of drowning in his heavy white jacket, White-Jacket takes a knife from his pocket and, as he says, "ripped my jacket straight up and down, as if I were ripping myself open. With a violent struggle I then burst out of it, and was free" (394). According to Otter, the scene "shows the reader how a white man was almost made a slave, and incredibly, made a man again." It does so, he goes on, by revealing the limits of the black slave/white sailor analogy: "In the comparative anatomy laid bare in *White-Jacket*, to be 'like' a slave is to be encased in skin that you cannot remove. To be unlike a slave is to possess a white jacket that is portable and divestible. *White-Jacket* ends with a vehement fantasy of erased marks and regenerated flesh: an emancipation from one's own skin."[37] The fantasy of "erased marks and regenerated flesh" goes beyond the divestiture of race, however. Rather, White-Jacket's final act is an attempt to shed the body itself — the physical incorporation that identifies men with other suffering souls but without transcending their individual, and raced, identities. Described on the first page of the novel as a "white duck frock . . . folded double at the bottom," White-Jacket's jacket resembles nothing so much as a straitjacket; his self-inflicted cesarean section from the jacket signifies his (re)birth out of the straitjacket of "the world in a man-of-war" and into heavenly peace and freedom. It is this concept of otherworldly communion — beyond the pains of earthly identifications — that I would argue constitutes the novel's true fantasy, a fantasy that Melville exposes as such in the final chapter of his novel.

"We mortals are all on board a fast-sailing, never-sinking, world-frigate," theorizes White-Jacket at the end of his narration, "of which God is the Lord High Admiral" (398). Although White-Jacket has earlier differentiated between man's justice and God's, his repeated rhetorical associations between captains and God reveal their fundamental connection. But if captains are analogous to slave masters and captains are analogous to God, so God, the metonymic connection goes, is also analogous to a "slave-driver" captain whose "infallible, unappealable dispensation and code" is impossible to fathom and whose wrath is therefore impossible to avoid. White-Jacket suggests as much when he refers to the "terrible . . . omnipotent authority" under which the sailor lives, in the chapter titled "A Flogging." "Indeed," says White-Jacket, continuing his thought, "the naval summons to witness punishment carries a thrill, somewhat akin to what we may impute to the quick and the dead, when they shall hear the Last Trump, that is to bid them all arise in their ranks, and behold the final penalties inflicted upon the sinners of our race" (135). Although ostensibly a social critique of man's inhumanity to man, *White-Jacket* is at the same time a comment on God's "martial law," which will someday find captains and sailors alike liable to, as well as beholding, God's "final penalties." There is no liberation, it seems, from the world of war. As the reading of the Articles of War reaches its climax, White-Jacket discovers that, even should his ship be destroyed, the law declares he will still be under the authority of its captain. "Hear you that, White-Jacket! I tell you there is no escape. Afloat or wrecked, the martial law relaxes not its gripe [*sic*]. And though . . . you were indeed to 'suffer death,' even then the martial law might hunt you straight through to the other world" (295–96). According to White-Jacket, there is no escape from the "terrible authority" that pursues one past the grave—past, that is, the dissolution of the body. Even there God, "the Lord High Admiral," can pick up the metaphorical whip that captains and slave masters have been forced to put down.

Ultimately, White-Jacket goes beyond condemning the rule of flogging that would "convert into slaves some of the citizens of the nation of freemen" (144) to comment on the existential drama of abuse, making connections between earthly punishment and divine retribution and locating man's salvation in his liability to be whipped. Men cannot bond, cannot be made equal, Melville suggests, until they are all in a position to be beaten, but then their bonding arises from a shared sense of their own powerlessness. As Ishmael declares in *Moby-Dick*, "Who ain't a slave? . . . Well, then, however the old sea-captains may . . . thump and punch me about, I have the satisfaction of knowing that . . . everybody else is one way or other served in much the same way. . . . The universal thump is passed around."[38] Ishmael finds solace in the idea that abuse is, sooner or later, universally and democratically experienced; in the meantime, there are moments of love as well as abuse to bring men together. In "A Squeeze of the Hand," Ishmael rhapsodizes on a moment of fraternal community when he and his brother seamen sit around a vat of whale sperm, squeezing the lumps out to get it ready for market: "I squeezed that sperm till I myself almost melted into it ... and I found myself unwittingly squeezing my co-laborers' hands in it.... Such an abounding, affectionate, friendly, loving feeling did this avocation beget; that at last I was continually squeezing their hands, and looking up into their eyes sentimentally; as much as to say, — Oh! My dear fellow beings, why should we longer cherish any social ascerbities, or know the slightest ill-humor or envy! Come; let us squeeze hands all round; nay, let us all squeeze ourselves into each other; let us squeeze ourselves universally into the very milk and sperm of kindness."[39] In a similar spirit of fraternity, White-Jacket asks his readers to "join hands with me ... and, in the name of that Being in whose image the flogged sailor is made," sympathize with sailors and demand that corporal punishment be abolished (142). The allusion here is telling: man is made in God's image, but God's image, through Christ, is also of "a flogged sailor," a whipping boy. Identification with mortal men will always involve, at some point, an awareness of their common crucifixion.

The allusion to Christ as a "flogged sailor" casts American sailor-sons as fellow sufferers with Christ. Yet suffering alone is no guarantee of redemption. As Melville makes clear, the redemptive effects of suffering are reserved for those observers, or narrators, sensitive enough to empathize with another's pain and make it his own. Such empathy is often dulled, it seems, by the false confidence of privilege: in contrast to the sailors, whose labor together might effect the dissolution of "social ascerbities," as Ishmael puts it, officers and captains seek to perpetuate hierarchy by inflicting their wills, quite concretely, on those deemed their inferiors. Likewise, in "Bartleby," the narrator's decision to abandon his "forlorn" employee stems from his belief that, in finally rejecting sympathy, his own suffering can be escaped. But in the end, White-Jacket concludes, self-deceiving men of privilege can only temporarily evade the inevitable and "universal thump" that will attend them in the next life, if not in this one, when God intercedes on behalf of the helpless: "Our Lord High Admiral will yet interpose; and though long ages should elapse, and leave [the sailor's] wrongs unredressed, yet ... let us never forget that, Whoever afflict us, whatever surround / Life is a voyage that's homeward-bound!" (400). White-Jacket ends his narrative with a reference to the heavenly home, but it is an ominous reference at best: this is a home where punishment awaits, and where men who now reject sympathy by refusing identification and allowing or perpetuating abuse will find themselves in the very position they authorized.

The disturbing irony, of course, is that Melville himself was no stranger to the strategy of inflicting pain in order to affirm what, according to White-Jacket, is always already a fictional sense of control. To return to where we began, home and its intimate relations was for Melville a site of punishment—punishment that he inflicted on his loved ones and punishment that he himself felt a victim of. Perhaps it is the very identification with family that allows Melville to see himself "held captive by," in Walker Cowen's words, those he seems to have tyrannized.[40] Certainly the power accorded to men in the mid-nineteenth century is qualified by Melville's rendering of the "sons of Adam" and the "sons" of America as equally helpless before "omnipotent authorities," including the power of their own feelings. The control that privileged, free, white men are meant to exemplify in antebellum America is undercut by the presence (or absence) of women, clerks, and black men, who reflect back to the sensitive man his own powerlessness. To the sensitive artist in particular, the recognition of his own face in the face of the other is but another source of pain. For Melville, the author who would "strike through the mask" to penetrate the truth of life is himself a victim of the pain he discovers, articulates, and inflicts.

To do justice to Melville's vision, then, Ishmael's paean to male bonding in "A Squeeze of the Hand" must be set side by side with his observation regarding that semiemasculated antihero, Ahab, that our "high mortal miseries" yet remind us "that the gods themselves are not forever glad. The ineffaceable, sad birth-mark in the brow of man, is but the stamp of sorrow in the signers."[41] Should one succeed in striking through the mask, in other words, one will discover that even God suffers melancholy and passes it down to his sons. If Melville appears at times to disavow this knowledge by highlighting, and celebrating, the bonds between men, the disavowal is temporary at best. His consistent return to the inability of empathetic sensibility to free men from their enslaved condition, as well as the depiction of identification itself as a form of enslavement, bears witness to that which Melville must personally have known: the hand that "squeezes" and the hand that whips is often one and the same, and the sympathy that binds men to family and to each other has as much potential to pain them as the ties that finally lash them to the mast.

CHAPTER 3

Fathers of Violence
*Frederick Douglass, John Brown, and the
Radical Reproduction of Sensibility*

*The humble and obedient slave exercises more or less control over the
most brutal and hard-hearted master. It is an invariable law of nature,
that weakness and dependence are elements of strength.... The moral and
physical world is but a series of subordinations, and the more perfect the
subordination, the greater the harmony and the happiness.*

*It is pleasing... to turn from the world of political economy, in which
"might makes right"... to that other world, in which weakness rules, clad
in the armor of affection and benevolence... the bosom of the family.*
— George Fitzhugh, "The Strength of Weakness," in Cannibals All! *(1857)*

In his infamous critique of northern capitalism, George Fitzhugh proposes southern slavery as evincing the most humane, most affectionate, and most liberating relationships to be found in the Western Hemisphere. Knowing their place in the hierarchy of human relations and protected by masters who act with the instinct of fathers, "negro slaves of the South are the happiest, and, in some sense, the freest people in the world." Although misguided abolitionists might succeed in eradicating slavery, observes Fitzhugh, "human law cannot beget benevolence, affection, maternal and paternal love.... It can never create between the capitalist and the laborer, between the employer and the employed, the kind and affectionate relations that usually exist between master and slave." In contrast to the free-market labor of the North, where owner-employers virtually "cannibalize" their workers in a greedy and heartless consumerism, in the patriarchal South, avers Fitzhugh, "the law of love prevails."[1]

According to Fitzhugh, such love is characterized by each person's willingness to surrender his rights to the interests of another. In the plantation "family," as in the nuclear one, "each [member] prefers the good of others to his own, and finds most happiness in sacrificing selfish pleasures, and ministering to others' enjoyments." Just as fathers abrogate their right to do as they please to the needs and desires of the family's "weaker" members, specifically wives and daughters, so slaveholders submit themselves to the interests of their dependents, or slaves: "Our hearts bleed at the robbing of a bird's nest," Fitzhugh offers by way of analogy, "and the little birds, because they are weak, subdue our strength and command our care."[2] Mutual subordination, that is, structures all successful domestic partnerships and renders master and slave a perfectly complementary relation. Displacing onto free-market capitalism the power dynamic that also holds slavery in place, Fitzhugh can argue that slaveholders are mastered, and slaves "in some sense" freed, by love.

In *Cannibals All!* Fitzhugh represents filial love as a vehicle to a power inversion; specifically, the translation of mastery into submission through sympathy with the weak. Such an inversion finds its apotheosis in Christ, whose teachings on, and example of, sacrificial love, argues Fitzhugh, exposes the limits of freedom in the free-labor system: "Christian morality can find little practical foothold in a [capitalist] community so constituted that to 'love one's neighbor as ourself' or 'to do unto others as we would they should do unto us' would be acts of suicidal self-sacrifice.... In the various family relations of husband, wife, parent, child, master, and slave," however, "the observance of these Christian precepts is often practiced, and almost always promotes the temporal well being of those who observe it."[3] According to Fitzhugh, what prevents self-sacrifice from being "suicidal" in the South is the recognition that freedom is achieved only through the mutual bond of love, an ideological blurring of freedom and bondage on which Christianity itself is founded: that is, according to the New Testament, the only true freedom is freedom from the "slavery" of sin (through Christ) that makes possible one's obedience to God.[4] In Fitzhugh's scheme, slaveholders are the truest, because most obedient, representatives of Christ.

Though Fitzhugh inverts the terms of freedom and slavery for his own proslavery ends, slavery apologists were not alone in declaring free-market society to be anything but free. In the famous abolitionist novel *Uncle Tom's Cabin* (1852), for example, Harriet Beecher Stowe joins a chorus of antislavery voices that claimed that "the American planter is 'only doing, in another form, what the English aristocracy and capitalists are doing by the lower classes'; that is . . . *appropriating them*, body and bone, soul and spirit, to their use and convenience." "Buying a man up," declares Stowe's reluctant slave owner, Augustine St. Clare, "sets the thing before the eyes of the civilized world in a more tangible form, though the thing done be, after all, in its nature, the same [in capitalism as in slavery]."[5] For Stowe, northern capitalists and southern slave owners alike mimic corrupt English aristocrats by attempting to produce a stratified, class-based society antithetical to American democratic, and Christian, values. Stowe's solution, akin to Fitzhugh's, is cross-racial sympathy born of parental love. Addressing the "men and women of America" who understand the power of parental feeling, Stowe asks her white readers to identify with the pain of slave mothers who have lost their children: "And you, mothers of America—you who have learned, by the cradles of your own children, to love and feel for all mankind . . . I beseech you, pity the mother who has all your affections, and not one legal right to protect, guide, or educate, the child of her bosom! By the sick hour of your child; by those dying eyes, which you can never forget . . . I beseech you, pity those mothers that are constantly made childless by the American slave trade!"[6] Though Stowe is working to abolish slavery and Fitzhugh to defend it, both Fitzhugh and Stowe present parents, and the self-sacrificing love that parenting engenders, as the only antidote to the competitive, acquisitive impulses destroying American liberty. But whereas Stowe posits family as essentially democratic in its vision of shared pain, Fitzhugh casts it as the embodiment of a loving hierarchy of relations that mirrors, rather than contradicts, the slave institution. In Fitzhugh's hands, family becomes another, though idealized, form of slavery.

My intention here is not to elide the real and material differences between proslavery and antislavery positions but instead to point out that Fitzhugh's model of love — one in which empathy equalizes power relations by having the "weak" "subdue [the] strength" and "command [the] care" of the privileged — is not confined to slavery apologists but serves as a broad-based paradigm for a nation defined in the 1850s by both its commitment to Christian principles and its agonized conflict over the institution of slavery. It is a model that disengages freedom from its concrete legal definition and aligns it with more abstract, if at times incompatible, ideas of sentiment, empathy, and submission. Such a model speaks to a white power base, I would contend, that was anxious about its privileges. Social inequities are obscured by putting social advantage in the service of making oneself into a more *feeling* human being.[7] "But, what can any individual do?" Stowe rhetorically asks her readers regarding the abolition of slavery: "They can see to it that *they feel right*.... See, then, to your sympathies in this matter! Are they in harmony with the sympathies of Christ?"[8] For Stowe, American liberty finds its hope and expression in the sympathetic, bereaved white mother whose own privileged status could not protect her from the loss of a child and whose consequent pain compels her to identify, like Christ, with the grief of the helpless. For Fitzhugh, by contrast, sympathy is embodied in the patriarchal master-father whose own submission to the weakness of others renders him Christlike. Without conflating Stowe's and Fitzhugh's radically different social agendas (or gender politics), one could argue that, for both writers, the ability to "feel right" is exemplified in the Christian empathy that converts "submission" to "strength" and vice versa. For both sides of the slavery debate, I am suggesting, family holds the key to an inversion of power that has the potential to set one, and others, "free."[9]

What remains so far unacknowledged in this arrangement of feeling is the extent to which the discourse of familial love recapitulates racial-based hierarchies, even slavery itself, by disavowing through inversion both the experiential difference between voluntary and obliged submission and the right to power on which that difference stands: only the individual with power, in other words, has the luxury to relinquish that power in sympathetic gestures and have it confirm his or her strength. As Eric Sundquist observes, power inversions are endemic to any slave society or nation. In such a nation, the concepts of freedom and bondage, mastery and slavery, necessarily inform and define each other. The question then becomes, Who is in a position to define such terms? In a work like Melville's *Benito Cereno*, Sundquist argues, the true power of the slave is revealed by the author's inversion of master-slave positions. The black slave Babo's psychological conquest of the Spanish captain, Don Benito, Sundquist notes, effectively dramatizes the inverted condition made famous by Hegel, where "the master's power is hedged by his discovery that his very identity *as a master* is bound to, and mediated through, another consciousness, that of the slave. The slave, in turn, although he is in thrall to the master and lives to a degree for his enhancement, nonetheless wields power over the master by refusing to grant him autonomy and forcing him into a psychological posture of dependence."[10] Thus, in the end, says Sundquist, Don Benito discovers that the slave owner is always already a slave to the servant who psychologically controls him.

    What I would like to note through Fitzhugh, however, is the way in which the master-slave inversion may be *doubled* to align masterfathers once again with the power they ostensibly accord to their dependents. Fitzhugh's formulation in effect takes back the power granted to the slave by Hegel and Melville by positioning the slave owner as already *consciously* identifying with, or "bound to," the consciousness of the slave; by virtue of their mutual attachment, suggests Fitzhugh, neither master nor slave is free to do anything but to love and to serve. Freedom is circumscribed, rhetorically at least, within a structure of empathy that renders the concepts of mastery and slavery interchangeable and forecloses the forward-looking dialectic of Hegelian theory — the idea that, in the fullness of time, "the truth of the independent consciousness" will prove "the consciousness of the bondsman."[11] In Fitzhugh's sentimental scenario, it is the slave owner who is not only conscious of his "bonds" but free enough to represent those bonds as further evidence of his power. The master becomes the slave to become the master again.

The rhetorical inversion by which writers like Fitzhugh translate mastery into submission through empathy, as we can see, may belie the true end of such power reversals: the conversion of submission back into control. Ultimately, Fitzhugh's manipulation of the concepts of freedom and bondage reaffirms white masculine supremacy even as it suggests that sympathy for others is one of the areas in which the white man reigns supreme. By claiming the slaveholder's submission to an ethics of emotion, one exemplified in filial love, Fitzhugh casts the southern slaveholder as the quintessential "man of feeling" — at once all-powerful, but too mindful of the needs of others to assert that power for his own individual good. While the master becomes, by his own hand and in his own words, both the subject *and* the object of sympathy — taking on the pain of his dependents ("our hearts bleed," he declares, at the plight of the weak) and making it his own — the slave serves only as an object of sympathy; he is a tool for the creation of the white master's feeling self. Empathy, submission, power, and authority thus *all* become the province of a particular, implicitly white, manhood. It belongs to men, that is, who are sensitive enough to identify with submission but free enough to transcend — or to convert back into agency — its otherwise enslaving effects.

It is the "master's" privilege, I am suggesting, to feel empathy, a privilege grounded not solely in his literal freedom (neither exploited northern workers nor their "cannibal"-owners share such a privilege) but also in the more abstract definition of freedom authorized and made popular by antebellum literature and culture: the ability to identify and to put oneself in a position to be identified with, without making oneself a slave to others.[12] It is a privilege granted, moreover, through that *other* inversion upon which both Fitzhugh's and Christianity's construction of freedom and paternal love implicitly rely, but which the work of radical abolitionists Frederick Douglass and John Brown will bring directly to the fore:

namely, the master-father's power to punish is the foundation of his willingness to submit. A man's recourse to violence enables his feelings of compassion. For Brown especially, mastery is coded as masculine by virtue of its basis in physical aggression and by the obfuscation of that fact in American Christian patriarchalism — the idea of the father/Father who "punishes those whom he loves."[13]

If, as we saw in the previous chapter, slavery is in part defined for Melville by the identities and feelings a man is compelled to bear, freedom for Douglass and Brown is achieved by the willingness to fight, quite literally, for the power to "master" the terms of empathy — to control, like Fitzhugh's slaveholder, how one will relate and be related to by others. Family, again, serves as a crucial but fraught concept in this fight: for Douglass and for Brown, as for Fitzhugh, family bespeaks identity (knowing one's relation to the world) *and* subordination (a love that compels one to submission). Fitzhugh's reading of slavery as part of a domestic institution may appear to be a patently self-serving lie, but Douglass, as a slave, knew that the tie between family and slavery was all too true. For example, the condition of the slave child follows the condition of his mother, even when he is fathered by his owner. For Douglass, to be a slave is to be liable to forms of identification that bind but rarely liberate. Thus, although one could argue that Douglass's second autobiography, *My Bondage and My Freedom* (1855), seeks to make meaningful the dichotomous terms (freedom and bondage, mastery and slavery) that proslavery writers like Fitzhugh render interchangeable, freedom appears in Douglass's work as in some ways inseparable from the struggle to enact a new form of kinship, one manifested in Douglass's compelling his readers to identify (with) him as white. In rejecting an identification with both slavery and family through acts of violence that align him with whites, Douglass re-creates himself, like a master, in relation to the slave he once was, "resurrecting," as he puts it, not only his manhood but the very sensibility that constitutes manhood and freedom in antebellum culture: "I felt as I had never felt before," Douglass writes after beating his overseer, Edward Covey, and though "I remained a slave in *form*," this "spirit made me a freeman in *fact*."[14]

If freedom is obtained through an individual's capacity to "feel right," right feeling must sometimes be preceded, Douglass suggests, by the right, or freedom, to feel. And such a right must literally be fought for. Like Douglass's, John Brown's abolitionist strategies rely on an inversion of racial identifications, a realignment or reconfiguration of familial identity meant to shift, through violence, antebellum America's balance of power. Brown's (in)famous pedagogical method of substitution—where Brown forces his son, John Jr., to beat *him* for the boy's domestic infractions—serves as a model for the disciplining of white manhood through acts of aggression that produce a new, more sympathetic sensibility. By forcing his son to handle the whip, Brown teaches him the lesson of the master-father: the feeling self is created in relation to the abject other over whom one chooses (or chooses not) to exercise one's power. It is a lesson that Brown's martyrdom will later perfect in relation to the state. Declaring on the eve of his execution for the raid on Harper's Ferry his willingness to "mingle my blood further with the blood of my children and with the blood of millions" of tortured slaves, Brown not only expands his family to include blacks as well as sons but also prefigures his cultural transformation into a "whipping boy" for the sins of the white fathers and imparts a Fitzhughian lesson to a nation of putative masters—that of "the strength of weakness" or the power of the abused.[15]

In John Brown's identification with black slaves and Frederick Douglass's identification with white men we find further evidence of the power inversions structuring antebellum ideas of family, empathy, and redemption, inversions that must be "mastered," or controlled to one's advantage, in order for "freedom," spiritual and/or material, to become possible. The difference between Douglass's and Brown's framing of mastery is apparent as well: Douglass, a black man, rejects the popular construction of slaves as worthy objects of sympathetic identification and positions black men and women who appear so as substitutes for a slave self he has already outgrown. Brown, a white man, offers himself as substitute for the sins of a white nation, finding power in his own objectification. But for both Brown and Douglass, I will argue, to be a man, finally, is to control, and sometimes create, the forms of punishment that will ultimately transform aggressors, including themselves, into Christ-like whipping boys for the salvation of a nation.

THE MAN OF FEELING

Rhetorical contests over the meaning of freedom in antebellum America coincide, as Cindy Weinstein has argued, with "the discursive battle over sympathy—who gets it, who gives it, who defines it." Both sides of the slavery debate locate the site of these battles in the family, an institution meant to embody the liberating possibilities of sympathy but whose promises for teaching and enacting love often went woefully unfulfilled: "One might . . . think of the question—what is a family—as, quite literally, a cultural *idee fixe* in which the idea of family is constantly trying to be 'fixed,' as if it were in need of definitional repair, as if idea and practice have become unhinged," writes Weinstein.[16] For proslavery writers, as we have seen, the expansion of family to include slaves and slaveholders, rather than epitomizing the destruction of sympathy, as many abolitionists had contended, was put forward as an opportunity for repairing the emotional gaps left open by a naive sanctification of freedom. Freedom, it was argued, was most fully realized in bonds of affection rather than bonds of blood, an argument that reflects, as Weinstein observes, the ideological shift taking place more generally in antebellum culture—from discussions of the traditional "family," or ties rooted in consanguinity, to a discourse of "kinship," in which attachments formed by mutual interest and like-mindedness are entered into freely.[17] I would like to suggest how an ex-slave and abolitionist like Frederick Douglass might make use of the discourse of choice and like-mindedness to free himself from an identity imposed upon him—to suggest, that is, the ways in which ideas of "kinship" as opposed to "family" become a potential form of liberation for *slaves* as well as slavery apologists through new identifications.

In *My Bondage and My Freedom* (1855) and "The Heroic Slave" (1853), Douglass portrays the biological family as an obstacle to the black man's achievement of selfhood precisely because the responsibility for sympathy and care attending antebellum ideas of manhood and fatherhood can only further enslave the man who has no choice but to submit. To care as a slave for loved ones who are also slaves is to confront one's own helplessness. Under slavery, therefore, feeling itself becomes, as we saw with Melville, another form of bondage, a debilitating condition from which the black man can only be freed, initially at least, by rejecting identifications with black men and women, whose enslaved condition reflects back his own. "A man, without force, is without the essential dignity of humanity," writes Douglass in *My Bondage*. "Human nature is so constituted, that it cannot *honor* a helpless man, although it can *pity* him; and even that it cannot do long, if the signs of power do not arise" (141).[18] For Douglass, the slave's submission is that which eventually precludes the very sympathy it should call up in observers (including himself), by virtue of the fact that no remedy is imaginable: should the "signs of power" not "arise" in the sufferer, the witness's pity must finally be withheld, lest he identify with an object whose helplessness threatens, as with Melville's narrators, to un-man him.

As Douglass will demonstrate, it is through the expression of mutual aggression, in which master and slave are "bound up together," that the black man re-creates himself in relation to the other — including the slave "other" that he once was — and in that creation finds the power to engage in identifications with free men. In making such a claim, I reject neither the scholarly arguments for Douglass's masculine individualism nor his investment in sympathy and sentiment. Rather, I am attempting to explain Douglass's emphasis on autonomy and the aggression through which it is achieved as necessary preconditions to the forms of feeling that testify to and enable one's ability to connect with others.[19] Although Robert Levine may be correct in arguing that "those whom [Douglass] believed possessed capacities for sympathy . . . were viewed as *nearly* transcending the limits of race," we will see that, for Douglass, the capacity for sympathy is worked through, rather than in transcendence of, a kinship with the masculine "force" he has learned from, and associates with, whites.[20] Implicitly participating in the construction of privilege and power as liberating for all concerned, Douglass aggressively demonstrates how a black man may become, like Fitzhugh's white southern slaveholder, a man of feeling.

The force with which subjectivity and, consequently, sensibility is initially brought into being is not Douglass's own. It belongs to his master and possible father, Aaron Anthony, whose whipping of Douglass's Aunt Esther the young Douglass witnesses and which becomes for him, in Saidiya Hartman's words, "an inaugural moment in the formation of the enslaved."[21] In his first autobiography, *Narrative of the Life of Frederick Douglass* (1845), Douglass names the woman as his Aunt Hester, and he views her beating through a crack in the floor boards of the closet where he sleeps: "I remember the first time I ever witnessed this horrible exhibition. I was quite a child, but . . . I never shall forget it whilst I remember any thing. . . . It struck me with awful force. It was the blood-stained gate, the entrance to the hell of slavery, through which I was about to pass."[22] The sight of his family member's whipping initiates Douglass into the slave condition, striking *him* "with awful force," even as his aunt is being beaten. Douglass rhetorically links Esther's condition to his own—he is "struck," just as she is, signifying both his identification with her and the violent means by which such familial identifications are introduced for the slave. When he recalls this incident in *My Bondage*, he calls his aunt "Esther" and notes that, although he "pitied her" from his heart, he is powerless to respond or object to the attack: "I was hushed, terrified, stunned, and could do nothing," imagining that "the fate of Esther might be mine next" (52). Rather than offering relief either to himself or to his aunt, Douglass's pity exacerbates the horror of his own situation; his identification with her renders him impotent, able to "do nothing."[23]

For Hartman and for Jenny Franchot, Esther's beating serves as a "primal scene" for the young Douglass, opening up a view into the secret interior of slavery's "diabolical" family relations. "A surrogate figure for Douglass's mother," writes Franchot, "Aunt Esther provides the author retrospective access to the recalcitrant interior of the past that closed within itself the parental relation. If slavery

Fathers of Violence (93)

leaves him 'without an intelligible beginning in the world,' Esther's punishment, 'struck ... with awful force,' ... obliterates any integral selfhood and imposes the new ontology of slavehood."[24] But if witnessing the master-father's brutalizing of his surrogate mother instantiates in Douglass a sense of his own objectification and powerlessness, a recognition of the "nothing" that he is or can do, it also causes him to question the seemingly arbitrary relations that led to this condition. Directly after his narration of the beating, Douglass writes, "The heart-rending incidents, related in the foregoing chapter, led me, thus early, to inquire into the nature and history of slavery. *Why am I a slave? Why are some people slaves, and others masters? . . . How did the relation commence?*" (52). These are questions of personal genealogy as much as they are a sociological inquiry. In essence, Douglass is asking, who has the power to decide who my "relations" are, and what they will mean to me? Included in those relations is not only biological family—the aunt with whom he identifies and the mother whose slave status determines his own—but the "relation" between master and slave. That is to say, Captain Anthony may in fact be Douglass's biological father, but his status as master is the critical one for Douglass. Douglass understands that he who is master can choose whom to identify, and/or identify with, as his "family"—that is, Anthony can renounce, or not, his paternal responsibility for Douglass. Thus, in a certain respect, the very perversity of the master-slave relationship—the right of the master to father or not father—endows Douglass with the knowledge of how unfixed, and thus open to manipulation, one's relations to others really are.

Esther's whipping, I am suggesting, while arguably the most brutalizing and degrading of the scenes of violence depicted in *My Bondage*, also stands (somewhat disturbingly) as one of the key incidents linking masculine violence to Douglass's liberation of consciousness. Hartman claims that by locating the "horrible exhibition" of his aunt's beating in the opening chapters of his first two autobiographies, Douglass "establishes the centrality of violence to the making of the slave and identifies it as an original generative act equivalent to the statement 'I was born.'"[25] What Douglass is born into, however, is enlightenment as well as objectification, a conflict of knowledge and feeling that signals the simultaneous birth and death of selfhood. On the one hand, the new perspective that Douglass gains allows him a view into the institutionalizing of abjection to which slavery reduces all its objects, a view that is tied for him to the dawning recognition of his relation to "family" and to slavery, themselves inextricably "bound up together." On the other hand, that knowledge becomes a vehicle for his eventual release, both from slavery and from the epistemological and sensible "nothingness" that the emasculating force of slavery has imposed upon him. In witnessing Anthony's violence, Douglass sees not only the master's power to dominate but also his power to (pro)create, to give birth to another man's identity as a slave. Through the whip, Anthony establishes his "relation" to Douglass as surely as, if not more than, the mother who bore him. In doing so, Anthony also gives Douglass the key to the means by which one may be born again. Referring to violence as the "original generative act" that "makes" the slave, Hartman unwittingly alludes to its corresponding potential to be the slave's *unmaking*—that is, it will become the means by which Douglass establishes a new relation to himself, to his biological family, and to the white men whose sympathy and identification he will, through violence, claim.

In a skillful counterpoint to the witnessed beating that turns Douglass from a boy into a slave, Douglass dates his transformation from slave into man to the day he beats his overseer, Edward Covey, many years later. Having been sent to the "negro breaker's" plantation for disciplinary correction, Douglass undergoes six months of humiliation and physical abuse. One day, however, Douglass decides he will be whipped no more: "I had brought my mind to a firm resolve, during that Sunday's reflection, viz: to obey every order, however unreasonable, if it were possible, and, if Mr. Covey should then undertake to beat me, to defend and protect myself to the best of my ability. My religious views on the subject of resisting my master, had suffered a serious shock, by the savage persecution to which I had been subjected, and my hands were no longer tied by my religion. . . . I had now to this extent 'backslidden' from this point in the slave's religious creed; and I soon had occasion to make my fallen state known to my Sunday-pious brother, Covey" (137–38). Since Christianity had "tied" his hands as effectively as his hypocritical "brother," Edward Covey, Douglass descends to his "fallen" state and resists any further attempts on the latter's part to whip him. After a two-hour brawl in which Covey, says Douglass, gets the worse end of the conflict, "Covey gave up the contest," and Douglass is "never fairly whipped" again. Douglass writes at length about this transforming experience, one that he describes as the "turning point" in his feelings about himself and his relation to the world. "I was a changed being after that fight," he declares. "I was *nothing* before; I was A MAN NOW" (141). In the next paragraph, Douglass refers to his change as a "resurrection," one prompted by his no longer fearing to die. In a self-conscious inversion of Christian terminology, Douglass represents his "fallen" state as the means of his redemption—by "resisting his master," Douglass becomes a (spiritually free) man.

Douglass has consistently linked the courage to be punished, even to death, to a psychological state of independence that transcends biology, even as it remains coded as masculine. In contrast to Esther's pleas before Anthony to "*Have mercy; Oh! have mercy.... I won't do so no more*" (51), Douglass offers an example of the slave woman Nelly's resistance to subjection through verbal abuse: "She was whipped—severely whipped," Douglass tells us, "but she was not subdued, for she continued to denounce the overseer, and to call him every vile name. He had bruised her flesh, but had left her invincible spirit undaunted." He then goes on: "The old doctrine that submission is the best cure for outrage and wrong, does not hold good on the slave plantation. He is whipped oftenest, who is whipped easiest; and that slave who has the courage to stand up for himself... becomes, in the end, a freeman, even though he sustain the formal relation of a slave" (55–56). Though he is talking about a woman rather than a "freeman," and one who cannot physically overpower her attacker, Douglass pays Nelly the highest compliment—that of granting her the status of a (free)man.

In contrast to the feminized abjection that, through Esther's body, becomes for Douglass the "entrance to the hell of slavery," Nelly represents masculine resistance. Though related to Esther by blood, he is more akin to Nelly, a likeness reflected in the almost identical language he employs to describe the aftereffects of his fight with Covey: "I was no longer a servile coward, trembling under the frown of a brother worm of the dust, but, my long-cowed spirit was roused to an attitude of manly independence.... This spirit made me a freeman in *fact*, while I remained a slave in *form*" (141). Partaking of antebellum constructions of the freedom found in spiritual liberation, Douglass locates his freedom in a *spirit* of rebellion, one potentially possessed by both women and men. But importantly, this spirit must be attained by first dissociating oneself from the tangle of earthly connections that potentially tether one to a degraded life. Contrary to the then-popular politics of sympathy that envisions freedom — the end of slavery — as the result of empathy and understanding, Douglass in this passage links fraternity to potential subjugation, a cowardly "trembling under the frown of a brother worm of the dust." Douglass has, a few sentences earlier, labeled Covey (before whom Douglass once trembled) a "cowardly" tyrant. What men too often have in common, Douglass implies, is fear — a fear of mortality, of death; they can be bonded, that is, in a perverse and debilitating fraternity that un-mans both the oppressor and the victim. By contrast, a real man feels and exerts his "independence" and, by exerting it, makes the feeling equivalent to fact. Rejecting both his aunt's model of begging for mercy and his "brother" Covey's cowardly abuse, Douglass claims what for him is new psychological territory: a "domain as broad as his own manly heart" that makes him "*a power on earth*" (141).

According to Douglass, the power of feeling that grants a man his own emotional and psychological "domain" is not something that can be borrowed from, or granted by, another who watches in sympathy. Though relational (arising out of productive, though aggressive, interactions with others), this domain relies on a man's willingness to be a subject, rather than an object, of sympathy. His declaration at the end of this pivotal chapter that "human nature ... cannot *honor* a helpless man," nor even pity him, "if the signs of power do not arise," suggests that both dignity and the sympathy it engenders must be fought for by oneself, and in that struggle, new sensations flow forth. Worthy of note in the "turning point" of Douglass's life and story, I am suggesting, is not only the association of manhood with rebellious self-assertion but also the figuring of manhood and the violence that precipitates it as an awakening to one's senses. Previous to this fight, the whippings Douglass bore had reduced him to an insensible object: "I was *nothing* before." Slavery's brutalizing tendencies led to a broken spirit and, emotionally speaking, to apathy: "Men accustomed to the lash and chain," Douglass later remarks, are "men whose sensibilities . . . have become more or less deadened by their bondage" (162). But by asserting the boundaries of self, Douglass experiences "[his] crushed self-respect and [his] self-confidence" "recalled to life." "I *felt* as I had never *felt* before" (emphasis mine) (141). Manhood, in other words, lies not only in a man's physical command of himself but in his ability to feel, and subsequently to manage, his *sense* of self. Such management is evinced in Douglass's writing of his life story, but also in his production of a sensible self capable of eliciting white readers' identification. Readers are to identify with him not as suffering slave but as master of a consciousness they recognize as akin to their own.

Douglass's transformation from an apathetic slave to a man of sensibility offers a provocative and useful variant on Adam Smith's theory of the importance of "propriety" or proportion in eliciting sympathy. Smith, whose *Theory of Moral Sentiments* (1759) influenced a century of Anglo-American thought on the relationship between sympathy and society, posits that the very violence of emotion the sufferer feels with regard to his own situation may actually present an *obstacle* to sympathy. A person may desire the "relief" that "complete sympathy" from others affords, but he will never obtain it, says Smith, except by "lowering his passion to that pitch, in which the spectators are capable of going along with him. He must flatten . . . the sharpness of its natural tone, in order to reduce it to harmony and concord with the emotions of those who are about him."[26] A person must already appear in emotional concord with his spectators if that person hopes to obtain sympathy. Douglass, too, sees the responsibility for appearing to be like his spectators, or his readers, as the slave's own.[27] Yet before the slave can "flatten" his natural passions to elicit identification, Douglass suggests, he must first be awakened to those passions. Once he has demonstrably acted in such a way that makes him *feel* himself, and appear to others like, a (free) (white) man, he may become a fit object of identification.

Reading Douglass's transformation from slave to man through Smith helps us to understand Douglass's comment on human nature's failure to pity a man without power as a gloss on the sympathetic imagination. Although one should grant sympathy where one is able, the object of sympathy must facilitate it by viewing himself from the other's perspective and acting accordingly.[28] In doing so, he is transformed from mere object to subject, "conceiving some degree of... coolness," as Smith puts it, "about his own fortune, with which he is sensible that [others] will view it."[29] Relating to oneself as object, then, allows one a degree of power to engage in identifications with others. Douglass attains that power only after he is "resurrected" to sensibility. Becoming a "man," rather than remaining a slave, Douglass can write a narrative about his own (prior) objectification, an autobiography related from the "coolness" of reflection and from the position of one whose "signs of power" justify the attention and empathy of other men like himself.

Had Douglass not become a man, in other words, his autobiography would never have been written. And to become a man, Douglass employs those means by which he has been taught men are made and slaves unmade: "I found my fingers attached to the throat of my cowardly tormentor," Douglass reports of his battle with Covey, "as heedless of consequences . . . as though we stood equals before the law. The very color of the man was forgotten. . . . I flung him on the ground several times, when he meant to have hurled me there. I held him so firmly by the throat, that his blood followed my nails. He held me, and I held him" (242–43). Because Covey is a "cowardly tormentor" rather than a man, the violence shared between them can only analogize, rather than truly represent, the emotional concord experienced by persons of like sensibility. What men should have in common is not fear but love—specifically, a love of liberty that each individual man is willing to fight for and can recognize and honor in the other. Put another way, violence can provide a common ground for masculine sensibility, one that, in Levine's words about sympathy, "nearly" or temporarily "transcends" race and social position. Bound together in the manly embrace of physical aggression ("He held me, and I held him"), Douglass and Covey become for a time "equal." Who is slave and who is master, like color, are momentarily "forgotten" in the reciprocal force that constitutes each man's un-raced identity. In the end, however, it is Covey's beaten body that proves the instrument of Douglass's redemption. It becomes the vehicle through which Douglass turns the tables to identify with the master, overpowering the "cowardly" other who is shown to be less than a man.

For Douglas, violence constitutes one of the primary ways that black men are redeemed from their emotional and psychological, as well as physical, bondage. It allows slaves the opportunity of identifying with forms of power that make and unmake men. After making Covey into the object that Douglass himself had been, Douglass's "fallen" state becomes synonymous with his "resurrection," a rhetorical paradox meant to exemplify the inversions of language and meaning that the slave institution engenders. In the hands of slaveholders, Douglass asserts, Christian concepts become distorted to the point of incoherence: "We had been taught from the pulpit of St. Michael's to recognize God as the author of our enslavement; to regard running away as an offense, alike against God and man; to deem our enslavement a merciful and beneficial arrangement . . . [and] that our work was not more serviceable to our masters, than our master's thinking was serviceable to us" (157). Echoing Fitzhugh, enslavement here is taught as freedom and work without pay as a virtual "service" for slaves. In light of such distortions, Douglass's equation of disobedience with salvation—the redemption of manhood and of feeling—can be read as a sign of his own ability to manipulate or reappropriate familiar Christian concepts, marshaling them in the cause of a sensibility to which his readers, he trusts, will relate. If that sensibility appears in Douglass's work as more akin to whites than to blacks, this can be attributed to an institution that consistently rewrites redemption into "devilry" and "independence" into isolation. In planning his escape to the North, for example, Douglass remarks on the love, even brotherhood, he feels for the black men going with him: "I must say, that I never loved, esteemed, or confided in men, more than I did these. They were as true as steel, and no band of brothers could have been more loving" (153). One of their party, however, in fear for his own safety, Douglass believes, betrays the rest, and Douglass is sent on his own to Baltimore to live with his master's brother. He eventually does escape to freedom, not just in spirit but in fact, but his journey is made alone — a sign of the emotional bonds that must be broken in order for slaves to become men and of slavery's ability to put family and liberty, not only rhetorically but literally, at odds.

Considerable critical debate has surrounded Douglass's apparent rejection of identifications with black men and women in favor of a masculine independence shaped by the forms of dominant white antebellum culture. As Sundquist observes, "The last chapters of *My Bondage and My Freedom* . . . certainly place somewhat more emphasis [than did his *Narrative*] on the fraternal bonds that are necessary to Douglass's theory of resistance, and it may be that this aspect of the revision was a reflection of Douglass's increasing need to work as an abolitionist within *black* circles, to stimulate political activity on behalf of and among 'my sable brothers.'" "But," Sundquist goes on, though "the sentiments are fraternal . . . Douglass himself remains paternally linked to the rhetoric and philosophy of the [white Founding] fathers, having identified himself as the single leader capable of espousing the right of revolution and planning the revolt." The question thus remains, says Sundquist, of whether Douglass, after representing his rebellious acts as signs of his independence, can himself "break free of the containing force of the revolutionary ethos."[30] Can he break free, Sundquist is asking, of the very structures of thinking and feeling that have simultaneously enslaved and liberated him? The question itself is perhaps rhetorical. Slavery has formed the bonds between black men and white men

Fathers of Violence (101)

on a foundation of violence as well as sympathy and made the sympathetic sensibility of each, as I have been arguing, a consequence of violence. To step outside the circle, or cycle, of violence is to be placed *back* within the biologically raced family whose embrace is, for Douglass, like the kiss of death. Within that family, direct aggression has no constructive place. Thus if, as we saw in Douglass's fight with Covey, violence provides men with a common ground of sensibility that temporarily transcends race, it is also true that in order to be redemptive the black man's violence must be directed at whites. After all (and somewhat ironically), it is precisely through his identification with the white father's aggression that Douglass has learned to be free.

Douglass's identification with white subjectivity is, as I have been arguing, an identification with both the white man's violence and his sensibility. No longer himself an object of pity, Douglass can write a narrative in which he empathizes with others. These "others" include, I would suggest, Douglass's Aunt Hester/Esther, whose beating ushers Douglass through the "blood-stained gate" of slavery. Recounting the incident from his perspective as a boy, Douglass emphasizes empathy's enslaving potential: he is "terrified" and "hushed" at the thought that he might be next. At the same time, however, the fact that Douglass can narrate the scene *at all* signals his transformed state. The stunned silence of youth is given voice by the man, who writes that he "pitied" his aunt from his heart. Douglass is now the subject, and Esther the object, of sympathy. Thus, in the end, Esther's subjugation proves not so much a reflection of Douglass's own powerlessness as a stand-in for it. She takes the whipping that Douglass as a child fears awaits him as well, but which in retrospect becomes the whipping that she takes instead of him. Her battered body signifies not only Douglass's initiation into but his ultimate redemption from slavery.[31]

That Esther's suffering ultimately provides a key to Douglass's way out of the deadening condition of slavery speaks to the inherently tangled, and ethically compromised, web of relations that slavery produces, where the potentially liberating effects of sympathy and identification may instead prove psychological weapons used against the beholder. Violence itself forms a strand of this ethical tangle: after all, by employing force to achieve his manhood, Douglass runs the risk of *over*-identifying with white masculinity — he runs the risk, that is, of denouncing tyranny only to reproduce it by taking up the metaphorical whip himself. Apparently sensitive to such a problem, Douglass consistently justifies his violence as a protection of rights rather than an attempt to oppress the other: "I was strictly on the defensive," writes Douglass of his fight with Covey, "preventing him from injuring me, rather than trying to injure him" (138).[32] In other words, Douglass's use of violence is self-consciously *not* represented as an identification with slave masters but as part of what Sundquist terms a "revolutionary ethos" — an identification with the American Founding Fathers whose spirit of aggression is inextricably tied to their love of liberty.

Perhaps nowhere does Douglass make the redemptive force of violence more explicit than in his only work of fiction, "The Heroic Slave." In this short story, the protagonist, Madison Washington, escapes slavery only to suffer both grief and guilt at leaving his wife behind. He returns to Virginia to free her, but upon reaching his former master's plantation, Washington is caught and his wife is killed. He is thereafter shipped off to New Orleans to be sold at auction, but once at sea Washington leads a slave revolt that results in the deaths of the white captain and much of the crew. Washington then steers the ship to the British-occupied Nassau, where, after an English trial, Washington and the other slaves are set free. Based on an actual slave rebellion on board the U.S.S. *Creole* in 1841, "The Heroic Slave" takes as its chief end the valorization of the rebellion's black leader, whose commitment to the revolutionary principles of 1776 aligns him with the white American Founding Fathers: "Let those account for it who can," writes Douglass about Washington's subsequent historical obscurity. "There stands the fact, that a man who loved liberty as well as did Patrick Henry, — who deserved it as much as Thomas Jefferson, — and who fought for it with a valor as high, an arm as strong, and against odds as great, as he who led all the armies of the American colonies through the great war for freedom and independence, lives now only in the chattel records of his native state."[33] Though he virtually embodies the white patriarchal father whose name he bears, the black Washington remains a slave to the white man's writing of U.S. history. "The Heroic Slave" is Douglass's attempt to rewrite that history, with the black man as revolutionary hero.

Written two years prior to *My Bondage*, "The Heroic Slave" looks forward to many of the themes and issues raised in the autobiography, the potential dangers of black familial bonding among them. After reaching Canada, Washington is haunted by the thought of his wife's reproachful suffering: "At times I could almost hear her voice, saying, 'O Madison! Madison! will you then leave me here? Can you leave me here to die? No! no! you will come! you will come!'" When admonished by his white interlocutor, Listwell, for the "madness" that led him to return and be recaptured, Washington replies, "Sir, I could not be free with the galling thought that my poor wife was still a slave. With her in slavery, my body, not my spirit, was free" (239). In a telling reversal of the transformation attending Douglass's violence against Covey ("This spirit made me a freeman in *fact*, while I remained a slave in *form*"), Douglass represents Washington's love for his wife as a kind of psychological bondage: "With her in slavery" he would never be free.

Perhaps the very illogic of this portion of the story—Washington escaping to Canada only to immediately return to Virginia—explains why critics tend to dismiss its importance. If mentioned at all, readers tend to concur with Krista Walter's assessment that, in Douglass's view, "the pursuit of freedom will only be hindered by the weak sentimentality that inheres in domestic relationships."[34] That family, slavery, and manhood prove an untenable combination to Douglass seems without doubt, but the dismissal of familial bonds as "weak sentimentality" does not, I think, do justice to the conflict Douglass is depicting. If Washington is "heroic" in his eventual rebellion aboard the *Creole*, an act that brings freedom to himself and the other slaves, he is meant to be heroic as well in his determination to return to family, knowing the folly of such a return. To be a (black) man, implies Douglass, is to be torn by opposing desires and responsibilities: to be a man, Washington must love liberty more than life, but to be a family man, he must also take care of his wife, whose liberty is in his hands. Caught in the grip of slavery, the claims of love and family can serve to endanger a man's freedom. This is an idea supported by the fact that Washington himself is finally free only once his wife is dead—that is, once his manhood is focused and founded on a single attainable goal, the liberation of his own person.

For Douglass, the dual roles of manhood—to serve one's self and to serve one's family—appear impossible for any but the free man, or master, to fulfill. Writing within and about slavery, Douglass thus often appears to envision women as a "hazard to [his] own liberty," just as Washington views his fellow slaves, "seated by a warm fire, merrily passing away the time," as representing a "treachery to freedom." To be truly free, a man must not only take control of his physical condition but also master those identifications that seduce him into complicity, or worse, "contentment with slavery" (226–27). It is precisely as a free man rather than as a slave that Washington rejects the identity assigned to him by the *Creole*'s white first mate at the end of the story: "You call me a *black murderer*. I am not a murderer. God is my witness that LIBERTY, not *malice*, is the motive for this night's work. I have done no more to those dead men yonder, than they would have done to me in like circumstances.... We have done that which you applaud your fathers for doing, and if we are murderers, *so were they*" (245). Washington frames his violence as an act of American patriotism, noting that Anglo-American men, of all people, must identify with it, given their revolutionary heritage.[35] The story concludes with the first mate's recitation of Washington's reception on the docks of Nassau, where he and the other rebels are greeted with the "deafening cheers of a multitude of sympathizing spectators" (247). This final scene signals the emancipation of the American slaves at the hands of the British, putting to shame, Douglass hopes, an American readership whose sympathetic identifications are so far misplaced. If the British, whom the Founding Fathers defeated, embrace Washington as a hero, certainly white

Americans should claim him as one of their own, recognizing in the violence done against them a kindred spirit who has learned from the white fathers what it takes to make oneself a free man of feeling.

BLOODY INSTRUCTIONS

Douglass's vindication of the historical Madison Washington in "The Heroic Slave" seeks to reframe for white readers "black" murder as American self-defense, justifying slave rebellions on the grounds that Anglo-Americans must find themselves, in Smith's words, sympathetically "bringing the case home to [themselves]."[36] The work of violence is thereby dislocated from its degrading purpose in the hands of slaveholders to become a redemptive means of attaining American sonship. As spiritually true descendants of American rebels, Douglass and Washington personify the sacrificial nature of radical abolition, where a man must be willing to give up all, even family, for the cause of freedom.

As many critics have noted, such a revolution in feeling comes for Douglass in his political shift from Garrisonian pacifism in the 1840s to radical abolitionism in the 1850s. By the time of his writing of "The Heroic Slave" and *My Bondage and My Freedom*, Douglass had eschewed the platform of nonviolent resistance in abolishing slavery and had broken ties with the peaceful white "father," William Lloyd Garrison, whose teachings in Christian love Douglass had once embraced and to whose patronage his first autobiography, *Narrative of the Life*, is somewhat indebted.[37] It is during the 1850s that Douglass becomes acquainted with John Brown, another radical abolitionist for whom "force" is the key to freedom. For Brown, as for Douglass, the sometimes necessary use of violence signals not so much a radical break from American culture's ethos of empathy as a masculinized, aggressive approach to how unity might be effected. Just as "the very color of the man is forgotten" in Douglass and Covey's violent embrace, so white Americans, John Brown believes, should be able to experience in the crucible of radical abolition the means of their own release and redemption from the grip of racial prejudice and strife.

"Though a white gentlemen [*sic*]," Douglass writes in a letter after first meeting him, Brown "is in sympathy, a black man, and as deeply interested in our cause, as though his own soul had been pierced with the iron of slavery."[38] Douglass's allusion to branding suggestively corporealizes Brown's commitment to the abolition of slavery, testifying to Brown's successful adoption of what John Stauffer has termed a "black heart"— the ability of a white person to "view the world as if [he] were black, shed [his] 'whiteness' as a sign of superiority, and renounce [his] belief in skin color as a marker of aptitude and social status."[39] Ever on the lookout, in Brown's own words, to do "something in a practical way for my poor fellow-men who are in bondage," Brown ultimately completes his task in two mutually reinforcing acts of sympathetic identification: he kills and he dies for the killing.[40] On October 16, 1859, Brown led a party of eighteen men, thirteen white and five black, in an assault on the government armory in Harper's Ferry, (West) Virginia, with the intent of freeing slaves in the surrounding area. The raid resulted in the deaths of four civilians, one Marine, and ten of Brown's own party, including two of his sons. He was captured and beaten, and on December 2, 1859, John Brown was hung. In the wake of the raid, Brown was denounced by proslavery proponents as a lunatic and a madman, a depiction Frederick Douglass rejects on the same grounds as those upon which he exalts Madison Washington: "It is an appalling fact in the history of the American people, that they have so far forgotten their own heroic age, as readily to accept the charge of insanity against a man who imitated the heroes of Lexington, Concord, and Bunker Hill. . . . It is an effeminate and cowardly age, which calls a man a lunatic because he rises to such self-forgetful heroism, as to count his own life as worth nothing in comparison with the freedom of millions of his fellows."[41] The "effeminate . . . age" is juxtaposed with Douglass's sense of Brown's attainment of manly sympathy. "As though his own soul had been pierced with the iron of slavery," Brown and his battered body brings black and white together in a symbol not of subjugation but of American force and courage.

The degree to which Brown is actually able to shed his white skin and adopt a "black heart" is, of course, open to debate. As Kimberly Rae Connor argues, Brown's self-alignment with blacks evinced at times more condescension than equality, as exemplified in his essay "Sambo's Mistakes," where Brown writes in the voice of a black man in order to instruct African Americans on how to lead more productive lives. "Brown's patronizing attempt to cast himself in blackface" in this essay, Connor goes on, "demonstrates how he was a man of his time," one who is unable to find a "dignified and effective mode of cross-racial discourse." Brown thus turns to violence, she says, as the only language "whites would hear and blacks would appreciate."[42] Brown's recourse to violence, however, rather than clarifying the color of his heart, further confuses it for white audiences of the time. According to Daniel C. Littlefield, Brown's aggressive methods in Kansas and at Harper's Ferry seemed on the one hand to bespeak his Anglo-Saxon manliness, a manliness in direct opposition to the supposed 'gentle docility' of African Americans. On the other hand, the black man was still regarded by many whites (at opportune moments) as irrational, fierce, and bloodthirsty — a "slave to his emotions." Brown's willingness to kill *for* blacks therefore rendered him, in the minds of some, as too "black" himself — that is, as too much akin to those he was attempting to free.[43] Even for many of those abolitionists in sympathy with Brown's politics, the violence of his methods distanced him from the popular image of the white liberal Christian whose sympathy was so complete it transcended race. Brown's aggressive actions, in other words, tended to exacerbate the racial divide rather than bridge it; his radical impulses threw into relief the seeming impassable gulf separating white men and black men and made manifest the problem of the model of aggressive manhood itself. After all, if black men adopted such a model, many whites believed, all hell would break loose.[44]

Brown's capacity to identify with blacks, then, ushered in its own set of social and moral problems, problems resolved, albeit uneasily, by way of the Christian paradigm of self-sacrifice. Brown's violence, many abolitionists contended, bespoke his willingness not only to kill but to *die* for others, and it was the latter point that eclipsed, or transformed, the former. Douglass's reference to Brown's "self-forgetful heroism" at Harper's Ferry importantly associates Brown not only with revolutionary force but with religious martyrdom. In the same spirit, Henry David Thoreau preaches on the day of Brown's execution that "some eighteen hundred years ago Christ was crucified; this morning, perchance, Captain Brown was hung. These are the two ends of a chain which are not without its links. He is not Old Brown any longer; he is an angel of light."[45] Ralph Waldo Emerson predicts that Brown's death will "make the gallows glorious, like the cross."[46] Brown's martyrdom translates his violence into a vehicle for, and a testament to, his sympathetic identification with the oppressed. He becomes, like Christ, a *victim* of violence and a symbol of its empathetic effects through suffering.

It was a popular New England refrain, born not only of white intellectuals' hatred for slavery but also of their own discomfort with Brown's radical methods. In her letter to Henry A. Wise, governor of Virginia, Lydia Maria Child writes that with regard to "Brown's recent attempt . . . I do [not] know of a single person who would have approved of it. . . . But . . . I will also say that if I believed our religion justified men in fighting for freedom, I should consider the enslaved everywhere as best entitled to that right."[47] Child's qualified "if I believed" speaks to the ambivalence that she and many other self-professed Christians felt about Brown's means of emancipating slaves. To vindicate his violent actions, it was necessary to explain and justify his motives. Very often that justification was grounded in what writers took to be Brown's quintessential demonstration of American Christian love. John Brown was a "Christian hero" of the Puritan type, declares the Reverend George B. Cheever: "It cannot be denied. It is the iniquity of Slavery . . . in opposition and defiance of which, John Brown, trusting in God . . . gathered up his strength, his life, and threw himself, in behalf of the enslaved, and against the enslaving government and law, even unto death." It is not the murder of men that Brown is after, argues Cheever, but their release from an "enslaving government."[48] In sacrificing his life for this purpose, he goes on, Brown proves his commitment to those God-given words "'Thou shalt love thy neighbor as thyself,' and 'Whatsoever ye would that men should do to you, do ye even so to them.'"⁴⁹ Of course, the ambiguous referent to what it is men "do" to each other—love or murder—epitomizes the problem Brown poses for his audience. The potential for reciprocating acts of violence rather than reciprocating acts of love is suggested in Child's allusion to Shakespeare in her letter to Wise. "Even if Captain Brown were as bad as you paint him," she comments to the governor, "I should suppose he must naturally remind you of the words of Macbeth: —'We but teach / Bloody instructions, which, being taught, return / To plague the inventor: this even-handed justice / Commends the ingredients of our poisoned chalice / To our own lips.'"⁵⁰ Though Brown can be said to have acted out of Godly motives, Child is saying, the actions themselves yet reflect the "bloody instructions" taught him by the abusive white fathers of a self-professed (but hypocritical) democratic nation.

As these contemporary responses indicate, both Brown's proactive violence and his execution for it loom large in the American imagination, a fact reinforced by Douglass in declaring Brown "THE MAN OF THIS NINETEENTH CENTURY."⁵¹ How John Brown comes to occupy this position can be accounted for, in part, as suggested above, by his dual embodiment of aggression and submissiveness, conflicting figurations that affiliate Brown simultaneously with black men and with white, themselves confusingly aligned with both characteristics. But if Brown's violence tends to confound his racial identity for contemporaries, his dying for that violence, I would argue, ultimately resignifies him as white. It is his status as a white man rather than as a black one, after all, that allows Brown's death to be read as a "sacrifice"—a payment made by one party on behalf of another. Moreover, the very sacrificial nature of his death (alluded to by Brown himself, as well as by others) invokes the masterful privileging of the white male body in pain—that is, the white master-father who not only appreciates the suffering of others but makes it his own. "What was his crime?" Theodore Tilton asks of his audience on the day of Brown's execution: "Guilty of what? Guilty of loving his fellow-men too well! . . . Guilty of too well 'remembering them that are in bonds as bound with them!'"[52] Brown's violent excesses are portrayed as an excess of love, one that whitewashes his own crimes even as it exposes the greater national crime of slavery, for which he, an ostensible innocent, pays with his life. Thus one could argue that Brown proves himself "THE MAN" precisely by the way in which he translates Anglo-America's paternal legacy of violence, so often and eloquently alluded to by Douglass, into a form of self-suffering. Although convicted for the murder of others, Brown's actions are ultimately represented by himself and other abolitionists as violence done against *him*: "I have been *whiped* [*sic*] as the saying is," Brown writes to his wife from his imprisonment, "but am sure I can recover all the lost capital occasioned by that disaster; by only hanging a few moments by the neck; & I feel quite determined to make the utmost possible out of a defeat."[53] Brown's choice of language exposes slavery as an essentially economic institution, one that he hopes to abolish with the "lost capital" of his body, now made in payment for future gains: making "the utmost possible" out of being "whiped." Through his own suffering white body, in other words, Brown hopes to exhibit to an intractable, insensible white nation the true cost of slavery.

It is tempting simply to read Brown's example, as many of his contemporaries did, as a testament to the power of cross-racial sympathy: "Remembering them that are in bonds as bound with them," Brown fights, and dies, for the freedom of his black brothers. His dying then ideally forces upon his white audience an identification with him, thereby effecting in them a new sensitivity toward the suffering of slaves. What I would like to pursue in the concluding pages of this chapter, however, is the reaffirmation of white manhood as the site of sensibility evinced in Brown's life and death, a sensibility only made possible, he implicitly posits, through the use of force. Although the liberation of black men and women is Brown's chief concern, to the extent that slaves remain *objects* rather than perpetrators of violence they also remain for Brown outside the cycle of aggression and love that is the white father's heritage and salvation.[54] Brown's analogous reference to his being "*whiped*" is, counterintuitively, indicative of the difference between his own position and those of black slaves. While the trope of whipping rhetorically links Brown with blacks, his representation of the salutary effects of his beating signals a radical disjunction between the whipping, or disciplining, of whites and the gratuitous beating of blacks. In contrast to those slaves with whom Brown's "whipping" is meant to identify him, Brown is able to make the "utmost possible" out of his suffering. He sees his pain, unlike the slave's, as part of an economy that produces new feeling: that is, his martyrdom will evoke an empathy that his violence alone failed to effect. Brown's logic speaks to a Christian disciplinary tradition in which suffering is equated with emotional correction and where the development of sensible personhood is brought about through the receiving, and the giving, of pain.

The racial implications of Brown's suffering sympathy can only be clearly understood in the context in which Brown himself viewed the efficacy of whipping—as a legacy of loving abuse handed down from (white) fathers to sons. As a Calvinist, Brown believed both in original human sin and in God's just punishment of that sin.[55] God does not punish without cause or design, however, but for the spiritual edification of his children. In a theology of punishment dating back to Augustine, as Theodore De Bruyn tells us, the "sufferings endured by humankind are construed as discipline from God who, like a father who beats his children precisely because he loves them, thereby prepares his heirs for eternal blessedness." This ritual of correction became known as "*pater flagellans*, or the father who 'whips' the son he loves (Proverbs 3.12/Hebrews 12.6)."[56] Though in Roman society, whipping or flogging was reserved for slaves, in the late fourth and early fifth centuries whipping was incorporated into domestic practice by Christians as a sign of the earthly father's obedience to, and imitation of, God. Brown himself was such a loving father, punishing his sons, as Stephen Oates writes, "with the wrath of a Hebrew patriarch at the slightest breach of good order and religious habits."[57] Yet, in one now-famous example of Brown's disciplinary tactics, Brown substitutes his own body for that of his son, impressing upon the boy through sympathetic identification the father's belief in a justice that hurts.

According to the memoirs of John Jr., his father "had a rule not to threaten one of his children." John Sr. did have a scrupulous way, however, of keeping track of his children's faults, and those of John Jr. were recorded in a book, along with the mounting cost of his transgressions:

> For disobeying mother . . . . 8 lashes
> unfaithfulness at work 3
> telling a lie 8

"On a certain Sunday morning," John Jr. remembers, his father concluded that "it was time for a settlement." He goes on:

> [Father] . . . showed me my account, which exhibited a fearful footing up of *debits*. I had no credits or off-sets, and was of course bankrupt. I then paid about *one-third* of the debt, reckoned in strokes from a nicely-prepared blue-beech switch, laid on "masterly." Then, to my utter astonishment, father stripped off his shirt, and, seating himself on a block, gave me the whip and bade me "lay it on" to his bare back. I dared not refuse to obey, but at first I did not strike hard. "Harder!" he said; "harder, harder!" until he *received the balance of the account*. Small drops of blood showed on his back where the tip end of the tingling beech cut through. Thus ended the account and the settlement, which was also my first practical illustration of the Doctrine of the Atonement. I was then too obtuse to perceive how Justice could be satisfied by inflicting penalty upon the back of the innocent instead of the guilty; but at that time I had not read the ponderous volumes of Jonathan Edwards's sermons which father owned.[58]

Here punishment is again represented in economic terms—a balance sheet of sin to lashes for which the transgressor is held to "account." The economics of punishment suggests, perhaps, Brown's attempt to rationalize—make objectively reasonable—his disciplinary methods, but it is a reasoning lost at the time on the son who, in his youth, is "too obtuse" to understand the calculations of "Justice."

Fathers of Violence

Reading the scene in retrospect, however, the adult John Jr. adopts his father's viewpoint and offers the moment as an example of Christian atonement: the shedding of an innocent's blood in payment for the crimes of the guilty. Even more to the point, I would argue, Brown's pedagogical method reveals the way in which, for Brown, boys become men by bearing the weight of other men's pain. And not just bearing it, but inflicting it. As Brown, who lays on his strokes "masterly," switches places with his son, he forces John Jr. to take the master's position. The boy does so reluctantly, and at first he "[does] not strike hard." But as Brown shouts at him to strike "harder! harder!" the evidence of the son's crime appears on the father's body: "Small drops of blood showed on his back where the tip end of the tingling beech cut through." As he does later in relation to a guilty, slaveholding nation, Brown here acts as a whipping boy, receiving the blows that he believes, in all "Justice," should rightly be aimed at another. In doing so, he offers a dramatic example not only of how the innocent may substitute for the guilty but of how the guilty may be spiritually corrected by learning sympathy for those they abuse. John Jr.'s punishment is to effect in him an emotional transformation — a compelled identification with his "victim" that forcefully impresses upon him the material consequences of his sin. The son's blows thus become, in a psychological sense, self-inflicted. What Brown seeks to teach his son, and by extension white America, is that, through identification, the abuse of others is a punishment in itself. Who holds the rod and who receives it is obscured in the suffering that both parties share.

Brown's voluntary sacrifice with respect to John Jr. provides us with not only a fascinating filial but a meaningful *cultural* moment in its manifestation of those power inversions we have traced in antebellum slavery debates and discourse. Central to the work of inversion are identifications that seek to distribute pain across a broad spectrum, putting masters in the position of slaves, fathers in the position of sons, and vice versa. Brown's sacrifice *for* his son (as well as, later, *of* his sons) foreshadows the identificatory work he sees for himself on a much grander scale many years later. Awaiting his sentence on the day of his conviction, Brown announces to the court, "Now, if it is deemed necessary that I forfeit my life for the furtherance of the ends of justice, and mingle my blood further with the *blood of my children and with the blood of millions in this slave country* whose rights are disregarded by wicked and unjust enactments, I say, let it be done!"[59] As he does for his son, Brown means to offer himself as a substitute, but one whose blood is shed along with, rather than instead of, those abused ones that he represents. In doing so, Brown represents himself not as aggressive father but as suffering son — a whipping boy whose martyrdom demonstrates that whites and blacks, fathers and sons, are always already one in their mutual, and potentially redemptive, experience of pain.

If such a reading of Brown's various martyrdoms seems to obscure the material difference in position between free whites and enslaved blacks, that is partly the point. I am arguing that part of Brown's cultural caché at the time resides in his ability to invoke for audiences both the manly "force" evident in white America's checkered history and its simultaneous disavowal through substitution and sentiment: that is, the popular, sentimental construction of power that envisions, in Fitzhugh's words, the plight of the weak "subduing the strength" and "commanding the care" of the privileged.[60] Insofar as Brown takes upon himself the role of the former, he demonstrates his capacity to become, like Christ, both father and son in one, both subject *and* object of sympathy, and he ironically aligns his sacrifice with the forms of dominant white culture he is so anxiously striving to reject.[61] That culture is manifested, moreover, in the very structures of discipline through which Brown imagines his sacrifice, a disciplinary model that posits male maturation as a consequence of abuse — both the abuse he gives and the abuse he receives. In antebellum America, such filial disciplinary intimacies are the dubious privilege of whites. Despite Fitzhugh's (among others') assertions that white masters are like fathers to their slaves, we know from Douglass's testimony that "punishments" under slavery are not applied for the purpose of the slave's personal development. The legacy of violence handed down from father to son, one on which the son's salvation as well as his majority depends, is, at this cultural moment, a particularly white legacy.

As perverse as it may sound to modern readers, in Brown's theology, whipping was part of the promise and privilege of inheritance. Like God, writes De Bruyn, "a father beats his son because he wants to ensure that his son will be a worthy and reliable heir. The father is motivated by love, not hatred, and is acting in the son's interest, since he desires that his son become a better person."[62] As Oates records, Brown believed that God was just such a father: "The rod became for [Brown] a symbol of the pain and terror—the inevitable doom—that awaited one who strayed from the path of righteousness."[63] Brown himself certainly felt chastened by God during his life. He endured the deaths of ten of his twenty-two children and the death of his first wife, Dianthe. With regard to the latter's death, Brown writes to his father, "We are again smarting under the rod of our Heavenly Father. Last night about eleven o'clock my affectionate, dutiful and faithful Dianthe (to use her own words) bade 'farewell to Earth.'" After the death of their daughter Amelia ("Kitty") by scalding, Brown writes to his second wife, Mary, that "notwithstanding God has chastised us *often, & sore*; yet he has not *himself* entirely withdrawn from us, nor forsaken us *utterly*. The sudden, & dreadful manner in which he has seen fit to call our *dear little Kitty* to take her leave of us, is I kneed not tell you how much on mind; but before *Him*; I will bow my head in submission, & hold my peace."[64] Though Brown obviously struggled with what he took to be God's method of dealing with a fallen world, he nonetheless trusted that God's punishments were for Brown's own good and thus submits to the Heavenly Father's "rod."

The legacy of a disciplinary violence motivated by love is not ideally reserved for whites alone—that is, I am not suggesting that Brown harbored exclusionary feelings with regard to his own family or his own race and their salvation. Rather, Brown saw blacks as already paying the price for sinful humanity, but for sins that were not their own. While still a young man, Brown encountered a black youth roughly his own age but "badly clothed" and "poorly fed." Brown felt sorry for him. But, in Oates's words, "contrition turned to horror when the master, right in front of John, beat the

Negro boy with an iron fire shovel. John returned [home] with an unrelenting anguish for the 'wretched, hopeless condition' of that *'Fatherless & Motherless'* slave boy."[65] Given Brown's religious beliefs, we may surmise that, for him, slavery was not unjust and inhumane simply because it employed the whip, but because it did so outside of a familial, pedagogical context. For beatings to be meaningful, they must be done in filial love; the intent must be to turn sinful sons into sensible men. Under slavery, however, "fatherless" black boys were denied an earthly inheritance, and perhaps even a heavenly one. Dehumanized rather than sensitized by the whip, slaves would never experience the redemptive effects of a father's punishing affection.[66]

For Brown, all men were sons before a Heavenly Father whose rod was employed to bring them to salvation. The deaths that accrued in holy wars were likewise viewed by Brown in this context — that is, as sacrifices that would bring white and black, oppressor and oppressed, together in God's crucible of pain. The idea is substantiated in Brown's own genealogical history, a history replete with the sufferings and sacrifices of sons. In his 1859 essay "A Visit to John Brown's Household," author and publisher T. W. Higginson sympathetically notes to his readers that "[Brown] had long before made up his mind to sacrifice every son he ever had, if necessary, in fighting slavery." Such men as Brown needed for his battle, Higginson goes on, "are not to be found ordinarily; they must be reared. John Brown did not merely look for men, therefore; he reared them in his sons."[67] By this account, Brown raised an army as much as a family, a view that accords with the story of the "Family Oath" that grew up around the Brown family years after John Brown's death. "According to the family tradition," writes historian Robert McGlone, "the antislavery sentiments of the oldest boys . . . were transformed into a sacred pledge in the late 1830s when their father conducted an impromptu lesson that culminated in a prayer and a formal oath of allegiance to the cause. . . . With profound seriousness, John, Jr. remembered, his father asked each son individually if he were willing to help free the slaves. After kneeling to pray, 'we all rose and with right hands raised, took upon us an obligation of secrecy, of fidelity and devotion to the work of a forcible resistance to slavery in our country.'"[68]

In the 1830s, Brown's oldest boys—John Jr., Frederick, Oliver, Watson, Jason—would have still been quite young, lending credibility to the idea that Brown "reared" his sons to be soldiers in the fight for freedom. It was, according to Higginson, a family legacy. Next to Brown's house, he reports, "is an old, mossy, time-worn tombstone.... It has a past duty and a future one. It bears the name of Captain John Brown, who died during the Revolution, eighty-three years ago; it was brought hither by his grandson bearing the same name and title; the latter caused to be inscribed upon it, also, the name of his son Frederick, 'murdered at Osawatomie [Kansas] for his adherence to the cause of freedom'... and he himself has said, for years, that no other tombstone should mark his own grave."[69] Like father, like son, like father. Brown's family, Higginson implies, is generationally linked through violence and blood, and by the love of liberty that renders both violence and blood an atonement for (another's) sin.

Remembering Brown's declaration to "mingle [his] blood with the blood of [his] children and with the blood of millions" of tortured slaves, we see in Brown's example not only the transcendence of blood over racial difference but the necessity of violence in creating a new, more expansive, familial sensibility. For the Browns, unlike for many, violence did not define the borders of family but instead the disintegration of its borders; individual families must be destroyed so that a larger, greater family might be born. "I have had thirteen children, and only four are left," Brown's second wife, Mary, purportedly tells Higginson, "but if I am to see the ruin of my house, I cannot but hope that Providence may bring out of it some benefit to the poor slaves." Brown writes in a similar spirit in his last letter to his wife and children before his death: "So my dear *shattered; & broken* family; be of good cheer.... And let me entreat you all to love *the whole remnant* of our once great family: 'with a pure *heart fervently*.'... It is the ground of the utmost comfort to *my mind*: to know that so many of you as have had *the opportunity*; have given full proof of your fidelity to the great family of man."[70]

For Brown, the shattering of the white family for the sake of the cross-raced national family, or the "great family of man," is the cost of freedom, as well as a labor of love. As we saw in Douglass's work, transcending racial prejudice involves transgressing familial categories, and in slaveholding America, Brown declares, the expansion of kinship ties cannot be achieved without sacrifice or bloodshed — the two are intimately tied together. As Fales Henry Newhall puts it in his funeral sermon for Brown, "For years and generations God has been bottling these tears [of slaves], and if he returns them to us in showers of blood, who will dare to murmur at his justice? The tears and the blood of the strong and of the weak, of the white and of the black, are alike to Him 'who hath made of one blood all nations of men.'"[71] The "great family of man" is delivered by turning tears into blood — or, perhaps more precisely, by turning "showers of blood" back into tears for *whites* as well as blacks, as their own families feel the pain of God's chastising justice. That John Brown was both the vehicle for, and the embodiment of, that pain for white men renders his a lesson not only in aggression but, by his own account, in self-flagellation. Both sacrificer and sacrificed, both whipper and "whiped," John Brown symbolizes the dual roles of white manhood, even white mastery, in antebellum culture. It is a mastery refracted through the lessons of Christianity, patriarchalism, and patriotism — a pedagogical Trinity of feeling by which sons are taught to emulate their fathers — divine, earthly, and Founding — by engaging in acts of aggression that will ultimately demonstrate their submission to the law of love.

The analysis offered here seeks neither to celebrate nor to dismiss the extent of the sacrifices Brown, his sons, and their families made for the abolition of slavery. Rather, it seeks to unpack and demystify some of the mechanisms through which those sacrifices are deployed and understood. One of those mechanisms, as I have been arguing, is the conversion of insensible men into men of feeling through acts of violence in which they are compelled to participate, acts that then become a vehicle for their empathetic identification with others. In Brown's case, those identifications are as overdetermined as they are critical to his cause. Brown's violent methods are read by his supporters, as we have seen, as a testament to his Christlike sympathy for African Americans—his "heroic" willingness to identify with, as Wendell Phillips puts it, "a race in whose blood he had no share."[72] Yet, as I have tried to show throughout this chapter, the enactment of the interracial family to which Brown's "mingled blood" would attest can hardly be imagined outside a paradigm of white Christian sensibility perpetuated, ironically, through the lash. In Brown's execution, white witnesses are asked to identify not only with black suffering through the sufferings of a white body like their own but also with the violent methods for which he dies. That is, whites are made complicit in a specific act of punishment (Brown's hanging) for which their own guilt, according to Brown, is responsible. Symbolically speaking, Brown thus stands as a whipping boy for the sins of a white nation whose violence, Newhall suggests, will come back to them in an inevitable, if unwelcome, identification with the "tears and ... blood" of their victims.

"I John Brown am now quite certain that the crimes of this guilty, land: will never be purged away; but with Blood. I had as I now think: vainly flattered myself that without verry much bloodshed; it might be done."[73] Brown's last words, scribbled on a piece of paper and handed to a guard on the morning of his execution, indicate the punishment to come he sees in store for a guilty nation, a view that Frederick Douglass shared: "Nature must cease to be nature; men become monsters; humanity must be transformed; christianity must be exterminated ... —ere a system [of slavery] so foul and infernal can escape condemnation, or this guilty republic can have a sound, enduring peace."[74] For both Douglass and Brown, Christianity itself required the purging brought on by an inevitable civil war, blood shed in testament to both God's justice and his love for an enslaved people. Having transgressed the boundaries of family through identification with the racial other, Brown and Douglass understand the violent foundation on which black men and white men become brothers. But whereas Douglass positions slave-others as substitutes for an objectification he has mastered, Brown embraces identification with powerlessness and converts it into another form of power. Through both force and submission, and the sacrificial mechanisms that conflate the two, Brown attempts to compel whites, including his sons, to "feel the pain" of those they abuse. As his final words, as well as his personal history, indicate, it is not just sympathy but violence that will finally free both blacks and whites. As Higginson soberly observes, the Brown tombstone "has a past duty and a future one." More deaths lie ahead. Brown's martyrdom must finally be seen then as more than a sacrifice on behalf of the millions of slaves whose blood has been shed. It is also a warning to those whites who have shed it: his pain will someday be their own. Though popularly hailed as a man with the capacity to inhabit another man's skin, Brown aims the force of his punishing affection primarily at whites like himself. His life and death signify the "even-handed justice" of violence and empathy, a double-edged identification that holds within it the future promise of self-flagellation. Though "in sympathy, a black man," Brown dies a white man, a material as well as symbolic testament to the chastening love he believes all whites will meet when, in the bloody days ahead, they are likewise "pierced with the iron of slavery."

CHAPTER 4

The Death of Boyhood
and the Making of *Little Women*

All wars are boyish, and are fought by boys,
The champions and enthusiasts of the state:
Turbid ardors and vain joys
Not barrenly abate—
Stimulants to the power mature,
Preparatives of fate.
—Herman Melville, "The March into Virginia," 1866

Written about the first major battle of the Civil War at Manassas, Virginia, Melville's poem "The March into Virginia" comments with critical but resigned admiration on the reckless and glorious audacity of youth. The battle of Bull Run, as it was popularly known in the North, was fought between young and inexperienced soldiers on both the Union and the Confederate sides, and Melville attempts to capture the spirit of boys whose martial ambition and ideological ardor will lead them into engagements that many older, and perhaps wiser, men have already put behind them.

"Did all the lets and bars appear / To every just or larger end / Whence should come the trust and cheer?" Melville asks at the poem's opening. He answers: "Youth must its ignorant impulse lend — / Age finds place in the rear."[1] The forty-two-year-old Melville undoubtedly aligned himself with "Age" at this point in his life. As a poet he records, rather than literally experiences, the con-

(123)

flict. Unlike Whitman, who, at the same age in the same year, describes with a certain envy the young men "falling in and arming" for war, throwing off "the costumes of peace with an indifferent hand,"[2] Melville portrays his scene as a sacrifice — though willing — of the naive and the impetuous: "Moloch's uninitiate" who "file toward Fate" in "Bacchic glee" (23).[3] Though these soldiers march toward their deaths, they feel neither fear nor dread. "All they feel," says Melville, "is this: 'tis glory / A rapture sharp, though transitory, / Yet lasting in belaureled story" (23). The brief, sharp pain of the bullet, in other words, is nothing compared to the glory of the moment and its long-lasting literary aftermath ("the belaureled story"). Older writers like himself, Melville implies, are complicit in the sacrifice of Youth through the very narratives that turn such a sacrifice into heroic fictions.[4]

Melville's claim that wars not only are fought by boys but are themselves "boyish" renders war an important site for an examination of the substitutions and identifications I have been tracing throughout this book: in particular, the ways in which, for Melville, boys serve as vehicles for the projections and displacements of both poetical and political "fathers." Though it was not only young men who fought in the American Civil War, the unreflective enthusiasm that Melville ascribes to his participants is characteristic of youth and innocence: it is their "trust" as well as their desire for glory that turns boys into "champions . . . of the state."[5] Representing the paternalistic state as its "champion," boys both stand in for father figures whose own period of youthful enthusiasm has passed and allow fathers to relive that enthusiasm through them. The boys' deaths by the poem's end thus mark more than the loss of individual lives; they mark the loss of boyhood itself. Such a loss is made palatable, I will argue in this chapter, only by the knowledge that boyhood's unreflective, unmediated aggression has no proper place "in the rear" — that is, in peaceful society.

At the end of the previous chapter, I attempted to outline one of the avenues through which youthful aggression is imagined as socially productive. In the religiously based pedagogical lessons of John Brown we have a model for the disciplinary violence that brings white sons to manhood through beating—both the beatings they give and those they receive. With respect to the former, Brown also represents the father's displacement of aggression onto a younger generation whose assumption of the whipper's role is meant to actively engage them in the mature personal and sociopolitical work of identification. A crucial element of such work, as I have been arguing, is the recognition of one's affinity to the things one harms. To grow up is to take on the burden of identification and feel another's pain as one's own.[6] As in Brown's case, Melville depicts aggressive boys doing their father's business, but doing it gladly. By the end, their ignorance turns to enlightenment through their deadly identification with their foes (23):

> But some who this blithe mood present,
> As on in lightsome files they fare
> Shall die experienced ere three days are spent—
> Perish enlightened by the vollied glare;
> Or shame survive, and, like to adamant,
> The throe of Second Manassas share.[7]

Death is the inevitable outcome of the boyish impulse for boys on both sides of the line, according to Melville: either literal death in battle or through "experience"—an "enlightened" state that converts once aggressively impetuous boys into shamed adults.

I open this chapter on Alcott's postwar narratives with Melville's poem because it reflects an ambivalence about the nature of boys—their aggression, their courage, and their inevitable demise—the cultural reverberations of which are felt for decades to come. In the popular U.S. boy-book genre appearing shortly after the Civil War, we find a nostalgic return to, and an implicit questioning of, the role of boyhood in postwar society.[8] If a boy's transition to manhood is most perfectly proven by his death in battle, what vision of manhood remains for the next generation? How is maturity to be gained in the absence of war? Yet if the boy's warring impulse is perpetuated, how are boys—or the communities in which boys reside outside of war—to survive at all? It is just such questions that undergird Alcott's popular postbellum trilogy of children's novels,

Little Women (1868–69), *Little Men* (1871), and *Jo's Boys* (1886), novels that sound a sympathetic echo of Melville's elegy for boyish exuberance even as they repeatedly resign such exuberance to its predetermined fate. Of course, this is partly literary design: as pedagogical coming-of-age stories, Alcott's trilogy of novels focuses on the development of its heroines and heroes from impetuous children to responsible adults. The boyish proclivities of both little men and little women are thus sacrificed to the sobering, and somewhat unevenly rewarded, wisdom of maturity. Written in the wake of war, however, Alcott's trilogy appears to be structured by something other than simple literary convention. Rather, depicting boyish aggression as simultaneously attractive and alarming, Alcott plays out what is both a personally inflected and a broad-based cultural ambivalence about the place of violence in America's postwar, Christian nation. Despite boyhood's charms, these novels suggest, boyish aggression must be curtailed—or, more precisely, redirected—lest it perpetuate the warring impulse on the home front.

The association of boyish aggression with *pleasure*, moreover, signals the particularly intractable problem posed by boyish impulses. Alcott's initial foray into examining this problem occurs in *Little Women*, where her famous tomboy, "Jo" March, confesses to her mother early on in the novel, "I get so savage, I could hurt any one and *enjoy* it" (79) (my emphasis). Her words resound throughout all three novels and capture the spirit of boyhood that, as Melville puts it, drives young men to battle in "Bacchic glee." *Little Women*'s foregrounding of Jo's struggle with the pleasures of aggression map Civil War issues of violence and stability onto the home even as it opens up those issues to the world of girls as well as boys. Set as it is during the early 1860s, *Little Women* and its Alcottian double, Jo, can be said to reflect, as Judith Fetterley has argued, the author's own internal "civil war"—a personal struggle with parental dictates about gender and behavior that calls for ceding boyish aggression to womanly self-control.[9] But if, as Fetterley also contends, *Little Women* rests on the paradox that "the figure [Jo March] who most resists the pressure to become a little woman is the most attractive" in the novel, Jo's resistance constitutes what is most dangerous as well as most appealing in the text.[10] Her propensity to battle threatens to keep war alive, in the home as in the world. The only resolution lies in growing up.

Instructed by her older sister, Meg, that she must "leave off boyish tricks" now that she is a young lady, Jo replies with bitter despondency over the process of maturation: "I hate to think I've got to grow up and be Miss March, and wear long gowns, and look as prim as a China-aster.... I can't get over my disappointment in not being a boy, and it's worse than ever now, for I'm dying to go and fight with papa, and I can only stay at home and knit like a poky old woman" (3). The equation of "female" employments (knitting) with old age and "male" pursuits (fighting) with youthful vigor in *Little Women* reproduces Melville's youth-age dichotomy in gendered terms: Jo's "dying" to go to war suggests that staying at home/growing up into womanhood is itself a kind of death, though not a glorious one. Jo's desire to join in her father's activities, however, is thwarted not only by her "not being a boy" but by the father himself. In his letter instructing Jo and her sisters to "*fight* their bosom enemies bravely" and "*conquer* themselves ... beautifully" while he is away at war, Mr. March essentially redraws the boundaries of conflict, shifting the site of battle from the southern plains to the heart and mind (my emphasis) (8). Rather than "fight with papa," Jo is instructed to fight (with) herself, allowing her father to establish his paternal authority over the domestic circle, and desire itself, even in his absence.

Jo's boyish impulse to go to war is a desire to be (like) the powerful, aggressive "father," an identification that Mr. March restages as an *interior* drama, thus effecting Jo's eventual transformation from a tomboy into a "little woman." Her example is but one of many internal "civil wars" occurring throughout Alcott's trilogy. In all three novels, the desire to hurt others is depicted as an impulse, and a pleasure, against which young people, especially boys and tomboys, must repeatedly fight. Thus we find Alcott's protagonists engaging in sadistic fantasies and play against toys, dolls, and their real-life counterparts: other children. Yet, as Mr. March's metaphor suggestively reveals, the sadistic impulse is not to be eradicated so

The Death of Boyhood (127)

much as redirected toward the self: in "conquering... themselves," Alcott's protagonists learn to internalize their aggression. Encouraged by fathers and father figures to embrace empathetic identification as a means of rerouting aggression inward, Alcott's little men and women come to see the pain they cause another as, essentially, a *self*-inflicted wound.

Of course, as Freud famously observes in "A Child Is Being Beaten," self-abuse holds its own kind of pleasure. Positing masochism as "sadism which has been turned round upon the self," Freud identifies the unconscious wish inhering in childhood fantasies of seeing others beaten: to be the child under the whip. In Alcott's trilogy, the conversion of sadistic into masochistic impulses occurs precisely through the condensation of aggression and affection about which Freud theorizes, where "I am beaten by my father" stands in the child's mind for "*I am loved by my father.*"[11] But whereas Freud reads masochism as indicative of a "regressive" Oedipal attachment to the father, Alcott sees it as a mark of mature Christian character. The protagonists' identification with the (imagined) powerful f/Father in Alcott's novels is refracted through a Christian framework that posits maturity as a recognition of one's affinity to the objects of one's abuse, an identification that affords its own form of pleasure by the child's understanding that the one who is "beaten" is the one who is loved.

In this respect, Alcott's trilogy perpetuates the pattern we have traced from *Wieland* to John Brown, one in which the impulse toward, and enactment of, violence catalyzes identifications that transform aggressors into "whipping boys" through their empathy with the things they harm. More than this, however, Alcott's novels virtually recapitulate the paradigm by tracing it through the child's development — that is, by examining its function in the child's experience of growing up. Part of a burgeoning literature for and about children in the United States, *Little Women*, *Little Men*, and *Jo's Boys* importantly tell the American story of the whipping boy from the child's vantage point. Yet it is a perspective nonetheless shaped by attachments to, and identifications with, the father. Rerouting the child's identification away from figures of power and toward objects of the child's violence, fathers initiate a dynamic wherein, as we will see, boyish aggression is marshaled in support of its own demise.

SPARING THE ROD

"I have made a plan for my life," Alcott writes in her journal as an adolescent. "I am going to be good. I've made many resolutions, and written sad notes, and cried over my sins, but it doesn't seem to do any good! Now I'm going to *work really*, for I feel a true desire to improve, and be a help and comfort, not a care, to my dear mother."[12] For the young Louisa, to "improve" was synonymous with controlling her anger. At age eleven, for example, Alcott confesses to her father that her bad temper is her worst fault.[13] Alcott's private writings reflect a preoccupation with her psychological faults, a fact unsurprising since, as Richard Brodhead notes, for Alcott, "life with father... was life with self-reformation as the continuing agenda."[14] A philosopher-educator intensely interested in child development, Amos Bronson Alcott fastened his attention early on to the maturation of his own daughters. His main objective as a father was to instill in his children a habit of self-control. Louisa's prospects in this regard, according to Bronson, were quite bleak: "There is a self-corroding nature [to Louisa] — a spirit not yet conformed to the conditions of enjoyment.... The will has gathered around itself a breastwork of *Inclinations*, and bids defiance to every attack that ventures against its purpose."[15] The martial imagery with which Bronson represents Louisa's behavior speaks to his own views of the parent-child relation as essentially a battle of wills. (It is not just the child who has gathered around herself a "breastwork of *Inclinations*" in his metaphor, after all, but also the parent, who is on the "attack.") And whereas with Louisa's older sister, Anna, Bronson saw an opportunity for winning this battle — that is, he sees the chance to "shape her," as he puts it, "into the image of [his] desires" — with Louisa, his ability to master the situation was far less assured. "[Louisa] refuses and that obstinately, whatever opposes her inclinations," Bronson writes when Alcott is barely two years old. "Her violence is at times alarming—father, mother, sister, objects, all are equally defied, and not infrequently, the menace terminates in blows."[16]

Whose "blows" are given and whose received is not made clear; what is clear, however, is the pattern of temper and violence that characterizes Alcott's early life with family and that puts father and daughter aggressively at odds. Although Alcott's life history is not the focal point of this chapter, her early experiences with her family, as well as her conception of her own character in relation to it, is key to understanding her literary trilogy's emphasis on selfhood as a construction of familial, identificatory dynamics. A truth made evident in all three novels is that children do not simply grow but are shaped and molded, molded both by their own desires *and* by the desires of those they love. One could say that Bronson helps define his daughter's character by producing in her an identification with *his* disappointment; his pain at Louisa's "violence" becomes hers. Noting more than once in her early journals her guilt and sorrow over being "cross," Alcott adds that once she had cried over her faults she "then felt better."[17] Alcott's mother, Abba, encouraged her daughter in this conversion of anger to passivity: "My Louy," she writes after one bitter fight between Bronson and Louisa, "I was grieved at your selfish behavior this morning, but also greatly pleased to find you bore so meekly Father's reproof for it. That is the way, dear; if you find you are wrong, take the discipline sweetly, and do so no more. It is not to be expected that children should always do right; but oh, how lovely to see a child penitent and patient when the passion is over."[18] Though Louisa may have begun life demanding her own way—defying "father, mother, sisters, all"—by adolescence she has learned to internalize her father's will and to see her "inclinations" as he does: as "bosom enemies" to be overcome.

The internalization of the parental perspective evident in Alcott's repeated self-reproofs would seem to exemplify the "disciplinary intimacy" that Richard Brodhead has famously argued begins to structure mid-nineteenth-century pedagogical models of correction. This new model eschews physical punishment for recalcitrant children in favor of emotional rehabilitation, one brought about by training the child, as early as possible, to associate authority with parental love. "From the child's perspective," writes Brodhead, "what the parent-figure believes in comes across indistinguishably from his love, so that the child imbibes what the parent stands for in a moral sense along with the parent's physical intimacy and affection." Authority figures can thus "spare the rod," in Brodhead's words, because a "nearer and surer enforcer" has been created: the child's desire to please and be loved by one whom s/he loves.[19] Notwithstanding Brodhead's persuasive claim for a virtual paradigm shift in disciplinary theory in the mid-nineteenth century, I argue that violence continues to play a crucial role—albeit in largely vicarious ways—in the disciplinary relation. In Alcott's fiction, violence proves central to the creation of empathetic bonds between parent figures and their children, as well as to the instantiation of an empathetic sensibility more generally in the child himself or herself. Although it is clear that new strategies of disciplinary intimacy have taken hold by the latter half of the century, that intimacy continues to be founded on the physical abuse of *some* body, though not necessarily the offending child's.

The predominant shift in emphasis from corporal to noncorporal forms of discipline in antebellum America can be attributed, at least in part, to the cultural association of whipping with slavery. Antislavery writings brought to the fore the evils of the lash, which in turn sparked debates not only about slavery but, as we saw with Melville, about naval flogging and, for our purposes here, about pedagogical practice. Typical of the educational reformist position were arguments like Lyman Cobb's, whose *The Evil Tendencies of Corporal Punishment* (1847) posits that physical punishment is not only immoral but inefficient. More effective is instilling in the child a proper sense of shame, so that ultimately "self-reproach" will become, as Cobb puts it, "the whip that scourges his faults."[20] Cobb's metaphor seeks to differentiate by analogy physical corrections from sentimental ones. The very comparison, however, underscores the extent to which the whip continues to serve as the dominating symbol of control and punishment, even in the reformist imagination. And it is not just symbolic. The previous chapter on

John Brown's disciplinary model — his embodiment, that is, of the *pater flagellans*, the father who, like God, whips the child he loves — demonstrates how the whip itself, and not just the psychological whip, gets incorporated into structures of Christian thought and discipline.

Brown is not anomalous in his pedagogical practice; his example of substitutionary violence with respect to his son — his demanding that John Jr. beat *him* for the boy's moral infractions — is a technique employed by Bronson Alcott in the mid-1830s during his running of the Temple School in Boston. In Elizabeth Palmer Peabody's *Record of a School* (1835), her chronicle of the school's first year, Peabody reports a "new mode" of disciplinary correction employed by Alcott.[21] Reminding his students of "the necessity of pain and punishment . . . in concentrating attention" and the spiritual usefulness of corporal punishment (doled out in strikes upon the palm of the hand), Alcott announces that he intends to have the punishment "administered upon his own hand for a time, instead of theirs; but that the guilty person must do it."[22] His decision is met with objections and dismay from the students, but Alcott is resolute, and upon the next incidence of disobedience Alcott takes the two offenders into a separate room and commands them to strike him. "At first," reports Peabody, "they were very unwilling, and . . . did it very lightly. He then asked them, if they thought that they deserved no more punishment than that? And so they were obliged to give it hard: but it was not without tears, which they never had shed when punished themselves." Like Brown, Alcott punishes his students through their identification with him. As Peabody puts it, "The children do not feel that they escape punishment; for it is taken for granted that they feel a greater pain, in seeing others suffer, than they would, in suffering themselves."[23] The "greater pain" experienced by the children surpasses that of the adult, in other words, solidifying the parent figure's authority through a transaction that reduces the offending, and empathetic, children to tears.

Louisa May Alcott certainly knew of her father's practice and undoubtedly read *Record of a School*. Much of Bronson Alcott's principles and methods structure the philosophy and practice of Jo

March's Plumfield, the "school for boys" (and girls) that provides the setting for *Little Men* and *Jo's Boys*.²⁴ One of the key scenes in *Little Men* involves an instance exactly parallel to the one reported by Peabody. However, in contrast to the examples of Bronson Alcott and John Brown—examples concerned primarily with the father figure's construction of the pedagogy of pain—Alcott's scene focuses on the psychological and emotional experiences of the children themselves. Their experiences provide a foundation for the dynamics of violence I will argue recur throughout Alcott's trilogy, a virtual circuitry of aggression in which violence toward others, and the suffering it engenders, is rerouted back to the youngster himself or herself.

In *Little Men*, Jo's husband, the Germanic Professor Bhaer, attempts to cure one of the boys at Plumfield of his habit of lying. He tells the orphan Nat that the next time Nat lies, "I shall not punish you, but you shall punish me. . . . You shall ferule me in the good old-fashioned way. I seldom do it myself, but it may make you remember better to give me pain than to feel it yourself."²⁵ Although Nat remains truthful for some time, one day he is caught off guard and tells a lie. Bhaer keeps true to his word and commands the boy to give him six strokes across the hand. Nat at first gives "two feeble blows," but Bhaer commands him to "strike harder." Then, after laying the sixth stroke, Nat "threw the rule across the room, and hugging the kind hand in both his own, laid his face down on it sobbing in a passion of love, shame and penitence: 'I will remember! Oh, I will!'" (58–59). The scene is witnessed by one boy, Tommy, who goes back to the group of boys "excited and sober" and reports the amazing event. "He made me do the same thing once," says Bhaer's nephew Emil, "as if confessing a crime of the deepest dye" (59). When asked how he could do such a thing, Emil explains: "I was hopping mad at the time, and thought I shouldn't mind a bit, rather like it, perhaps. But when I'd hit uncle one good crack, everything he had ever done for me came into my head all at once somehow, and I couldn't go on. No, sir! If he'd laid me down and walked on me, I wouldn't have minded. I felt so mean" (59).

Like Bronson's students, Nat and Emil are made to feel the

weight of an innocent's suffering, an identification that affirms, by contrast, their own *guilt*. In Nat's case, the identification also serves to reinforce his already feminine nature. Prior to Nat's punishment, readers are told that Professor Bhaer finds him "as docile and affectionate as a girl. He often called Nat his 'daughter' when speaking of him to Mrs. Jo, and she used to laugh at his fancy, for Madame liked manly boys, and thought Nat amiable but weak" (56). Nat's weakness is not cured by the ostensible transfer of power that Bhaer accords him. A "shy feeble boy" (55) in temperament, Nat's blows are equally "feeble," resulting in Bhaer's demand that Nat "strike harder." The coerced manliness only succeeds in making Nat cry, however, and like the "daughter" he is, he pours out his wretchedness in a "passion of love, shame and penitence." Interestingly enough, the more "manly" Emil fares no better. Though, as he says, he thought he might "rather like [hitting Bhaer]," the act itself leaves him feeling "mean." What begins as anger ("I was hopping mad at the time") ends in abjection — a willingness to be "laid down and walked on" by his uncle. Bhaer's method of punishment thus not only effects in the boys a greater sensitivity toward others but also circumvents a possible childish rebellion against paternal authority (and authority's "rod"). Aggression's potential pleasure (the possibility that the child might "rather like it") is subverted by the child's forced expression of aggression and pleasure's subsequent association with "a crime of the deepest dye."

Although Alcott explicitly focuses on the children's experience of inflicting violence in this scene, one could argue that Bhaer's aggression is equally in play. Like Bronson Alcott, Bhaer seeks not to obviate but to displace the father's authority to punish onto the children, an act that in its very displacement serves to reinforce paternal control. Bhaer explicitly contrasts his method of discipline with an "old school" approach of direct aggression, which he himself was subject to as a boy. As he tells Nat, "When I was a little lad I used to tell such lies! . . . My parents had talked, and cried, and punished, but still did I forget as you. Then said the dear old grandmother, 'I shall help you to remember, and put a check on this unruly part' and with that she drew out my tongue and snipped the end with her scissors till the blood ran." According to Bhaer, this was all for the best, because, as his tongue was sore for days, "every word I said came so slowly that I had time to think. After that I was more careful, and got on better, for I feared the big scissors" (56–57). The old ways of discipline, practiced by "dear old grandmother," attest to the castrating effects of corporal punishment, here represented by "the big scissors." Bhaer's reformation from unruly boy to sensitive man is evidenced not only by his empathy with Nat (putting himself, literally, in Nat's place) but by the transfer of aggressive agency into the boy's hands. The result is Nat's own empathetic transformation. At the end of this incident, readers are told, Nat never again tells lies, nor does he ever touch "the kind hand" of Professor Bhaer "without remembering that it had willingly borne pain for his sake" (61). Bhaer's hand is made "kind" precisely by his having made Nat's hand cruel.

Whereas in much nineteenth-century domestic fiction, as G. M. Goshgarian argues, children learn to kiss the hand that beats them, *Little Men* teaches children to kiss the hand that they have beaten.[26] Its lesson is nevertheless equally an affliction, one that touches the "feeble" and the "manly" alike. This scene from *Little Men* helps demonstrate that material bodies and the violence done to them remain key components of the new progressive "disciplinary intimacy" characterizing mid- to late nineteenth-century educational reforms. In the translation of educational practice to pedagogical fiction (from Bronson's classroom, that is, to Louisa's), aggression still holds sway. Thus if, as Brodhead claims, Alcott's trilogy is representative in its depiction of children who "imbibe the parent's moral sense along with the parent's . . . affection," it also and importantly proves instructive in its vision of children taking on the parent's role (and vice versa) through acts of aggression. The parent-child relationship, in other words, is more a dynamic of cross-identifications than a passive "imbibing" of parental values; its pedagogical power resides in the displacement of violence onto children, who thereby recognize their own criminality. In their demonstrations of violence, Louisa, Bronson's students, and Nat and Emil all feel the pain of their "victims." But, like Melville's boy soldiers, the children's suffering arises from the guilt and shame of exercising (and momentarily enjoying) their power. That girls as well as boys are involved in this dynamic suggests that biology matters less in Alcott's world than the "inclinations" that gender a person: it is the desire to handle the whip — to terminate conflicts by "menace" and "blows" — that makes a child boyish, and that implicates the child in a cycle of violence that proves both the cause and the cure for what ails her/him.

THE CHILDREN OF BOSTON: *LITTLE MEN*

If, as I have been arguing, the love that disciplines Alcott's little women and men is manifested and engendered through acts of violence performed on a body with which the children identify, it is also true that the object of abuse signifies the love object. Professor Bhaer, for example, already a beloved father figure for the boys, becomes invested with kindness and generosity by Nat and Emil when they strike him. Likewise, in Bronson Alcott's case, no sooner have his students hit him than "a new sense of the worth and importance" of what Mr. Alcott represents "seemed to spring up all around" the children, writes Peabody, "while the unquestionable generosity of it, was not only understood, but felt to be contagious."[27] For Bronson's and Bhaer's sacrificial acts to work (that is, to produce in the children an empathetic identification), they must be valued persons to begin with. Their value, and their influence, then increases by their willingness to suffer for the children's sake. Through violence, in other words, child aggressors learn to appreciate the worth of those they harm, and even, as we will see, to seek to emulate them in their suffering.

In *Little Men*, Alcott presents the emotionally transformative work of violence not only as serious business but as child's play. Although the beating scene with Nat and Emil evinces humiliation and shame — a serious subject indeed — in the chapter "Pranks and Plays" Alcott examines childish aggression in a quite different context: as an expression of the natural "freaks and fancies that originate in the lively minds of little people" (112). At the beginning of this chapter, Alcott's narrator announces her intention to "describe a few scenes in the life at Plumfield for the amusement of little persons." She then goes on to detail one such humorous scene involving the "Naughty Kitty-mouse," an invisible sprite "whom the children had believed in, feared, and served for a long time" (112). Though an invention of the children's own, the Kitty-mouse is nonetheless conscientiously obeyed, and one day young Demi ominously informs his twin sister, Daisy, that "the Kitty-mouse wants us this afternoon" (113).

"What for?" asked Daisy anxiously.

"A *sackerryfice*," answered Demi solemnly. "There must be a fire behind the big rock at two o'clock, and we must all bring the things we like best, and burn them!" he added, with an awful emphasis on the last words.

"Oh, dear! I love the new paper dollies Aunt Amy painted for me best of anything. Must I burn them up?" cried Daisy, who never thought of denying the unseen tyrant anything it demanded.

"Every one. I shall burn my boat, my best scrapbook, and all my soldiers," said Demi firmly.

"Well, I will: but it's too bad of Kitty-mouse to want our very nicest things," sighed Daisy.

"A *sackerryfice* means to give up what you are fond of so we *must*," explained Demi, to whom the new idea had been suggested by hearing Uncle Fritz describe the customs of the Greeks to the big boys who were reading about them in school.

Although Demi fails in his command of the "big boy" terminology, his understanding of the basic principle of sacrifice hits the mark. In Demi's mind, it is the very attachment one has to a thing that singles it out for relinquishment; the fonder one is of something, the more necessary that it be given up. Such a logic is indebted not only to Greek custom but also to Judeo-Christian myth. It calls up the Old Testament story of Abraham, the father who is willing to kill his beloved only son as a sign of his fear and obedience and whose willing sacrifice serves as a foreshadowing of God's eventual sacrifice of *His* son, Jesus. Nicknamed the "Preacher" by his schoolmates, young Demi resurrects not only the pagan habits of the Greeks but also the Christian foundation of substitutionary violence, where the thing that is killed is the thing one loves best and the thing with which (sooner or later) one identifies.

Of course, since the beloved objects laid on the altar of obedience in this case are mere toys, it is tempting to dismiss this incident from *Little Men* as part of the "pranks and plays" that children are prone to. Certainly, Alcott attempts to present it in such a light, narrating with adult bemusement and ironic gravity the unhappy fate of Demi's soldiers, who one by one marched heroically to their deaths until "all vanished in the flames and mingled in one common pool of melted lead" (114). Equally seriocomic is the narrator's description of the children's savage delight over the destruction of an entire toy village. "Charmed" by Demi's suggestion that the town be burned, Daisy and the other children "arranged the doomed village . . . and then sat down to watch the conflagration": "It was somewhat slow to kindle owing to the paint, but at last one ambitious little cottage blazed up, fired a tree of the palm species, which fell onto the roof of a large family mansion, and in a few minutes the entire town was burning merrily. The wooden population stood and stared at the destruction like blockheads, as they were, till they also caught and blazed away without a cry. It took some time to reduce the town to ashes, and the lookers-on enjoyed the spectacle immensely, cheering as each house fell, dancing like wild Indians when the steeple flamed aloft, and actually casting one wretched little churn-shaped lady, who had escaped to the suburbs, into the very heart of the fire" (115). If the "whimsical and tyrannical" god (112) whom the children serve is pleased with the sacrifice, that pleasure, Alcott implies, is nothing compared with the children's own, whose "enjoy[ment of] the spectacle" identifies them not with Christians or even with Greeks, but with the "wild Indians," who apparently revel in the heathen destruction of people and property.

Daisy, Demi, Rob, and Teddy might have been left in their savage state but for the overzealousness of the youngest member of the tribe, Teddy, who, "excited to such a degree" by the "superb success of the last offering," decides to make a sacrifice of his own. First throwing his stuffed lamb into the fire, the narrator tells us, Teddy then plants the children's favorite doll, "dear old Annabella" (116), onto the funeral pyre. Unlike the wooden "blockheads," who "blazed away without a cry," however, Annabella "expressed her anguish and resentment in a way that terrified her infant destroyer." In a passage noteworthy for its graphic content, Alcott describes Annabella's demise: "Being covered with kid, [Annabella] did not blaze, but did what was worse, she *squirmed*. First one leg curled up, then the other, in a very awful and lifelike manner; next she flung her arms over her head as if in great agony; her head itself turned on her shoulders, her glass eyes fell out, and with one final writhe of her whole body, she sank down a blackened mass on the ruins of the town" (115–16). While this unexpected demonstration upsets everyone, it so frightens Teddy that he runs screaming to his mother, Jo, for reassurance and protection. Mrs. Jo takes the long view, mildly chiding the children for the "ruin that [they] have made." "I shall have to write up in the nursery the verse that used to come in the boxes of toys," she goes on. "'The children of Holland take pleasure in making / What the children of Boston take pleasure in breaking.' . . . 'We never will again, truly, truly!' cried the repentant little sinners, much abashed at this reproof" (116).

As Madeline Stern notes in her afterword to *Little Men*, contemporary reaction to the doll burning, represented by the review in the *Overland Monthly* of September 1871, was "simply that the sacrifice was 'a capital bit of fun, and a truthful illustration of the wonderful power of imagination in children.'"[28] An appreciation for the "capital bit of fun" Alcott offers her readers, however, is dependent upon the reader's understanding of the absurdity of taking seriously the "deaths" of inanimate objects—the absurdity, that is, of imbuing leaden soldiers, wooden villagers, and paper dolls with human feeling. And, despite the narrator's reference at the opening of the chapter to the "little persons" she aims to amuse, that understanding, we must assume, belongs to adults like Mrs. Jo. "The power of imagination in children," by contrast, renders the ontological status of beloved objects, however insentient, ambiguous.

The Death of Boyhood (139)

The mature narrator describes Annabella's burning, for example, in similes ("she flung her arms over her head as if in great agony") meant to depict the "lifelike *manner*" of the doll's destruction, but young Teddy apprehends the scene not as metaphor but as real life. In the comfort of his mother's arms, Teddy pours out "in his broken way something about 'poor Bella hurted,'" making clear his confusion as to whether or not toys are capable of experiencing pain. And while the older children seem aware that this cannot be the case, the torturous verisimilitude of Annabella's agony calls into question, even for them, the possibility that their play contains within it some unnamed horror — the possibility, that is, that the "pleasure" they take in "breaking" is actually the pleasure of inflicting pain. The freedom that Johan Huizinga has famously defined as "the first main characteristic of play" — freedom from consequence, including the consequence of guilt or shame — relies on the cognitive suppression of just such correlations.[29] Once confronted with the potential connection between pleasure and (causing) pain, the children's play is no longer "fun."[30]

What begins for Demi and Daisy as a sacrifice of material pleasure — the renunciation and destruction of the things they like best — becomes for them another kind of pleasure (the pleasure of breaking), for which the children must atone. It is this very progression that signals for Alcott the children's transformation from "wild" pagans and heathens (Greeks and Indians) to Christian "little men" and "women": that is, "repentant little sinners" capable of an adultlike empathy. Of course, as noted above, Christianity contains within it structures of violence as well as of feeling. In God the Father's sacrifice of his Son (with whom, as part of the Trinity, He is always already identified), we have a model for identifications that render aggressors the victims of their own violence. Following this model, Alcott's *Little Men* portrays sadistic impulses converted to masochistic ones through the children's identification with the objects of their abuse.

Although obviously not synonymous, the targets of the children's aggression and the children themselves are rendered *analogous* in Alcott's fiction, as evidenced not only by the doll Annabella's "lifelike" suffering but also by Alcott's repeated comparisons of children to dolls. In *Little Men*, for example, Amy's daughter Bess is referred to as a "sort of doll" whom the other children "dared not touch... lest she should break" (155). Likewise, Teddy is said to be in "real danger" from the violent play of Daisy and Nan (who try to hang Teddy from a tree as a "robber"), for often those "excited ladies were apt to forget that he was not of the same stuff as their long-suffering dolls" (122). And in *Little Women*, Alcott likens the younger sisters, Amy and Beth, to dolls, remarking that the older sisters, Meg and Jo, "watched over them in their own way, 'playing mother' they called it, and put their sisters in the places of discarded dolls, with the maternal instinct of little women" (41). It may be that the superficial likeness between children and dolls to which Alcott draws our attention is meant to alert us to an even more profound connection between them: that is, the idea that children, like dolls, represent an approximation of personhood — not (yet) fully human because still not masters of the empathetic attachments that constitute true Christian adulthood. That development, and those attachments, are then worked out in the children's relation to "dolls" (including other children), who excite both the children's solicitude (they "dared not touch" Bess, "lest she should break") and their aggression.

If the children's treatment of toys corresponds in some degree to their treatment of persons, boyish children prove the more aggressive. In *Little Men*, the ladylike Daisy is said to tend to her "many dolls with an expression of dreamy attachment on her face" (55), but in *Little Women*, tomboy Jo's relationship to her dolls is characterized alternately by physical torture and neglect. Though credited with "maternal instinct" above, Jo's history with dolls does not suggest it: her headless and otherwise amputated dolls rather attest to the "tempestuous life" to which she has subjected them until the feminine Beth takes them "to her refuge" (39). Jo's (mis)treatment of dolls is matched only by her alter ego, the tomboy "Naughty Nan" of *Little Men*, whose own behavior with respect to dolls evinced "a most unmaternal carelessness" (104). Frustrated by the late arrival of her belongings to Plumfield, for example, Nan is said to have "fretted and fumed, and whipped her doll till Daisy was shocked" (107). The prim Daisy should hardly have been surprised. On a previous visit, Nan had insisted on washing the doll Blanche-Matilda's "plaster face, which spoiled the poor dear's complexion forever" (104). Later on, we are told that Nan "buried her big doll and forgot it for a week, and found it well mildewed when she dug it up." Although Daisy "was in despair," Nan remedies the situation by investing the neglected toy with new aggressive power: "Nan took it to the painter who was at work about the house, got him to paint it brick red, with staring black eyes, then she dressed it up with feathers, and scarlet flannel, and one of Ned's lead hatchets; and in the character of an Indian chief the late Poppydilla tomahawked all the other dolls, and caused the nursery to run red with imaginary gore" (110). Nan's identification with the bloodthirsty Poppydilla is evidenced in the latter's "tomahawking" of all the other dolls, as if Poppydilla-turned-Indian were but acting out its "mother's" own wishes by getting rid of the nursery's pseudo-children. This idea is made explicit when Nan, in another fiasco involving her charges, finally surrenders all attempts at "playing mother": "'Never mind; I'm tired of dolls, and I guess I shall put them all away and attend to my farm; I like it rather better than playing house,' said [Nan], unconsciously expressing the desire of many older ladies, who cannot dispose of their families so easily however" (224).

Just as the children are likened to Indians in their delight over the burning of the toy village, Nan has her doll take on the persona of a ravaging Indian chief, exemplifying what Kenneth Kidd notes is nineteenth-century American boyhood's attraction to "playing Indian" as a way of temporarily evading the inevitable incorporation into civilized life.[31] The algebraic equation that says that if children are (like) Indians and dolls are (like) Indians then children are (like) dolls reinforces the analogy between dolls and little persons Alcott has alluded to throughout *Little Men* and *Little Women*. The analogy reveals children, like dolls, to be both the objects *and* the agents of violence in Alcott's novels. In the latter respect, child's play serves as a site not only for the expression but for the displacement of aggression, where dolls and children imitate their "parents" (who also implicitly or explicitly resemble Indians) in their aggressive fantasies: as Alcott's narrator tells us, in refusing any longer to "play house," Nan unconsciously expresses the desire of many mothers who cannot so easily "dispose of their families."

Importantly, then, we can see that childish aggression mirrors and mimics the parent's. Yet it is also clear that children alone represent the victims of the violence they employ. Identified with the objects of their aggressive play, Alcott's children can be said to engage in fantasies of their own destruction. Of course, as Freud will theorize years later, masochism has its own reward by condensing pain's "unpleasure" into the pleasure of its unconscious meaning: "*I am the child loved by the father.*"[32] In Freud's reading, the masochistic impulse is generated by the child's "sexual love" for the father, for which whipping or beating becomes a "regressive substitute." Substituting whipping for the father's (sexual) love s/he desires but is denied, the child both atones for that forbidden desire and sublimates it through masochistic imaginings in which s/he is the child being beaten.[33] Alcott, by contrast, depicts aggression-turned-inward as the attainment of an empathetic maturity (rather than regressive fantasy) representative of Christian character. By taking on another's pain as their own, children learn to be, like Christ, self-sacrificing. Whereas Freud sees the condensation of violence and love as Oedipal in nature, Alcott locates it in Christian rituals of child sacrifice, where to be the abused object is to be the loved object, a psychological substitution that underlies both Alcott's, and Christianity's, transformational identifications.

Thus to return to where we began: we can see in Demi's ritual of "sackerryfice" both the conscious and the unconscious meanings contained in his play. As Demi tells his Aunt Jo, "I wanted to be like [the Greeks], only I hadn't any live creatures to sackerryfice, so we burnt up our toys" (117). Demi's replacement of toys for live creatures replicates on a childish scale adult versions of sacrifice, ones in which "live creatures" substitute for people. Again, the structure alludes not only to Greek but also to Judeo-Christian sacrifice: in Abraham's case, a ram is finally (and fortunately) substituted for the young Isaac as an offering to God, but the sacrifice that it foretells —

The Death of Boyhood (143)

Christ, the "Lamb of God," dying on the cross — reverses the objects yet again, substituting a man for a lamb.[34] Playfully mimicking the religious analogy by which lambs stand in for children and children for lambs, Alcott has Teddy first throw his toy lamb into the conflagration, only to follow it with a doll that burns as if she were a child. It is not only children's best-loved toys, we are reminded, but fathers' best-loved sons who are slain, reinforcing the substitutionary value of "violence" for "love" in the masochistic (and Christian) imagination.

The Judeo-Christian allusion in "sackerryfice" makes explicit the extent to which the violence these children inflict is patterned after *adult* models — not only the "Greeks," "big boys," and Indians whom Demi wants to emulate but the Christian God's sacrifice of his son. What follows is then a childish emulation of devotion to the "Kitty-mouse" that reinscribes the vulnerability of children, even as it offers these particular children a momentary sense of domination. While Demi, Daisy, and the others destroy what they love best for the sake of an omniscient power that (they imagine) demands such offerings, the children realize their *own* sense of power in the act of destruction. Their act of propitiation becomes an act of imitation of the "father," an imitation that gives the children access to, for a time at least, an adult form of power. Yet, as we have seen, the manifestation of this adult power is a sacrifice of the very objects (dolls, lambs, toy soldiers) with which children identify and are themselves identified.[35] One of the paradoxes in *Little Men* is the attainment of maturity through the adoption of a victimized object-identification: to grow up, as *Little Men* presents it, is to identify with the object that one abuses.

Perhaps Alcott means to suggest such a double bind in the very name the children give to their god: the "Kitty-mouse." Denoting both aggressor and victim, both agent and object of violence, the Kitty-mouse epitomizes the children's precarious position in the postwar world of adults. In the end, the tyrannies of the Kitty-mouse point to the same lesson as the sentimental pedagogy of the kind-hearted, kind-handed Professor Bhaer: children cannot exert power without inevitably suffering the effects of it. If such a lesson leads Alcott's children to a masochistic pleasure of dubious reward, well this, Alcott seems to say, is all part of the process of growing up.

AGGRESSION AND ATONEMENT: *LITTLE WOMEN*

Though written three years after the immensely popular *Little Women*, *Little Men*, with its rituals of aggression and identification, makes manifest the complicated psychological negotiations attending the development of Alcott's most beloved little woman, Jo. Particularly in young Jo's struggle with anger against her living "dolls," Amy and Beth, we find the veritable incarnation of (tom) boyish play: that is, the savage desire to "dispose" of one's family. As a young adult (she is fifteen at the start of *Little Women*), Jo is beyond the "pranks and plays" of childhood. Her manifestations of violence therefore have serious repercussions. The fact that Jo's anger and independence are ultimately converted to a quiescent domesticity by the end of the trilogy has baffled many readers over the years. But if *Little Men* has taught us anything, it is how to read *Little Women*. Unable to disentangle her love for her sisters from her pleasure in hurting them, Jo ultimately converts her sadistic impulses into masochistic ones, thereby becoming not only a loved object but a "little *woman*."

In the chapter titled "Jo Meets Apollyon," Jo returns home from an outing with her friend Laurie to discover that her little sister Amy, in a fit of jealous pique, has burned the only copy of Jo's literary manuscript. Though Amy regrets her rash act and begs for Jo's mercy, Jo refuses to forgive her. "No one spoke of the great trouble," writes Alcott's narrator, "for all had learned by experience that when Jo was in that mood words were wasted; and the wisest course was to wait till some little accident, or her own generous nature, softened Jo's resentment, and healed the breach" (76). Some "little accident" is precisely what follows: trailing after Jo and Laurie when they next go skating on the pond, Amy, ignored by her sister, falls through the ice and nearly drowns. Though Amy is brought home safely, Jo sees her own "hardness of heart" as responsible for the accident and announces to her mother, Marmee, that "if [Amy] *should* die, it

The Death of Boyhood (145)

would be my fault." Jo then sobs out her gratitude "for being spared the heavy punishment which might have come upon her" (78–79). Worthy of note is not only Jo's assumption of responsibility for Amy's accident but her identification with the abused object: that is, Amy's accident, a result of Jo's desire to punish her sister, becomes Jo's own "punishment." Jo takes on the painful experience that belongs to Amy, viewing it as part of a larger design that casts Jo's emotions as the source of all suffering: "It's my dreadful temper! I try to cure it; I think I have, and then it breaks out worse than ever. Oh, mother! what shall I do! what shall I do?" (79). In a fantasy of animate anger, Jo's temper becomes for her a live, physical force, "breaking out" to destroy everything in its path, including Jo herself.

A similar egotism appears in relation to Beth's contraction of scarlet fever. When Marmee goes to visit her ailing husband in the army hospital, she enjoins her daughters not to forget their impoverished neighbors, the Hummels. Beth, the "angel of the house," takes up the responsibility, but on one particular day she asks that one of the other girls go. All three claim previous engagements. When Beth returns from her visit, she reports in a shaky voice that the Hummel children are sick and that the Hummel baby, whom Beth had been tending, is dead. "[The doctor] . . . told me to go home and take belladonna right away," Beth tells Jo, "or I'd have the fever." "No you won't!" cried Jo, hugging her close, with a frightened look. "Oh, Beth, if you should be sick I never could forgive myself!" (177). Beth does indeed come down with the fever, and Jo suffers the pangs of self-remorse: "Serve me right" to catch the fever again, mutters Jo. "Selfish pig, to let you go, and stay writing rubbish myself!" (178). Reading the March history as Jo reads it, Jo herself is the author of events; her "selfish" and aggressive impulses write the story of her sisters' experiences, experiences that have the potential to be returned upon Jo — to "serve [her] right."

Fetterley's claim that the Civil War serves as "an obvious metaphor for internal conflict" in *Little Women* suggests that war operates as a displacement for battles closer to home, battles whose stakes are, for Jo, like the soldiers she emulates, a matter of life and death. Jo's disappointment in "not being a boy" and her desire to "go and fight with papa" is thus converted, argues Fetterley, into a struggle against her own inclinations.[36] I am suggesting further, however, that the inclinations Jo combats include what *she* fears is the temptation to cause her sisters harm—a temptation rooted in the pleasure of her aggression. Having experienced the joys of an escalating anger—"the more I say the worse I get," says Jo, "til it's a *pleasure* to hurt people's feelings" (my emphasis) (80)—Jo becomes afraid of her own capacity to inflict pain. It is after Amy's accident on the ice, for example, that Jo confesses to her mother: "You don't know; you can't guess how bad it is! It seems as if I could do anything when I'm in a passion; I get so savage, I could hurt any one and enjoy it." Jo's confession is then followed by her fearful prediction of passion's consequences, for herself as well as for others: "I'm afraid I *shall* do something dreadful some day, and spoil my life, and make everybody hate me" (79). For Jo, "savagery" leads to ruin and ostracism, themselves, for all practical purposes, synonymous. What Jo fears most, in other words, is not the short-term effects of an unguarded moment of temper but the "spoil[ing]" of an entire existence: a future wiped out in one violent, if pleasurable, gesture.

Conscious of the problem of aggression and feeling at a loss to eliminate it, Jo turns to her mother for advice about her violent proclivities. Marmee then tutors Jo in the conversion of sadistic into masochistic impulses (79):

> "You think your temper is the worst in the world; but mine used to be just like it."
> "Yours, mother? Why, you are never angry!" and, for the moment, Jo forgot remorse in surprise.
> "I've been trying to cure it for forty years, and have only succeeded in controlling it. I am angry nearly every day of my life, Jo; but I have learned not to show it; and I still hope to learn not to feel it, though it may take me another forty years to do so."

The reader suspects that another forty years will in fact *not* do the trick, since the first forty have been insufficient. But the point, we might gather, is in fighting the battle rather than in winning the war. Thus Jo asks, "Mother, are you angry when you fold your lips tight together, and go out of the room sometimes, when Aunt March scolds, or people worry you?" And Marmee replies, "Yes, I've learned to check the hasty words that rise to my lips; and when I feel that they mean to break out against my will, I just go away a minute, and give myself a little shake, for being so weak and wicked" (79–80). Like Jo, Marmee represents her aggressive impulses as if they have lives of their own—her "hasty words" mean to "break out" against her will. The personification of anger speaks to the power of Marmee's unconscious desires, desires with which she dis-identifies: though Marmee *wants* to speak, she constructs her words as enemies fighting *against* her. Her only recourse, as she represents it, is to fight aggression with more aggression: to "give herself a little shake." If anger cannot be defeated, Marmee implies, it must be redirected at oneself.

Marmee's solution to dealing with her temper suggests that maturation involves internalizing one's aggression. It is to sacrifice the "pleasure to hurt people's feelings," as Jo describes it, and to hurt one's own instead. And although Jo will eventually be successful in the sacrifice, Alcott renders Jo's success as troubling as it is necessary. After all, to become like Marmee, Jo must renounce a spirit of boyishness that, for better and for worse, represents a certain freedom of thought and expression—a liberation from the very social conventions that cause women like Marmee to "fold [their] lips tight together." Jo's use of the word "savage" to describe herself in fact serves as a kind of code for the untutored and antisocial spirit thought to characterize boys at this time. "By the 1860s," notes Kidd, "the boy-savage association ... was axiomatic in American letters," so that for many writers, "an African savage" (or, for Alcott, a "wild Indian") "became boyish, and the boy [became] ... savage."[37] Whereas Marmee has spent forty years being socialized to keep her mouth shut, Jo represents the desire of children, especially boys, to express themselves openly—to let their words, as Jo puts it about her own speech, "fly out before I know what I'm about" (80). To lose this is, in effect, to grow up into a Christian man or woman;

it is also to lose the very aggression that characterizes Jo's independence from her family.

Jo's anger is not her only source of pleasure, of course. Rather, it typifies a broader-based desire for liberation, a freedom from convention and domestic responsibility—"playing house," as Alcott puts it in *Little Men*. The fact that such freedom is consistently linked with boyhood—a state-of-being contrasted both with adulthood and with femininity—signals its ephemerality. Though Jo evades for a time the strict confines of true womanhood, first by refusing Laurie in marriage and then by moving to New York to become a professional writer, she is eventually forced to inhabit the very person(a) she has for so long resisted. After several months in New York, Jo is called home to attend to her dying sister, Beth, who makes of Jo one final demand: "You must take my place, Jo, and be everything to father and mother when I'm gone. They will turn to you—don't fail them; and if it's hard to work alone, remember that I don't forget you, and that you'll be happier in doing that, than writing splendid books, or seeing all the world; for love is the only thing that we can carry with us when we go, and it makes the end so easy" (418). To be happy is to be loved, Beth suggests, and to be either, Jo must identify with Beth rather than cling to her own selfish/independent desires—that is, "writing splendid books" and "seeing all the world." Jo's reward is to be loved (rather than hated, as Jo has always feared) as Beth is loved.

Like *Little Men*, *Little Women* represents identification as a form of "punishment" and maturation through which its protagonist attains the status of love object. To be that object, Alcott consistently affirms, is to die to self and be reborn in the image of those one has "beaten." Having been (what Jo believes is) the precipitate cause of Beth's illness and eventual death, Jo does indeed "take [Beth's] place." She renounces her "old ambition" and "pledges herself to a new and better one, acknowledging the poverty of other desires, and feeling the blessed solace of a belief in the immortality of love" (418–19). And though Jo's success is not immediate (the narrator tells us that Jo "tried in a blind hopeless way to do her duty" while "secretly rebelling against it all the while"), the substitution is ultimately accomplished. Jo asks her father to talk to her as he used to talk to Beth, and, sitting in Beth's chair, Jo discovers a "recovered cheerfulness, and a more submissive spirit" (433–34). She also takes on Beth's duties in the home, for now "brooms and dishcloths never could be as distasteful as they once had been, for Beth had presided over both; and something of her housewifely spirit seemed to linger" around them (434). As she used these articles, Jo "found herself humming the songs Beth used to hum, imitating Beth's orderly ways, and giving the little touches here and there" that made the "home happy" (434).

By identifying with Beth, Jo atones for the independent and often angry spirit that once threatened to "break" apart her family. That such an extreme turnaround is rendered as a happy ending by Alcott can be accounted for by the ambiguity all along surrounding what the true objects of Jo's affection really are: her sisters or her freedom. Jo herself never seems sure whether by indulging her aggressive impulses — subconsciously killing off her sisters one by one, we might say — she will be left empty or made whole. It is a conflict that Beth herself appears to intuit and capitalize on. Prior to their final conversation, in which Beth asks Jo to "take her place," Beth finds a poem Jo has written about her and, in one of the stanzas, sees that Jo has made a request of her own:

> Oh, my sister, passing from me,
> Out of human care and strife,
> Leave me, as a gift, those virtues
> Which have beautified your life.
> Dear, bequeath me that great patience
> Which has power to sustain
> A cheerful, uncomplaining spirit
> In its prison-house of pain.

Being bequeathed Beth's virtues, as the poem goes on to say, Jo's "great loss" will become "[her] gain" (417). The idea that one's loss (of a sister *and* of an old self) may become one's gain (of a new self) returns us to the paradigm of "sackerryfice" that structures both life and play in *Little Women* and *Little Men*, a paradigm in which one's attachment to an object (or a feeling or a lifestyle) becomes the foundation for its destruction, even as the object's destruction becomes the basis for a new sensibility. As this implies, Alcott's Christian lessons don't call for a cessation of violence altogether, but rather they encourage identifications that render the abuse of a loved one as a vehicle through which the protagonist herself becomes loved. And Jo does indeed become loved. In a plot twist suggestive of pre-Freudian fantasy, Jo marries the fatherly Professor Bhaer. Thus viewed optimistically, Alcott's lessons imply that nothing is ever truly forfeited. One's loss in one sense will be one's gain in another. But if Jo is able to recuperate her lost sister by identifying with her, it is a bittersweet recovery; after all, Jo has lost herself in the process, along with her boyish pleasures.

JO'S (LAST) BOYS

Jo's story, of course, does not end with *Little Women*. At the end of that novel, Jo and Fritz Bhaer settle at the boys' school, Plumfield, where "a family of six or seven boys sprung up like mushrooms," to be followed by two biological sons of her own (484). Jo delights in her "wilderness of boys," and, as the narrator notes in *Little Men*, she "always took part in whatever [activity] was going on, and enjoyed it as much as any boy among them" (102, 43). Notwithstanding her participation in their frolics, however, Jo's boyish pleasures in *Little Men* are now largely vicarious; they are lived out through the boys and tomboys whose youthful indiscretions poignantly remind her of her own. One character in particular stands out in this regard: Dan, a teenage orphan whose "rough life" has made him "hard and careless, willful and suspicious" (92). As Jo tells her husband early on in *Little Men*, "I seem to know by instinct how [Dan] feels, to understand what will win and touch him, and to sympathize with his temptations and faults. I am glad I do, for it will help me to help him; and if I can make a good man of this wild boy, it will be the best work of my life" (142). Dan has rightly been referred to by critics as Jo's alter ego, for Dan evinces the internal struggle with a "rough and wild" nature that Jo herself battles throughout

Little Women (9).³⁸ Unlike Jo, however, Dan never fully succeeds in sacrificing those aggressive impulses that would allow him to settle down to a white, Anglo-Saxon domesticity. Though he tries with Jo's help to subdue the savage nature that the latter understands all too well, the "wild boy" Dan ends up killing a man and, as Jo once feared for herself, "spoil[ing] [his] life."³⁹ His fate suggests the alternative ending possible for Jo and her ilk, a fate that has Dan settle, and die, among what is for Alcott a very different "wilderness of boys" — the Montana Indians.⁴⁰

The associative link between boys and Indians that first appears in *Little Men* is characteristic of boy-books in this period, books that tend to stress the importance of boys "playing Indian" as a precursor to their eventual mastery of the "primitive" impulse. In *Jo's Boys*, however, Alcott embues this association with tragic implications. Written fifteen years after *Little Men*, *Jo's Boys* takes boyishness out of the realm of "play" to locate it in a contemporary crisis: U.S. Indian removal. Dan's identification with the American Indian ends with the sacrifice of both to the forward march of white "civilization." Whereas I began this American narrative with a story of powerful, aggressive white fathers represented as perpetual "sons," I conclude with the white father figure's displacement of aggression onto objects of "wildness" whose passing secures the safety of middle-class, empathetic life. Dan's inability to move beyond the boyhood phase of development ultimately signals the loss of something larger than an individual. It marks what is for Alcott the regrettable, but apparently inevitable, death of boyhood, of "savagery," and of Native life in American culture.

We first encounter Dan in *Little Men* when he comes to Plumfield at his young friend Nat's urging, and Jo initially finds the fifteen-year-old "a bad specimen" (82). It is not boyish exuberance or boyish aggression that earns Dan this evaluation but rather a singular coolness of disposition. In the "big black eyes" that were "fixed" on her, Mrs. Jo finds a "hard, suspicious expression, sorrowfully unboyish" (83). It is Dan's *lack* of boyishness — a certain "fixed"-ness of character unrelieved by joy or flexibility — that warrants concern. The loving lessons of Plumfield, then, are in Dan's case meant not so much to usher him into manhood as to regress him back to boyhood, and to a state of vulnerable impressionability from which Mrs. Jo and Professor Bhaer can create Dan anew.

The parents of Plumfield find this difficult going, however. Already having gotten some of the other boys to play poker and smoke cigars like the older men that orphan Dan has been associating with, Dan continues to spread discord by initiating a boxing match between himself and Emil, soon followed by his tormenting the family cow, Buttercup. It is this last that brings him before the judgment of Professor Bhaer, who reprimands him with words designed to indoctrinate him into the ways of white, middle-class compassion: "One of the first and most important of our few laws [at Plumfield] is the law of kindness to every dumb creature on the place. I want everybody and everything to be happy here, to love, and trust, and serve us as we try to love and trust and serve them faithfully and willingly. I have often said that you were kinder to the animals than any of the other boys, and Mrs. Bhaer liked that trait in you very much, because she thought that it showed a good heart. But you have disappointed us in that, and we are sorry, for we hoped to make you quite one of us. Shall we try again?" (93). It is not Dan's behavior so much as his "good heart" that is in question. Although Dan's latter two infractions are, like Demi's worship of the Kittymouse, essentially games (in the first instance, playing "gladiators" and in the second, "bullfighting"), Dan's imagination is deemed too aggressive, and perhaps too worldly, to go undisciplined. His games, it seems, are not playful *enough* to vouch for their innocence. Whereas Demi's antics never threaten to compromise his place in the family—his right to be "one of us"—Dan must earn his place by proving himself capable of being touched by the love extended to him. And, for a time, he succeeds. Dan, we are told, was "more tamed by kindness than he would have been by the good whipping which Asia [the cook] had strongly recommended" (93).

Like every other "dumb creature on the place," Dan is to be "tamed" by kindness, a concept that suggests both youthful tractability and the distinctively unworldly, uncivilized state to which he must return in order to begin anew the stages of maturation. That return is to be accomplished through love: that is, the Bhaers' kindness is meant to initiate Dan into the innocently boyish ways of the white Anglo-Saxon Protestant family (a family to which "Asia," who recommends whipping, apparently has not the sensibility to belong). His taming continues throughout *Little Men*. Learning to "trust and serve" his friends, especially Nat, Dan comes to demonstrate his potential to be domesticated, epitomized in the chapter "Taming the Colt," in which Dan's successful work with Charlie, a young, unbroken horse, is rendered analogous to Mrs. Jo's breaking of her "wild boy": "'I am taming a colt too, and I think I shall succeed as well as you if I am as patient and persevering,' said Mrs. Jo, smiling so significantly at him that Dan understood and answered, laughing, yet in earnest: 'We won't jump over the fence and run away, but stay and let them make a handsome, useful span of us, hey Charlie?'" (251).[41] Dan's response testifies to the Bhaers' measure of success in winning Dan back from the world—now he "won't run away." However, it also equates him with the very animal he has successfully broken. Put another way, though Dan has shown talent, and a manful superiority, in taming the colt, he is repositioned (by both Jo and himself) as yet another of Plumfield's animals to be subdued, even as it emphasizes the care that must be taken if wild creatures are to be made "useful."

Of course, Dan is not the only boy at Plumfield likened to an animal. As Caroline Levander observes, Plumfield's at-risk boys in *Little Men* "are equated variously with 'colts,' 'owls,' 'squirrels,' 'wild hawks,' 'beavers' and 'robins.'" Such equations, notes Levander, signal Alcott's imaginative consonance with the "newly established scientific fact that 'boys are animals,'" an idea itself grounded in the popular evolutionary theory of recapitulation.[42] If, as the theory goes, children inevitably repeat or "recapitulate" the evolutionary stages of human development, manipulation of that development—through early training or, increasingly, through children's literature—allows a parent (or a nation) to, in Alexander Chamberlain's words, "'suppress' its nation's 'useless past' and to 'purify' its ancestors' 'animal nature.'"[43] The point of books like *Little Men*, argues Levander, is not to suppress but to *acknowledge* boys' "animal natures" — to recognize their primitive impulses and to reorient those impulses toward more productive, more "useful" ends. Levander sees all of Alcott's little men, including Dan, eventually progressing to the point where they evince "the whiteness that indicates their social evolution from 'savage' to citizen."[44] I would argue, however, that Dan is never "purified" of his ancestors' "animal nature." Rather, like the Native Americans that he is repeatedly compared to and whose "vanishing" is always already assumed, Dan represents the vanishing American, both in terms of his primitive traits and of his perpetual boyhood, themselves linked together.[45] Unlike the other Plumfield creatures, Dan never moves beyond the boyhood phase of development. Having successfully regressed Dan to a state where he can be managed in *Little Men*, Alcott leaves him there in *Jo's Boys*, neither a "sorrowfully unboyish" (83) youngster who will protect himself at all costs, nor a civilized man capable of domesticity and reproduction.

Chapter 4 of *Jo's Boys* opens with the observation that "Mrs. Jo often thought that Dan had Indian blood in him, not only because of his love of a wild, wandering life, but his appearance," an appearance that includes "sinewy limbs" and "eyes full of . . . fire," a "keen, dark face" and "strong brown hand[s]" (54). The references to Dan's brownness (face, hands, and skin) are repeated throughout *Little Men* and *Jo's Boys*, signaling Dan's racial difference from the other boys, like Nat, whose face, in contrast to Dan's, is described in *Little Men* as "long, and fair, and rather weak, but very amiable with its mild eyes and good forehead" (157).[46] What begins in *Little Men* as an interest in Indians — "Dan knows lots about them," says Nat (158) — becomes in *Jo's Boys* an absolute affiliation. Not only does Jo conjecture in *Jo's Boys* that Dan had "Indian blood in him," but Dan himself jokes that he may bring an "Indian squaw" home as a wife (56), tells Nan that he'll "scalp a few red fellows or smash up a dozen or so cowboys" for her benefit (61), and indeed spends much of the novel living among what Alcott makes clear are his own kind of people: the "wronged" and dispossessed "Montana Indians" (62–63). Though Dan's actual parentage is veiled in mystery (all we know is that Dan's mother escaped an abusive husband with her

The Death of Boyhood (155)

son and then died), his "lawless spirit" appears to come from his father, a man whom Jo, in *Jo's Boys*, suspects had been "handsome, unprincipled, and dangerous" (310). To Dan's mother, by contrast, Jo ascribes Dan's innate, though untutored, love of good things: "As [Jo] looked... she remembered the streak of sentiment and refinement that lay concealed in Dan like the gold vein in a rock, making him quick to feel and to enjoy fine colour in a flower, grace in an animal, sweetness in women, heroism in men, and all the tender ties that bind heart to heart; though he was slow to show it, having no words to express the tastes and instincts which he inherited from his mother" (305). Dan's very blood, these observations suggest, put him at odds with himself, explaining his earlier desire in *Little Men* to "burst out somehow... to smash something, or pitch into somebody" as the natural consequence of a warring disposition (242).

In associating Dan with American Indians, Alcott might appear to be rather conventionally participating in the late nineteenth-century boy-book genre, a genre that "first identifies boys with, and then distinguishes them from, the savage."[47] But unlike the middle-class boys of Thomas Bailey Aldrich's *The Story of a Bad Boy* (1869) and William Dean Howells's *A Boy's Town* (1890), Dan is not "*playing* Indian" at all; to Jo, he may *be* Indian. He is thus excluded from the "evolutionary logic" that necessarily converts white boys' "savage virtues" into productive, manly ones.[48] Nor do the "tastes and instincts" inherited from his mother and fostered by Mrs. Jo guarantee that Dan will cross over into the white world of the March clan. On the contrary, they ultimately work against him. Unable to deny his "blood" but compelled by his adopted middle-class family to try, Dan becomes a victim of the sentimental lessons that teach him to long for that civilized end that Alcott repeatedly suggests he can never attain. Thus even though Mrs. Jo attempts to explain away the impulse to "smash" and "burst" and "pitch" as "the very natural desire of all young people for liberty" ("I used to feel just so," she sympathetically adds in *Little Men* [242]), what is "natural" for Dan has far different consequences than it does for Jo's other boys, or for Jo herself. Unlike author Jo, Dan has "no words to express" the tastes and instincts that Mrs. Jo imagines are lurking "like a gold vein" beneath the surface. Those tastes and instincts, characterized by Dan's ability to feel "the tender ties that bind heart to heart," thus manifest themselves in deeds, and often aggressive ones. Put another way, Dan's better nature often expresses itself through his lesser one, so that smashing and pitching become Dan's way of demonstrating his care. He among all of Jo's boys is unable to renounce aggression; it becomes the means by which his explicitly heathen love and empathy are put into action.

Although Mrs. Jo exclaims in *Jo's Boys* that "I always knew [Dan would] do something fine and brave, if he didn't get shot or hung for some wild prank instead" (289), it becomes clear that for "adventurous fellows" like Dan, "something fine and brave" proves inextricable from "some wild prank" and leads to the same result. Mrs. Jo's remark references Dan's heroic actions after a mining disaster, when he saves the lives of twenty men. But as Dan himself says, those twenty lives are meant to pay for the one life he has already taken (295), a crime for which he goes to prison and comes out "alive, but scarred for life" (297). The crime he commits is both noble and impulsive, like Dan himself. On his way out west to his "old friends the Montana Indians" (62), Dan meets a young man who has fallen in with some card sharps who fleece the boy of his life savings. When Dan comes to the young man's aid, he accidentally kills one of the men and is convicted of manslaughter. Dan's actions are prompted by his identifying the boy with his adopted brother: "Dan always had a soft spot in his heart for any younger, weaker creature whom he met, and something about the lad reminded him of Teddy" (183). Though spurred on by familial love, Dan's good deed nevertheless manifests itself in violence, the consequences of which, the narrator in *Jo's Boys* informs us, are Dan's responsibility to bear: "Yes, Dan was in prison; but no cry for help from him as he faced the terrible strait he was in with the dumb despair of an Indian at the stake; for his own bosom sin had brought him there, and this was to be the bitter lesson that tamed the lawless spirit and taught him self-control" (182).

Dan's good intentions are rendered inseparable from his heathen tendencies, those "dangerous energies" (67) that consistently undermine his Christian upbringing. Dan's incarceration, we might surmise, was always already a foregone conclusion. Dan himself seems to intuit the fated nature of his life and choices, and in "dumb despair" (tellingly compared to "an Indian at the stake"), Dan reflects upon "his ruined life": "[Dan] gave up all his happy hopes and plans, felt that he could never face dear old Plumfield again, or touch those friendly hands, with the stain of blood upon his own.... 'It's all over with me; I've spoilt my life, now let it go. I'll give up the fight and get what pleasure I can anywhere, anyhow.... Poor Mother Bhaer! She tried to help me, but it's no use; the firebrand can't be saved'" (186). Dan's words echo Jo's youthful prophecy years before, in *Little Women*, with respect to her own temper, when she laments to her mother that her "passion" will drive her to "do something dreadful, and spoil [her] life, and make everybody hate [her]" (79). But whereas Jo's dire future is diverted by her identification with true womanhood, Dan enacts the "something dreadful" that Jo once foresaw for herself. Through him we see the consequences of a boyish spirit that goes untamed.

Jo is helped in *Little Women* by her mother and father, who advocate fighting oneself rather than turning one's aggression upon others. And though Dan is alone and despondent in prison, the spirit of parental care nonetheless quickly becomes evident. In the place of "Mother Bhaer," Alcott offers a substitute, in *Jo's Boys*, one who again makes clear the role of Christian self-sacrifice in ameliorating, or redirecting, the effects of aggression. "A middle-aged woman in black, with a sympathetic face, eyes full of compassion and a voice" whose "motherly tones ... reminded Dan of Mrs. Jo," makes a philanthropic visit to the prison and manages to "break up the ice of despair which was blighting all the good impulses of [Dan's] nature" (188). Her influence is extended through a sermon of sorts, beginning with a "simple little story" about two soldiers in a hospital during "the late war," both of whom are badly wounded in the arm. "One was patient, docile and cheerfully obeyed orders, even when told that his arm must go." The other soldier, however, "rebelled, would listen to no advice, and having delayed too long, died a lingering death, bitterly regretting his folly when it was too late." The woman concludes: "'This [prison] is a hospital for soldiers wounded in life's battle; here are sick souls, weak wills, insane passions, blind consciences, all the ills that come from broken laws, bringing their inevitable pain and punishment with them.... Pay the forfeit manfully, for it is just; but from the suffering and shame wring new strength for a nobler life. The scar will remain, but it is better for a man to lose both arms than his soul; and these hard years, instead of being lost, may be made the most precious of your lives, if they teach you to rule yourselves.... And... never forget the Father whose arms are always open to receive, forgive, and comfort His prodigal sons, even at the eleventh hour'" (189).

The analogy of a prison to a hospital positions young men like Dan in the role of wounded soldiers, maimed in "life's battle" by their own "weak wills" and "insane passions." But though the analogy suggests Alcott's continuing belief in restoration rather than retribution, it is telling that her anonymous parent figure can only imagine that restoration occurring through amputation. Both the woman's story and the "little moral" with which she concludes it foreground arms: God's "arms... open to receive" the prodigal sons and the wounded arms of the soldiers. The story and moral thus present a disturbing juxtaposition: in contrast to the Father's arms, which are open, the soldier-son's arm has been literally cut off in the soldier's prime. Criminals like Dan, though forgiven, will remain "scarred for life." That scar, of course, is depicted as being in the soldier's best interest: better to lose an arm than a life, moralizes the woman, and better to lose both arms than one's soul. But though couched in metaphor, the woman's words have tangible implications; the metaphor's symbolism points beyond the loss of limbs. Since Dan's real "crime" lies in his blood, its treatment can only be effected through a wholesale amputation—specifically, through the cutting off of Dan's genetic line lest his criminal nature be reproduced in future generations. Dan himself is the limb to be amputated in order to preserve the integrity of the white national body.[49]

This fact is evidenced upon Dan's return to Plumfield the following summer. In the penultimate chapter of *Jo's Boys*, Dan confesses his crime and punishment to Mrs. Jo, who listens to his secret with anguish and with sympathy. Almost at the same time, however, Jo discovers Dan's *other*, and more catastrophic, secret: his romantic love for Amy's daughter, Bess. Alcott frames this love not as a boyhood crush but as a newly awakening manhood that finds itself beginning to "hunger for the food neglected or denied for so long." In his "all too expressive face," Dan tells "the longing after beauty, peace, and happiness embodied for him in the innocent fair girl before him" (305). No sooner is Dan's progress toward manhood revealed, however, than it is foreclosed: "The conviction of this sad yet natural fact came to Mrs. Jo with a pang, for she felt how utterly hopeless such a longing was; since light and darkness were not farther apart than snow-white Bess and sin-stained Dan" (305). Nature itself, according to Jo, has conspired to attract Dan to Bess even as it has ensured that his attraction remains "hopeless" — that is, as Dan surmised, his "stain" will never be made clean. When Jo confronts Dan shortly thereafter with her suspicions, Dan admits his feelings. "A man must love something," says Dan to Jo, "and I'd better love a spirit like [Bess] than any of the poor common girls who would care for me" (310). But, as Alcott's narrator tells us, "there was no hope and [Mrs. Jo] gave none.... Few women would care to marry Dan now, except such as would hinder, not help, him in the struggle which life would always be to him; and it was better to go solitary to his grave than become what she suspected his father had been — a handsome, unprincipled, and dangerous man, with more than one broken heart to answer for" (310). Having been taught to hunger after the middle-class ideal (as opposed to the "common" girls who would want him), Dan is then denied its fulfillment, leaving him, in Jo's words, "to go solitary to his grave."

As has been evident from her very first encounter with the young "firebrand," in *Jo's Boys*, Jo is not without sympathy for Dan's various passions. On the contrary, she has both identified with Dan's wild ways and admired them.[50] This is evidenced not only in her declaration that she always knew Dan would do something "fine and brave" but also in her initial response to Dan's idea of fighting for the Indians: "Do it! Do it! cried Mrs. Jo . . . for misfortune was much more interesting to her than good luck" (63). One could argue that it is not only the Native Americans' misfortune in which Jo is interested but Dan's as well. Unable or unwilling to roam like a free spirit herself, Jo lives this life vicariously through Dan. The unfortunate consequences of that liberty recur to Dan, whose travels abroad consistently get him into trouble. After pronouncing her judgment on Dan's future (a judgment that includes sending Bess away and letting Dan return to the Indians), Jo watches as Dan struggles to "speak again in the manly tone of resignation to the inevitable," a struggle "that showed how honest was his effort to give up everything but the pale shadow of what, for another, might have been a happy possibility" (311). Those others for whom happiness is a possibility include virtually all of Alcott's white boys and tomboys—temporary "primitives" whose sense of the "inevitable" is not exclusion from, but adoption into, white, Christian middle-class life.

Dan's response to Mrs. Jo's dashing of his hopes signals a derailment of Dan's sexual maturity. His coming-of-age is converted from a "hunger" for Bess to a "manly . . . resignation," implying that it is Dan's ability to face hard facts, rather than his physical or even emotional yearnings, that constitutes his manhood. One of those hard facts is the unbridgeable difference between his blood and Bess's, represented not only by the respective moral states that Jo assigns to them—"snow-white Bess and sin-stained Dan"—but also by the contrasting "light and darkness" that Dan himself sees written on their bodies. "Poor Dan looked with a shudder at the brown fist he clenched involuntarily as he remembered what he had done since a certain little white hand [Bess's] had laid in it confidingly" (229). Though he will never grow up to marry into the "snow-white" March family, Dan's recompense is to find a different kind of manliness in the recognition of his otherness. His maturity, in other words, is constituted by his internalization of the very middle-class values that he himself will never embody, an internalization that teaches him to see himself as the tainted, racial Other, inevitably

The Death of Boyhood (161)

doomed, in Mrs. Jo's words, to a "hard life and a lonely future" (311). While his resignation is meant to signify a certain salvation, that salvation is contingent upon his decision never to reproduce — never to become a legitimate father or, like his own father, a man "with more than one broken heart to answer for." Thus we are told in the last paragraph of *Jo's Boys* that Dan "never married, but lived, bravely and usefully, among his chosen people till he was shot defending them, and at last lay quietly asleep in the green wilderness he loved so well, with a lock of golden hair upon his breast, and a smile on his face which seemed to say that [Dan] had fought his last fight and was at peace" (322).

As I have traced throughout this book, American innocence and the suffering that characterizes it is located in the image of American boyhood and sonship that generations of nineteenth-century fathers aspired, through identification, to (re)claim. In Alcott's post–Civil War trilogy, that image appears to exist only in memory. Having become the symbols not of innocence but of the pleasures of aggression, boys are sacrificed to the empathetic structure of civilized Christian living, one in which masochism, or "sadism turned round upon the self," marks the precondition for postwar maturity. To resist (or be refused) such transformation leads to death. Writing of the late nineteenth-century boy-book genre, John Crowley comes to a similar conclusion, observing that "the cost of becoming a man is the irrecoverable loss of the boy-world, and the sense of this loss accounts for the frequently elegiac tone of the boy-book, which typically ends before the passage into manhood or just as it is beginning."[51] Alcott's elegiac tone at the end of *Jo's Boys* derives equally from what is lost and what was never found. If, as Kidd claims, "the subjectivity of American boyhood... was constituted in the late nineteenth century according to a social biology that designates the Other as permanently primitive, in contradistinction to the temporarily primitive or juvenile white male self," Dan is representative of the boy who never grows up.[52] His fate foreshadows those other Americans whose vanishing appears to be for Alcott as inevitable as it is mournful. Speaking of the Montana Indians with whom he lived, Dan tells Mrs. Jo early on in *Jo's Boys*, "They are a peaceful tribe, and need help awfully; hundreds have died of starvation because they don't get their share. The Sioux are fighters, thirty thousand strong, so the Government fears 'em, and gives 'em all they want. I call that a damned shame!" (62).[53] Identified not with the "fighters" but with the starving, Dan ominously foreshadows his life, and his life's work, as something of a lost cause. At the time of Alcott's writing (1885–86), thousands of American Indians had already died in battle or through starvation or disease, suggesting that Dan is not the only one who is to die "in the green wilderness." His death thus marks the passing not only of his own boyhood but of a people in whom many white writers had invested, both ignorantly and arrogantly, their late nineteenth-century ideas of what "boyhood" means.

In *Jo's Boys*, that death is figured as both tragic and predictable. The language and imagery surrounding Dan's death reminds us of the anonymous woman's sermon to the prisoners, one that positions Dan as a "wounded soldier." It also returns us to Melville's "March into Virginia," where boys willingly sacrifice themselves for the greater good, venturing into "that leafy neighborhood" until a "rapture sharp" translates them into "belaureled story." Dan's story, as I have argued, stages his death as the end of an era — an era as full of promise as it was of pain.[54] And to this extent, *Jo's Boys* is representative of the late nineteenth-century boy-book, a genre that looks back nostalgically to a rebellious spirit left behind, one that now can only be recaptured in play.[55] But whereas Melville is quite literal in his claim that "all wars are boyish and are fought by boys," Alcott imagines war simultaneously as a concrete event and as a spiritual condition. For perpetual boyish aggressors like Dan, another war lies within: only death will finally put him "at peace."

It is just such an interiorizing of conflict that ultimately differentiates Alcott's novels from other boy-books of the period. Her consistent portrayal of children as identified with (their) objects of abuse both locates maturity within an empathetic Christian frame-

The Death of Boyhood (163)

work and signals its cost for generations to come. For while the brown-skinned Dan, the boy whom Jo both loved and admired, dies a lonely death in the wilderness, the fair-faced Nat Blake, "amiable but weak," lives on to marry Daisy and usher in the next generation of Marches. Characterized throughout *Little Men* and *Jo's Boys* as of doubtful evolutionary promise, with a "weak mouth," a "rather weak" face, and "the sensitive nerves belonging to a music-loving nature" (*Jo's Boys*, 270; *Little Men*, 157, 132), Nat is summed up by Jo early on in *Jo's Boys* as "not man enough" to marry Daisy and "never would be" (28). There is thus little to account for Nat's ascendancy but his spotless ancestry. Unlike Dan, Nat appears to have no skeletons in his family closet. "The Blakes are a good lot," Nat tells Mrs. Jo in *Jo's Boys*. "I looked 'em up, and not one was ever in prison, hanged, or disgraced in any way" (100). Though Nat will never be the man that Dan might have been, neither he nor his forebears was ever in prison. Thus Nat lives on to father a new, more "sensitive" generation.

Perhaps it is just such evolutionary twists — that is, the weak procreate while the strong fight themselves to death — that causes Alcott at the end of *Jo's Boys* to state, somewhat sullenly and with the self-confessed air of a "weary historian," her temptation to "close the present tale with an earthquake which should engulf Plumfield and its environs so deeply in the bowels of the earth that no youthful Schliemann could ever find a vestige of it" (322). Such vehemence suggests not only "weariness" but a barely suppressed rage on the author's part against the March family "history" and what that history signifies: the ineluctable conversion of aggressive energies into domestic quiescence. Having lived her entire life with a father who preached the necessity of renunciation and self-sacrifice, Alcott knew firsthand the cost of such conversions. Her own fantasy of burying Plumfield so deeply that no archaeologist should ever unearth it thus beautifully captures both the expression and the repression of aggression with which her trilogy has all along been concerned. Given what Mrs. Jo describes in *Jo's Boys* as her own dubious talent for playing "literary nursemaid" and providing "moral pap for the young" (40), it is with possible relief that Alcott finishes this, her last novel, and lets "the music stop, the lights die out, and the curtain fall for ever on the March family" (323).[56] In doing so, Alcott accomplishes what the "savage" and boyish Jo never could: she disposes of the March family, and all that they represent, once and for all.

Afterword

This book grew out of a question: If, as one might safely say, nineteenth-century American culture distinguished itself by being tremendously sentimental and relentlessly violent at the same time, what was it about Christianity in particular — as the locus of both America's national sense of justice and its commitment to pursue that justice to its most aggressive ends — that allowed this apparent contradiction to flourish?[1] In the aftermath of 9/11, critical questions of America's investment in the redemptive logic of violence have surfaced with a vengeance, and, perhaps usefully, these questions return us to America's roots of war. Michael Warner's powerful essay, "What Like a Bullet Can Undeceive?," for example, examines perceptions of violence and redemption in post-9/11 America through a reading of Herman Melville's Civil War poem "Shiloh," subtitled "A Requiem," in memory of those soldiers who lost their lives in the stunningly destructive battle of 1862. A pastoral lyric of sorts, Melville's poem, as Warner notes, conventionally "answers to the expectation of redemption through art" — a process whereby violence is translated into beauty through the words and images that give it coherent meaning. Yet the poem presents, even more interestingly, Warner goes on to say, a "paradox in its redemptive language — one that says as much about how violence comes to be scandalous, about the traps of redemption, and about the dilemmas of liberal culture."[2] One of those dilemmas is the use of violence in the cause of ending it.

Cradled in the bookends of its beginning and ending image — swallows peacefully skimming over the dead and dying bodies on the field at Shiloh — is the poem's assurance that the men who fought each other as "foes" in the morning have, by virtue of their "mingled bodies," become "friends at eve." "Fame or country" are now "least their care," having discovered to their mutual amazement and horror the limits of redemptive possibility in their own deaths.[3] Focusing on Melville's next climactic, yet ironically parenthetical line in the poem — "What like a bullet can undeceive!" — Warner cites Melville's implicit critique of violence, especially state-sanctioned violence, as a means of achieving an end, even a righteous end. Framed by the North as a salvific vehicle for the United States as "redeemer" nation to bring all lost sheep back to its fold, war and its atrocities were often seen as a necessary evil for an ultimate good. "Human cruelty is remediated in this [earthly] world," writes Warner, "by the delegated human violence of the state and in the next world by [God's] judgment for which the American state is an instrument and a foreshadowing type" (43). But Melville didn't buy it. "In Melville's parenthesis," Warner goes on, "the whole idea of a war fought for a cause, any cause, is made to seem absurd" (44).

In the end, Warner argues, Melville's soldiers "outlive, however briefly and uselessly, their redemptive frameworks; and this window of injury-registration is ironically their most authentic life. What had been sacred justice becomes mere violence, in part because it stands in visible contrast to that which had been violated—a deep subjectivity" (53–54). In the preceding chapters, I have offered an alternative reading of that which appears to be "mere violence," to suggest the ways in which, for nineteenth-century authors writing in the shadow of war, violence appears impossibly bound up with the recognition, and construction, of authenticity and subjectivity. Although Warner is undoubtedly right that Melville means us to see his soldiers as undeceived about the all-too-simple motivations for war—"fame" and "country"—his readers are nonetheless thrown back on the redemptive possibilities of violence in the personal, and intersubjective, nature of attachments produced by battle—that is, the conversion of "foes" into "friends." That such a transformation occurs only at the moment of death points to Melville's belief in the necessity of suffering in effecting subjectivity—selves imaginatively connected to and embedded in other selves by virtue of their mutual experience of pain. Even more pessimistic, it suggests that the deceptions imposed by a redemptive view of violence exceed the soldiers' ability to stand apart from those deceptions and live.

Warner's own point in the essay is to unmask the ways in which violence has come to be seen, both in the normal workings of the state and in the categories of liberal ethics, as an "aberration" (45), a "scandal." "Violence," he writes, "is always the violence of another" (44). The act of naming violence involves a disavowal of sorts. It is a disavowal that, as I have tried to show, gains traction through the mediating operations of empathy. In my view, then, the dilemma posed by Melville's poem is not, Will we or won't we be deceived by the redemptive rhetoric of violence? but, To what extent can we recognize and experience the intra- and intersubjective nature of our worlds without the penetrating aid of violent enactments?

This is not to say that Melville, among others, considered violence as in and of itself redemptive, but it is to acknowledge the ways in which aggression is represented as fostering emotional attachments that are themselves given meaning through secular and sacred forms of knowledge and understanding. In nineteenth-century U.S. culture, as in the twenty-first, one of those key forms is identification with others. Authors and literary critics even today can write with confidence, as John Michael does, that the "imaginative placing of oneself in the embodied place of the other ... forms justice's essential requirement." Ethical living, he goes on, "requires not merely the power of rational abstraction to universal principles but the force of imaginative identification with concrete particularities, with actual positions, and with the people in them."[4] Melville, I think, would agree. But he might also ask us to consider the ways in which the structures of liberal, Protestant Christianity — structures that idealize and attempt to promote empathetic identifications, turning "foes" into "friends" — are rendered unimaginable outside of the violence, both psychological and material, that attends and makes possible the identifications that Christianity so valorizes.

To place this disturbing paradox in a contemporary context we need only think about how the issue of U.S. compassion has been shaped by political rhetoric in the wake of the war on Iraq. In his 2004 presidential stump speech, George W. Bush announced that "the strength of this country is in the hearts and souls of its citizens. That's the true strength of America. If you really think about it, you don't find it in the halls of government; you find it in the hearts of people. And the President [of the United States] must understand that. And one of my most important jobs is to rally the armies of compassion, to call upon people to love their neighbor just like you would like to be loved yourself."[5] President Bush's words to the American people underscore a prevailing idea in U.S. culture—the representation of America as first and foremost a sympathetic nation, a nation composed of people attuned to their own emotions and sensitive to the needs and sufferings of others. The very promise that sympathy offers, as well as the identifiable limits to its idealized goals, may help explain its conflicted persistence in American political discourse. For both proponents and detractors of sympathetic interventions, the concept itself carries enormous ideological weight. In the last two decades, Republicans and Democrats alike have engaged in what Kathleen Woodward calls "the presidential politics of empathy," but author Mickey Kaus explicitly warns against the use of compassion as a platform for social policy: "Compassion is a miserable basis for American politics," writes Kaus. It carries "the condescending implication of charity, inferiority, and helplessness," even as it renders social justice dependent on the whims of people's "charitable impulses."[6] Lauren Berlant critiques the call to compassion on similar grounds, claiming that the Right's embracing of "compassionate conservatism" opens up yet another avenue for people of privilege to institute social controls over the underprivileged: "By insisting that society's poorest members can achieve the good life through work, family, community participation, and faith, compassionate conservatives rephrase the embodied indignities of structural inequality as opportunities for individuals to reach out to each other, to build concrete human relations."[7] As these statements suggest, critics of compassion often base their skepticism over its social efficacy largely on the unequal power relations they see inhering in its practice. As Berlant puts it, "In operation, compassion is a term denoting privilege: the sufferer is *over there*."[8]

I would like to resituate Bush's use of "compassion" within its etymological context to argue for the importance of reading the word as, like sympathy, a matter of people "suffering together."[9] I do so not to invalidate the argument that real, material differences exist between sufferers and nonsufferers, nor to deny the hierarchical implications inhering in the political rhetoric of compassion, but to illuminate the ways in which Bush's particular phrasing reveals a long-standing, and arguably even more problematic, rendering of empathy in U.S. literature and culture. If, as Bush's reference to the Golden Rule implies, compassion involves "loving one's neighbor as oneself," that love is tellingly linked to expressions of aggression — "armies" — that are thought to manifest and engender love. In contrast to the feminine connotations raised in Bill Clinton's well-known catchphrase, "I feel your pain," Bush's determination to rally the "armies of compassion" invests the latter with masculine, even muscular energy.[10] The metaphor's appositional placement in relation to Christianity's injunction to "love one's neighbor," moreover, gives the latter the feel of a crusade. What might otherwise appear as an abstract, liberal call to *feel right* (in Harriet Beecher Stowe's now well-known exhortation to her readers) is cast in weighty, forceful terms.[11] Yet ultimately it is not simply the masculinizing of compassion that characterizes Bush's vision, but the idea that force itself can help bring compassion into being. If loving one's neighbor takes the "strength" of compassion, that strength, Bush implies, is inextricable from the conditions of violence through which compassion and empathy are incarnated in the world.

As this last statement suggests, I believe we can read the subtext of Bush's rallying cry for the "armies of compassion" as an attempt to legitimize American military action in foreign lands. His metaphor indicates that it is not just U.S. citizens who will benefit from American compassion, but America's worldwide "neighbors" as well — that is, those developed and developing nations with which American armies are often literally engaged. Importantly, however, Bush's speech obscures national involvements by subsuming them in personal ones. Strategically disavowing the power of the state, or "the halls of government," to represent the "strength of America," Bush locates it instead in the "hearts of people." There, in the "hearts and souls of its citizens," American "strength" is dislodged from its impersonal and potentially oppressive connotations by its association with interpersonal, empathetic feeling: the power of compassion. Bush thus links compassion to a religiously encoded identification ("loving one's neighbor as oneself") and tethers both to a metaphor that legitimizes U.S. force at home and abroad: the "armies" of compassion that nominally express not aggression — but Christian love.

Bush's representation of American character as essentially empathetic relies on a cultural understanding of the position of the United States as national martyr in the wake of 9/11. Every American, Bush implies, is a real or potential victim, identified with those "other" victims (Iraqi civilians, for example) who stand in need of America's neighborly love. Against, or side by side with, this characterization of American compassion we might place the torture of prisoners at Abu Ghraib, a scandal that came to light in the same year that Bush was stumping his speech. The tortures glaringly reveal not American innocence but U.S. brutality. Yet, in one widely circulated picture brought to public view during the scandal, we get a glimpse, once again, of the imaginative power of Christian martyrdom.

The infamous "Hooded Man" photo depicts a hooded prisoner standing on a pedestal, arms stretched wide with his fingers connected to wires in an imitation of crucifixion.[12] The intentionality of the photo's composition is difficult to determine. That is, it is unclear whether the man was posed in the act of martyrdom or whether the camera caught a signifying moment. What is clear is that this photo became an icon of the "scandal" of violence — an "othering" of unnatural force by virtue both of its subject matter (a Muslim depicted in the attitude of Christ) and its implication that the soldiers engaged in the torture were somehow renegades. At the same time, I would argue, the photo works to confront Americans with their own guilt and aggression; it gains its cultural power from the identification of Americans with the ones they abuse. This idea is supported by the words of the foreign minister of the Vatican, Archbishop Giovanni Lajolo, who observed that the photos in general represent "a more serious blow to the United States than [the] September 11, 2001 attacks. Except that the blow was not inflicted by terrorists but by Americans against themselves."[13] Aptly, if unconsciously, articulating the U.S. cultural identification of abusers with their abused, Archbishop Lajolo represents the torture of others as a self-inflicted *American* wound.

The very dislocation of symbol and meaning in the "Hooded Man" photo suggests a breakdown in the central signifiers of Christian American exceptionalism — a bankruptcy in understanding of the very terms the United States employs to foster its self-created image. Melville seemed to point to such a bankruptcy, not only in his Civil War poetry but in his last work, *Billy Budd* (1886–91). There, in the sacrifice of the Christlike "Baby" Budd to the martial law of the Godlike Captain Vere, Melville makes clear the perverse ideological confusion between God and state, a confusion in which earthly sons die for the ostensibly redemptive work of their warlike fathers. In fact, it is precisely as a father figure that Melville represents his hawkish captain, underscoring the personal attachments and identifications through which the state both operates and obscures its power. "[Captain Vere] was old enough to have been Billy's father. The austere devotee of military duty, letting himself melt back into what remains primeval in our formalized humanity, may in end have caught Billy to his heart, even as Abraham may have caught young Isaac on the brink of resolutely offering him up in obedience to the exacting behest."[14] Comparing Vere and Billy's relationship to that of Abraham and Isaac, Melville brings to the end of an epoch a religious myth that, as I have been arguing, informs so much of nineteenth-century U.S. fiction in its depiction of American innocence subtending arrangements of power. The sentimentalizing of this dynamic, moreover, is made apparent in the father figure's co-option of the son's pain. As Melville's narrator tells readers, evidence of Vere's "agony," written on his face, indicates that "the condemned one [Billy] suffered less than he who mainly had effected the condemnation [Vere]."[15]

Of course, as Melville has it, Billy is complicit in, if not responsible for, the sanctification of his oppressor. Meeting his death with the pacifying words "God bless Captain Vere!" (and thereby deterring a possible mutiny), Billy is positioned as the consummate whipping boy; his ironic declaration revisits the blessings of the innocent son on the aggressive father, who himself suffers, vicariously, for the son's sake.[16] Thus we are reminded that in the American paradigm of the whipping boy, emotional transformations belong not to the objects of abuse but to the perpetrators of it. Like Melville's soldiers, Vere becomes identified with his victim, to become, imaginatively speaking, "one" with the object he harms. As Melville knew, identification comes with a high price. Its reparative ends are too often bought with some body's blood. Yet implicit in this work, as in "Shiloh," is the question of how we are to be redeemed — from selfishness, apathy, and/or existential estrangement — without it? That is the dilemma that America yet faces.

NOTES

INTRODUCTION

1 The sustained critique of sentimental culture began in earnest with Ann Douglas's groundbreaking *The Feminization of American Culture* (New York: Anchor Press, 1977). More recently, it is exemplified in Lauren Berlant's influential article "Poor Eliza," *American Literature* 70 (September 1998): 635–68. For a sympathetic reading of sentimental literature's egalitarian goals, see Philip Fisher, *Hard Facts: Setting and Form in the American Novel* (New York: Oxford University Press, 1987); and Jane Tompkins, *Sensational Designs: The Cultural Work of American Fiction, 1790–1860* (New York: Oxford University Press, 1985).
2 Lori Merish, *Sentimental Materialism: Gender, Commodity Culture, and Nineteenth-Century American Literature* (Durham: Duke University Press, 2000), 3.
3 Ibid.
4 See Philip Fisher, *The Vehement Passions* (Princeton: Princeton University Press, 2002).
5 For the role of women in the creation of U.S. sentimental culture, see especially Tompkins, *Sensational Designs*; Shirley Samuels, ed., *The Culture of Sentiment: Race, Gender, and Sentimentality in Nineteenth-Century America* (New York: Oxford University Press, 1992); and Karen Sánchez-Eppler, *Touching Liberty: Abolition, Feminism, and the Politics of the Body* (Berkeley: University of California Press, 1993). On the politics of male sentimentalism, see Mary Chapman and Glenn Hendler, eds., *Sentimental Men: Masculinity and the Politics of Affect in American Culture* (Berkeley: University of California Press, 1999); Caleb Crain, *American Sympathy: Men, Friendship, and Literature in the New Nation* (New Haven: Yale University Press, 2001); and Jennifer Travis and Milette Shamir, eds., *Boys Don't Cry? Rethinking Narratives of Masculinity and Emotion in the U.S.* (New York: Columbia University Press, 2002).
6 Such an idea has its roots in what I have elsewhere argued is a postrevolutionary, national ethos infused with and informed by the sentimental ideals of its day. At the turn of the nineteenth century, democracy and

empathy appear to go hand in hand, fashioning a popular image of the American individual as one whose politics are inextricably bound up with his or her ability to feel another's pain. See Elizabeth Barnes, *States of Sympathy: Seduction and Democracy in the American Novel* (New York: Columbia University Press, 1997).

7 "Roger Malvin's Burial" first appeared in *The Token* (1832) and was later included in Hawthorne's story collection *Mosses from an Old Manse* (1846).

8 Nathaniel Hawthorne, *Mosses from an Old Manse*, ed. William Charvat, Roy Harvey Pearce, and Claude M. Simpson (Columbus: Ohio State University Press, 1974), 356, 360. All citations hereafter appear in parentheses following the quotation.

9 Freud sees identification as a compensation for the loss of a love-object, the "most obvious reaction" to which "is to identify oneself with it, to replace it from within, as it were, by identification." Sigmund Freud, "An Outline of Psycho-analysis" (1940), in *The Standard Edition of the Complete Psychological Works of Sigmund Freud*, trans. and ed. James Strachey, 24 vols. (London: Hogarth Press, 1953–74), 23:193.

10 See Eve Kosofsky Sedgwick, *Between Men: English Literature and Male Homosocial Desire* (New York: Columbia University Press, 1985); René Girard, *Deceit, Desire, and the Novel: Self and Other in Literary Structure*, trans. Yvonne Freccero (Baltimore: Johns Hopkins University Press, 1961); and Diana Fuss, *Identification Papers* (New York: Routledge, 1995).

11 Fuss, *Identification Papers*, 2.

12 The relationship between violence and redemption in American culture has perhaps been most famously articulated by Richard Slotkin, who argues that the idea of "regeneration through violence" proved a "structuring metaphor of the American experience." According to Slotkin, the early colonists' fraught relationship to nature—specifically, the American wilderness and the indigenous inhabits of that wilderness, the American Indians—was ultimately made beneficial to colonists through a frontier myth that posited violent exchange as a means of initiation into new life. Slotkin's theory of the colonial experience is supported more recently by the work of Hent de Vries and Samuel Weber, whose summation of transnational modernist and postmodernist reevaluations of violence leads them to conclude "what thinkers from Nietzsche through Adorno to Levinas and Derrida have long suspected: that violence is not necessarily the exclusive characteristic of the other but rather, and perhaps even above all, a means through which the self, whether individual or

collective, is constituted and maintained." My study seeks to complicate, as well as contextualize, this notion of selfhood and self-determination made possible through violence by attending to the American sentimental structures that render selfhood a fluid, and fraught, dynamic. Richard Slotkin, *Regeneration through Violence: The Mythology of the American Frontier, 1600–1800* (Middletown, Conn.: Wesleyan University Press, 1973), 5; Hent de Vries and Samuel Weber, eds., *Violence, Identity, and Self-Determination* (Stanford, Calif.: Stanford University Press, 1997), 1–2.

13 Richard Brodhead, *Cultures of Letters: Scenes of Reading and Writing in Nineteenth-Century America* (Chicago: University of Chicago Press, 1993), 17–18. I address Brodhead's ideas more fully in chapter 4.

14 Gail Bederman, *Manliness and Civilization: A Cultural History of Gender and Race in the United States, 1880–1917* (Chicago: University of Chicago Press, 1995), 11.

15 The term is first recorded during the reign of Charles I (1625–49), by John Trapp, in *A Commentary or Exposition upon the Five Books of Moses*: "Rebuke before all: yet not as if they were whipping boyes." Following the belief in the Divine Right of Kings, Prince Edward (son of Henry VIII) and Prince Charles (son of James I) were considered beyond physical correction by their tutors. In the place of each stood what became known as a "whipping boy." Charles I's stand-in was his best friend, William Murray, a high-born noble whose proximity to Charles (in terms of both position and affection) presumably strengthened his disciplinary value.

16 The term "empathy," translated from the German word *Einfühlung* ("feeling as one") and coined by Rudolf Lotze in 1858, did not become a part of Anglo-American discourse until the early twentieth century, when, as Ann Mikkelsen observes, it became associated with the German tradition of aesthetics through philosophers like Theodore Lipps. "According to Lipps' reflections on sculpture and architecture," writes Mikkelsen, "empathy refers to a state of 'aesthetic imitation' in which distinctions between subject and object disappear. . . . Upon observing the aesthetic representation of a human or structural form, an 'ideal self' or ego that 'objectifies itself' is formed, 'bound up with the sensuously perceived figure' and creating a state in which 'the object is myself and by the very same token this self of mine is the object. Empathy is the fact that the antithesis between myself and the object disappears, or rather does not yet exist.'" Ann Mikkelsen, "From Sympathy to Empathy: Anzia Yezierska and the Transformation of the American Subject," *American Litera-*

ture 82, no. 2 (June 2010): 369. In my view, nineteenth-century authors' use of the term "sympathy" anticipates the objectification of self through identification to which Lipps refers. One might say that the innocent victim, or whipping boy, represents a virtual work of art — an object created by the aggressive father-figure who then views himself, through empathy, as simultaneously the subject and object of violence.

17 Harriet Beecher Stowe, *Uncle Tom's Cabin, or Life among the Lowly* (New York: Penguin Books, 1986), 211. The ideas I am outlining here are specifically Protestant ones. In a recent study, Tracy Fessenden importantly attends to the ways in which American religious history promotes a developmental narrative in which the practice of "good" religion — that is, a certain form of Protestantism — emerges as coincident with, and the facilitator for, the new, redeemed American nation. All other religious practices are deemed "irrational, regressive, or inscrutable," and their practitioners are ostracized or victimized with unreflective impunity." *Culture and Redemption: Religion, the Secular, and American Literature* (Princeton: Princeton University Press, 2007), 2.

18 The idea of God and Christ as universally empathetic is not confined to the nineteenth century. In a book I read recently on grief, the writer states: "Finally, in some mysterious way, God grieves and suffers with you. I say mysterious because I can't explain how it works. God's ways are not our ways. Yet God has entered our lives in his Son Jesus, and Jesus was all about helping those who suffer. Jesus cared deeply for people whose hearts were broken by sorrow. *When you cry, Jesus cries. Your tears are his tears. Your pain, his pain.* This is a total mystery to me, but I believe it: God doesn't take away our pain, but shares it. That's the way God's love works." Kenneth C. Haugk, *A Time to Grieve: Journeying through Grief, Book One* (St. Louis: Stephen Ministries St. Louis, 2004), 40–41 (emphasis mine).

19 See Theodore De Bruyn, "Flogging a Son: The Emergence of the *Pater Flagellans* in Latin Christian Discourse," *Journal of Early Christian Studies* 7, no. 2 (1999): 249–90. This philosophy, as I discuss in chapter 3, is grounded in such biblical verses as Proverbs 3:12: "For the Lord reproves him whom he loves, as a father the son in whom he delights"; Hebrews 12:6: "For the Lord disciplines him whom he loves, and chastises every son whom he receives"; and Revelation 3:18: "Those whom I love, I reprove and chasten."

20 Judith Butler, *Bodies That Matter* (New York: Routledge, 1993), 112. The context for Butler's assertion is the fear of likeness underlying homopho-

bia. Although sexual identity is not the focus of my argument, Butler's observation about the work of disavowal is nonetheless useful.
21 Herman Melville, *White-Jacket, or The World in a Man-of-War*, ed. Harrison Hayford, Hershel Parker, and G. Thomas Tanselle (Evanston: Northwestern University Press, 2000), 144; Frederick Douglass, *Narrative of the Life of Frederick Douglass, An American Slave* (New York: Anchor Books, 1973), 5; Louis DeCaro, "Black People's Ally, White People's Bogeyman: A John Brown Story," in *The Afterlife of John Brown*, ed. Andrew Taylor and Eldrid Herrington (New York: Palgrave Macmillan, 2005), 13; Richard Scheidenhelm, ed., *The Response to John Brown* (Belmont, Calif.: Wadsworth, 1972), 37.
22 Fisher, *Hard Facts*, 99.
23 Franny Nudelman, *John Brown's Body: Slavery, Violence, and the Culture of War* (Chapel Hill: University of North Carolina Press, 2004), n182. See Laura Wexler, *Tender Violence: Domestic Visions in an Age of U.S. Imperialism* (Chapel Hill: University of North Carolina Press, 2000), 104–5.
24 Berlant, "Poor Eliza," 641. See also Nudelman, *John Brown's Body*, nn182–83.
25 The phrase "sentimental wounding" comes from Marianne Noble's chapter on *Uncle Tom's Cabin*, where she argues that the white reader's "longing to heal the wounds of an internalized otherness" produces an ecstatic, erotic response in the reader in relation to abused others. See Marianne Noble, *The Masochistic Pleasures of Sentimental Literature* (Princeton: Princeton University Press, 2000), 139.
26 For an excellent study of the role of submission in American democratic practice, see Christopher Newfield, *The Emerson Effect: Individualism and Submission in America* (Chicago: University of Chicago Press, 1996). For my early formulations of elite, white male sensitivity and its implications for the U.S. citizenry, I am especially indebted to Julie Ellison's *Cato's Tears and the Making of Anglo-American Emotion* (Chicago: University of Chicago Press, 1999).
27 George W. Bush, September 16, 2001.
28 Donald Pease, "Re-thinking 'American Studies after US Exceptionalism,'" *American Literary History* 21, no. 1 (Spring 2009): 22.
29 Amy Kaplan, "The Tenacious Grasp of American Exceptionalism," *Comparative American Studies* 2, no. 2 (2004): 154.
30 As Fisher observes, the coexistence of institutionalized brutality and committed humanitarianism makes sense if one considers Rousseau's theory in *Discourse on the Origins of Inequality* — that at the historical moment at

which society reaches the "maximum" of historical inequality—namely, slavery—it will "also reach the maximum of sensibility or sentimentality, the maximum of complex sympathetic relations between people." This is so, argues Rousseau, because compassion is a "'species preserving' rather than individual preserving feeling." By attending to the needs and feelings of others less fortunate, privileged men and women also save themselves, their families, and their way of life. Quoted in Fisher, *Hard Facts*, 105.

31 Charles Brockden Brown, *Wieland & Memoirs of Carwin*, ed. Sydney J. Krause and S. W. Reid (Kent, Ohio: Kent State University Press, 1977), 230.

32 Herman Melville, *Correspondence*, ed. Lynn Horth (Evanston, Ill.: Northwestern University Press and the Newberry Library, 1993), vol. 13 of the Northwestern–Newberry Library Series, 212–13.

33 Herman Melville, "Bartleby, the Scrivener," in *Melville's Short Novels*, ed. Dan McCall (New York: Norton, 2002), 17.

34 Melville, "Bartleby, the Scrivener," 19.

35 Melville, *White-Jacket*, 135.

36 Frederick Douglass, *My Bondage and My Freedom*, vol. 2 of *The Frederick Douglass Papers*, ed. John W. Blassingame, John R. McKivigan, and Peter P. Hinks (New Haven: Yale University Press, 1999), 141.

37 Ibid. (emphasis mine).

38 Scheidenhelm, *Response to John Brown*, 37.

39 As John Stauffer notes, Brown was fond of the biblical verse Hebrews 9:22: "Without the shedding of blood there is no remission of sin." See *The Black Hearts of Men: Radical Abolitionists and the Transformation of Race* (Cambridge: Harvard University Press, 2002), 13.

40 Melville, *White-Jacket*, 219.

41 Michael Paul Rogin, *Subversive Genealogy: The Politics and Art of Herman Melville* (Berkeley: University of California Press, 1979), 92–93.

42 Sigmund Freud, "'A Child Is Being Beaten': A Contribution to the Study of the Origin of Sexual Perversions" (1919), in Strachey, *Complete Psychological Works of Sigmund Freud*, 17:194.

43 Ibid. Freud writes that the child's assurance that the father loves only him/her (because he is beating the other child) "was meant in a genital sense; owing to the regression it is turned into 'My father is beating me (I am being beaten by my father).' This being beaten is now a convergence of the sense of guilt and sexual love. *It is not only the punishment for the forbidden genital relation, but also the regressive substitute for that relation,*

and from this latter source it derives the libidinal excitation which is from this time forward attached to it, and which finds its outlet in masturbatory acts. Here for the first time we have the essence of masochism." It is precisely the sexual component of the beating fantasy that led Freud to see it as — irrespective of gender — a paradigm of feminine masochism (189). See also David Savran, *Taking It Like a Man: White Masculinity, Masochism, and Contemporary American Culture* (Princeton: Princeton University Press, 1998), 30.

44 "After all," Freud writes, "all of the many unspecified children who are beaten . . . are . . . nothing more than substitutes for the child itself." Freud, "A Child Is Being Beaten," 191.

45 Louisa May Alcott, *Little Women* (New York: Penguin Classics, 1989), 79 (emphasis mine). Part I of *Little Women* was originally published in 1868. Part II, entitled *Good Wives*, was published in 1869.

46 Noble's *Masochistic Pleasures* also argues for the potential pleasures inhering in a "fantasized submission to power," but her work focuses almost exclusively on women.

47 In chapter 4, I situate Alcott's *Little Men* and *Jo's Boys* within the "boy-book" genre made popular in the 1870s. While the genre certainly reflects a preoccupation with boyhood, I argue that its nostalgic, even elegiac, representation of boyhood suggests the end, rather than the beginning, of an era celebrating boyish pleasure.

48 Quoted in Savran, *Taking It Like a Man*, 35–36.

CHAPTER ONE

1 Adam Cohen, "It's a Bad Trading Day . . . and It's About to Get Worse," *Newsweek*, August 9, 1999, 22.

2 Evan Thomas and T. Trent Gegax, "The Atlanta Massacre," *Time*, August 9, 1999, 26. Other reports told a similar story: "Day Trading: It's a Brutal World" read one section of *Time* magazine's coverage of the serial murders; the *San Francisco Chronicle's Nation* section headlined its article "Volatile Business of Day Trading," explicitly correlating the financial volatility of active stock trading with the psychological volatility of this man who practiced it.

3 The entire letter of confession is reprinted in *Newsweek*, August 9, 1999, 27.

4 See Charles Patrick Ewing, *Fatal Families: The Dynamics of Intrafamilial*

Homicide (Thousand Oaks, Calif.: Sage Publications, 1997), 134. According to statistics in the national archives of Canada and Wales, from the 1970s to 1990, men were responsible for 95 percent of all familicides. See Margo Wilson, Martin Daly, and Antoinetta Daniele, "Familicide: The Killing of Spouse and Children," *Aggressive Behavior* 21 (1995): 279–80.

5. Ewing, *Fatal Families*, 134–36.
6. In fact, his daughter, Mychelle, accused him herself, in 1994, at the age of twenty-two, but authorities decided that she was probably experiencing trauma from her mother's death. Adam Cohen, "It's a Bad Trading Day," 27.
7. Ibid., 28.
8. Daniel A. Cohen, "Homicidal Compulsion and the Conditions of Freedom: The Social and Psychological Origins of Familicide in America's Early Republic," *Journal of Social History* 28 (Summer 1995): 725. See also Wilson, Daly, and Daniele, "Familicide." Daniel Cohen cites Thomas M. McDade's *The Annals of Murder* (Norman, Okla., 1961) as a bibliographic source for publications on familicide from 1680 to 1900. He also observes that Neil King Fitzgerald locates a total of eleven family murders between 1780 and 1839 but notes that Fitzgerald defines that category more broadly than Cohen himself does (Daniel A. Cohen, "Homicidal Compulsion," 753). See Neil King Fitzgerald, "Towards an American Abraham: Multiple Parricide and the Rejection of Revelation in the Early National Period" (master's thesis, Brown University, 1971).
9. John Cowan, *The Life and Confession*, ed. James Allen (Cincinnati, Ohio, 1835), quoted in Daniel A. Cohen, "Homicidal Compulsion," 739; Abel Clemmens, *Cruel Murder!! A True Account of the Life and Character of Abel Clemmens* (Morgantown, W.Va.: 1805?), quoted in Daniel A. Cohen, "Homicidal Compulsion," 734.
10. "An Account of a Murder Committed by Mr. J[ames] Yates, upon his family, in December, A.D. 1781," quoted in Daniel A. Cohen, "Homicidal Compulsion," 728.
11. In his "Advertisement" (preface), Brockden Brown reminds skeptical readers of "an authentic case, remarkably similar to that of Wieland," a case that Alan Axelrod takes to be James Yates's murder of his family at what he claimed was God's command in 1781. Shirley Samuels makes the argument that Brockden Brown would probably also have known about the Beadle murders of 1782. See Shirley Samuels, *Romances of the Republic: Women, the Family, and Violence in the Literature of the Early American Nation* (New York: Oxford University Press, 1996), 52–53; and Alan

Axelrod, *Charles Brockden Brown: An American Tale* (Austin: University of Texas Press, 1983), 61.

12 Charles Brockden Brown, *Wieland & Memoirs of Carwin*, ed. Sydney J. Krause and S. W. Reid (Kent, Ohio: Kent State University Press, 1977), 244. All citations hereafter will appear in parentheses following the quotation.

13 Myron Tuman, *Melville's Gay Father and the Knot of Filicidal Desire: On Men and Their Demons* (Christchurch, New Zealand: Cybereditions, 2005), 89.

14 See Søren Kierkegaard, *Fear and Trembling, and the Sickness unto Death* (1954) (Princeton: Princeton University Press, 1968); René Girard, *Violence and the Sacred* (Baltimore: Johns Hopkins University Press, 1972); René Girard, *The Scapegoat* (Baltimore: Johns Hopkins University Press, 1986); and Susan L. Mizruchi, *The Science of Sacrifice: American Literature and Modern Social Thought* (Princeton: Princeton University Press, 1998).

15 Matthew 26:39.
16 Genesis 22:7–8.
17 Genesis 22:2, 22:16–17.
18 John 3:16.
19 Daniel A. Cohen, "Homicidal Compulsion," 728, 729, 736, 739.
20 See Karen Halttunen, *Murder Most Foul: The Killer and the American Gothic Imagination* (Cambridge: Harvard University Press, 1998), especially chapter 5.
21 Stephen Mix Mitchell, *A Narrative of the Life of William Beadle* (Hartford, Conn.: Webster, 1783), 14.
22 These accounts do not concern themselves with the crime alone; rather, they aim to help guide readers toward a proper interpretation of the material by delineating for their audience the bounds of appropriate feeling and response. Thus the *New-York Weekly Magazine* included an essay entitled "The Fatal Effects of Indulging the Passions" in its 1796 issue, reprinting the account of James Yates's murder of his family. Various editions of Mitchell's *Narrative of the Life of William Beadle*, published from 1783 to 1805, concluded with extracts from John Marsh's sermon preached at the Beadle family funeral, "The Great Sin and Danger of Striving with God." *Sketches of the Life of James Purrinton* (1806) was published with "Remarks on the Fatal Tendency of Erroneous Principles, and Motives for Receiving and Obeying the Pure and Salutary Precepts of the Gospel."
23 "The following is a particular account of a horrid murder. Abel Clem-

mons [that is, Clemmens] murdered his wife and eight children." Clarksburg, Virginia, November 11, 1805.

24 Ibid.

25 "Horrid Massacre!! Sketches of the Life of Captain James Purrinton, Who on the Night of the Eighth of July, 1806, Murdered His Wife, Six Children and Himself" (Augusta, Maine: Peter Edes, 1806), 8.

26 "Remarks," 13.

27 James Dana, "Men's Sins Not Chargeable on God, but on Themselves: A Discourse Delivered at Wallingford, December 22, 1782, Occasioned by the Tragical Exit of William Beadle, His Wife, and Four Children, at Wethersfield, on the Morning of the 11th Instant, by His Own Hands" (New Haven, Conn.: T. and S. Green, 1783), title page.

28 Ibid., 9, 11, 19, 22.

29 Ibid., 21, 22.

30 *Pennsylvania Packet*, January 2, 1783. Mitchell notes that Beadle felt that the murder of his wife, which he had not previously planned, was a necessary kindness: "He finally concludes it would be unmerciful to leave her behind to languish out a life in misery and wretchedness, which must be the consequence of the suprizing [sic] death of the rest of the family." Mitchell, *Narrative of the Life of William Beadle*, 14.

31 Dana, "Men's Sins," 22.

32 "Horrid Massacre," 21–22.

33 John Marsh, "The Great Sin and Danger of Striving with God" (Hartford, Conn.: Hudson and Goodwin, 1783), 6, 16.

34 Dana, "Men's Sins," 5, 9.

35 Ibid., 10.

36 Ibid., 11.

37 Ibid., 17.

38 John Leland, "A True Account, How Matthew Womble Murdered His Wife (Who Was Pregnant) and His Four Sons, on June the 9th, 1784" (Stockbridge, Mass.: Richard Lee, 1793), 7.

39 Ibid., 8.

40 Axelrod, *Charles Brockden Brown*, 61.

41 Ibid., 57.

42 Jane Tompkins, *Sensational Designs: The Cultural Work of American Fiction, 1790–1860* (New York: Oxford University Press, 1985), 53, 44.

43 See Jay Fliegelman, *Prodigals and Pilgrims: The American Revolution against Patriarchal Authority, 1750–1800* (Cambridge: Cambridge University Press, 1982).

44 He later tells her that this was a lie concocted so that he wouldn't have to explain his gift of ventriloquism.
45 David Brion Davis, *Homicide in American Fiction, 1798–1860: A Study in Social Values* (Ithaca: Cornell University Press, 1957), 90.
46 Diana Fuss, *Identification Papers* (New York: Routledge, 1995), 9.
47 Norman Grabo asserts that the incestuous desire between Wieland and Clara is mutual, and that Clara's fear of her brother and all he represents is actually projection. He sees in Clara's narrative the "movement toward a kind of identity with Theodore attainable only over the bodies of Theodore's wife and children." Norman S. Grabo, *The Coincidental Art of Charles Brockden Brown* (Chapel Hill: University of North Carolina Press, 1981), 27. If Grabo's reading is correct, Clara not only desires her brother but also identifies with his desire to possess and to kill her, the latter fantasy accounted for by Clara's guilt about her own incestuous desire.

CHAPTER TWO

1 Herman Melville, *White-Jacket, or The World in a Man-of-War*, ed. Harrison Hayford, Hershel Parker, and G. Thomas Tanselle (Evanston: Northwestern University Press, 2000), 144. All references hereafter will appear in parentheses following the quotation.
2 Charles Olson, *Call Me Ishmael* (San Francisco: City Light Books, 1947), 92.
3 Edwin S. Shneidman, "Some Psychological Reflections on the Death of Malcolm Melville," *Suicide and Life Threatening Behavior* 6 (1976): 233; Herman Melville, *Moby-Dick*, ed. Hershel Parker and Harrison Hayford (New York: W. W. Norton, 2002), 140. Elizabeth Renker, *Strike through the Mask: Herman Melville and the Scene of Writing* (Baltimore: Johns Hopkins University Press, 1996), 62–68. Renker's chapter 3 synthesizes biographical material previously published on Melville's domestic situation, including an article from the *Proceedings of the Massachusetts Historical Society*, which brought to light "some newly discovered letters, dated May 1867, that suggest Herman Melville physically and emotionally abused his wife. One letter reveals that Elizabeth Shaw Melville's minister proposed a feigned kidnapping to get her out of the house and away from her husband." As Renker goes on to note, except for one publication in 1981 by the Melville Society on the subject, "the discovery has received astonishingly little sustained attention" (49).

4 Leon Howard, *Herman Melville* (Minneapolis: University of Minnesota Press, 1961), 93.
5 Renker, *Strike through the Mask*, 65.
6 Ibid., 67. Renker links the theme of "blankness" associated with women in Melville's fiction to the blankness of the page, both of which present barriers to the apprehension of truth. "The pasteboard mask that can't be struck through," writes Renker, is but one tangible referent in Melville's "dramas of composition in which paper acts as a material site of blockage, frustrating the author's desire to penetrate and so to transcend material conditions" (67).
7 Murray, quoted by Forrest G. Robinson in his biography of Murray, *Love's Story Told: A Life of Henry A. Murray* (Cambridge: Harvard University Press, 1992), 240–41.
8 Hershel Parker, "Damned by Dollars: *Moby-Dick* and the Price of Genius," in Melville, *Moby-Dick*, 722.
9 Lewis Mumford, *Herman Melville* (New York: Harcourt, Brace, 1929), 230.
10 Herman Melville, *The Piazza Tales and Other Prose Pieces, 1839–1860*, ed. Harrison Hayford, Alma A. MacDougall, and G. Thomas Tanselle (Evanston, Ill.: Northwestern University Press and the Newberry Library, 1987), vol. 9 of the Northwestern–Newberry Library Series, 250.
11 Herman Melville, *Correspondence*, ed. Lynn Horth (Evanston, Ill.: Northwestern University Press and the Newberry Library, 1993), vol. 13 of the Northwestern–Newberry Library Series, 212–13.
12 Herman Melville, "Bartleby, the Scrivener," in *Melville's Short Novels*, ed. Dan McCall (New York: Norton, 2002), 34. All references hereafter will appear in parentheses following the quotation.
13 Adam Smith, *The Theory of Moral Sentiments*, ed. D. D. Raphael and A. L. Macfie (Oxford: Oxford University Press, 1976), 140. *Moral Sentiments* was originally published in 1759, but the source text now commonly used is the expanded sixth edition, which Smith published in 1790. For an excellent reading of Smith's passage, see Julie Ellison's *Cato's Tears and the Making of Anglo-American Emotion* (Chicago: University of Chicago Press, 1999), 11–12.
14 The seminal essay on this subject is Louise K. Barnett's "Bartleby as Alienated Worker," *Studies in Short Fiction* 11 (Fall 1974): 379–85. For other Marxist readings, see Barbara Foley, "From Wall Street to Astor Place: Historicizing Melville's 'Bartleby,'" *American Literature* 72 (March 2000): 87–116, and James C. Wilson, "'Bartleby': The Walls of Wall Street," *Arizona Quarterly* 37 (Winter 1981): 335–46.

15 Susan Ryan, *The Grammar of Good Intentions: Race and the Antebellum Culture of Benevolence* (Ithaca: Cornell University Press, 2003), 9.
16 Ibid., 11.
17 George B. Cheever, "An Article in the North American Review on the Removal of the Indians: The Letters of William Penn," *American Monthly Magazine*, January 1830, 704.
18 Rev. S. D. Clark, *The Faithful Steward; or, Systematic Beneficence: An Essential of Christian Character* (New York: M. W. Dodd, 1850; republished by Doctrinal Tract and Book Society, 1853), 55, 140. Clark's was one of four chosen as winners of a contest in New York for "the best approved treatise on the importance of Systematic Beneficence" (giving money in a systematic way).
19 Ibid., 2.
20 Smith, *Theory of Moral Sentiments*, 9.
21 Leo Marx, "Melville's Parable of the Walls," reprinted in McCall, *Melville's Short Novels*, 239. Marx, like Renker, notes Melville's preoccupation with the "pasteboard masks" that Ahab complains that "all visible objects," including men, wear. How can an individual, Ahab continues, "strike through the mask," or how can the prisoner "reach outside" the prison of his own mind, "except by thrusting through that wall?" (*Moby-Dick*, 140). Marx applies the passage to "Bartleby," remarking, "Like the whale, the wall will destroy the man who tries too obstinately to penetrate it. Bartleby had become so obsessed by the problem of the dead-wall that his removal to prison hardly changed his condition, or, for that matter, the state of his being; even in the walled street he had allowed his life to become suffused by death" (Marx, "Melville's Parable of the Walls," 253). To argue, as I am doing, that the story tells us more about the narrator than his employee is not to deny the significance of Bartleby's alienation but to suggest that, rather than confronting the wall of human or theological inscrutability, Bartleby represents it. He is himself the "mask" that the narrator fails to "strike through."
22 H. Bruce Franklin, *The Wake of the Gods: Melville's Mythology* (Palo Alto, Calif.: Stanford University Press, 1963), 126–27.
23 Elizabeth Margaret Chandler, "Mental Metempsychosis," in *Essays, Philanthropic and Moral, Principally Relating to the Abolition of Slavery in America* (New York: Baker, Crane, & Day, 1845), 117.
24 William McNally, *Evils and Abuses in the Naval and Merchant Service Exposed; with Proposals for Their Remedy and Redress* (Boston: Cassady and March, 1839), 128.

25 Samuel Otter, "Race in *Typee* and *White-Jacket*," in *The Cambridge Companion to Herman Melville*, ed. Robert S. Levine (Cambridge: Cambridge University Press, 1998), 24.
26 McNally, *Evils and Abuses*, 129 (emphasis mine).
27 Ibid.
28 Frederick Douglass, *My Bondage and My Freedom*, vol. 2 of *The Frederick Douglass Papers*, ed. John W. Blassingame, John R. McKivigan, and Peter P. Hinks (New Haven: Yale University Press, 1999), 309.
29 Ibid., 310.
30 Ibid., 310–11.
31 Ibid., 310.
32 These next three chapters are titled "Some of the Evil Effects of Flogging," "Flogging Not Lawful," and "Flogging Not Necessary."
33 See James D. Hart, "Melville and Dana," *American Literature* 9, no. 1 (March 1937): 53.
34 Richard Henry Dana, *Two Years before the Mast: A Personal Narrative of Life at Sea* (New York: Penguin Classics, 1986), 152, 155, 156, 153.
35 See Peter Bellis, "Discipline and the Lash in Melville's *White-Jacket*," *A Journal of Melville Studies* 7, no. 2 (October 2005): 30. Bellis contends that Melville is less interested in racial analogies than in holding Americans to their republican ideals. I see the two issues as inseparable.
36 The infraction that leads to White-Jacket's arraignment hardly seems commensurate with mutiny, but, as Robert Levine explains, White-Jacket's rebellious reaction to his sentence fosters a feeling of kinship with the *Somers* sailors—and possible guilt over the urge to resist. See Robert Levine, *Conspiracy and Romance: Studies in Brockden Brown, Cooper, Hawthorne, and Melville* (New York: Cambridge University Press, 1989), 184–88.
37 Otter, "Race in *Typee* and *White-Jacket*," 32.
38 Melville, *Moby-Dick*, 21.
39 Ibid., 322–23.
40 Walker Cowen, *Melville's Marginalia*, 2 vols. (New York: Garland, 1987), 1:xx.
41. Melville, *Moby-Dick*, 355.

CHAPTER THREE

1 George Fitzhugh, *Cannibals All! or, Slaves without Masters* (1857) (Cambridge: Harvard University Press, 1960), 18, 205–6.

2. Ibid., 204, 205.
3. Ibid., 30.
4. In Romans 6:16-18, for example, Paul writes, "Do you not know that if you yield yourself to any one as obedient slaves, you are slaves of the one whom you obey, either of sin, which leads to death, or of obedience, which leads to righteousness? But thanks be to God, that you who were once slaves of sin have become obedient from the heart to the standard of teaching to which you were committed, and, having been set free from sin, have become slaves of righteousness."
5. Harriet Beecher Stowe, *Uncle Tom's Cabin, or Life among the Lowly* (New York: Penguin Books, 1986), 340–41.
6. Ibid., 623–24.
7. My point is not that empathy never can nor ever does help foster true social justice — clearly, it can — but that it may also *appear* to equalize social relations through a concept of shared submission and shared pain.
8. Stowe, *Uncle Tom's Cabin*, 624.
9. As Cindy Weinstein points out, Stowe should not be accused of advocating an approach to slavery that makes feeling alone the arbiter of right and wrong, an approach that would render sympathy relative. In fact, in Stowe's *Key to Uncle Tom's Cabin*, Weinstein writes, "Stowe savages . . . pro-slavery positions with ruthless irony, arguing that they can only be maintained at the expense of the facts, and getting the facts wrong is an expression of one's *lack* of sympathy" (emphasis mine). Cindy Weinstein, *Family, Kinship, and Sympathy in Nineteenth-Century American Literature* (New York: Cambridge University Press, 2004), 67. I agree with Weinstein that one cannot ignore the progressive force of Stowe's novel simply because proslavery writers used that position to justify their own ends. Nevertheless, I believe it is important to recognize the similarity of strategy in these otherwise antipathetic views of slavery.
10. Eric J. Sundquist, *To Wake the Nations: Race in the Making of American Literature* (Cambridge: Harvard University Press, 1993), 40–41.
11. Quoted in ibid., 41.
12. Or, as Fitzhugh puts it, without a "suicidal" sacrifice of self. Fitzhugh, *Cannibals All!*, 30.
13. Proverbs 3:12: "For the Lord reproves him whom he loves, as a father the son in whom he delights"; Hebrews 12:6: "For the Lord disciplines him whom he loves, and chastises every son whom he receives"; Revelation 3:18: "Those whom I love, I reprove and chasten."
14. Frederick Douglass, *My Bondage and My Freedom*, vol. 2 of *The Fred-*

erick Douglass Papers, ed. John W. Blassingame, John R. McKivigan, and Peter P Hinks (New Haven: Yale University Press, 1999), 141. All references hereafter will appear in parentheses following the quotation.

15 Richard Scheidenhelm, ed., *The Response to John Brown* (Belmont, Calif.: Wadsworth, 1972), 37.

16 Weinstein, *Family, Kinship, and Sympathy*, 68, 19–20.

17 In a plethora of mid-century sentimental novels that promote and celebrate adoption, Weinstein points out, "the family's vulnerabilities are the consequences of blood; its strengths are the result of choice." Ibid., 29.

18 Douglass here effectively rewrites abolition's best-known sentimental construction, made famous in *Uncle Tom's Cabin*, of the suffering slave as the paradigmatic object of sympathy. For Douglass, any form of sympathy that seeks to be personally or socially productive must work from the perspective of demonstrable like strengths rather than from shared weaknesses.

19 For provocative and insightful readings of Douglass's masculinist strategies and ethics, see especially Sundquist, *To Wake the Nations*; and Jenny Franchot, "The Punishment of Esther: Frederick Douglass and the Construction of the Feminine," in *Frederick Douglass: New Literary and Historical Essays* (New York: Cambridge University Press, 1990). Gabrielle Foreman also sees Douglass as advocating an American individualism with which readers would be familiar, but she importantly notes Douglass's self-conscious deployment of sentimental strategies—strategies made popular by Stowe with *Uncle Tom's Cabin*—to make the case for abolition to a white readership. See P. Gabrielle Foreman, "Sentimental Abolition in Douglass's Decade: Revision, Erotic Conversion, and the Politics of Witnessing in *The Heroic Slave* and *My Bondage and My Freedom*," in *Sentimental Men: Masculinity and the Politics of Affect in American Culture*, ed. Mary Chapman and Glenn Hendler (Berkeley: University of California Press, 1999). I agree with Foreman that Douglass "explore[s] emotive arenas in order to energize political protest" (150), but I believe that what all of these critics have missed is the extent to which, for Douglass, the ability to feel is explicitly linked to the ability to punish. In a slave society, violence and sentiment go hand in hand.

20 Robert S. Levine, "*Uncle Tom's Cabin* in *Frederick Douglass' Paper*: An Analysis of Reception," *American Literature* 64, no. 1 (March 1992): 71–93.

21 Saidiya V. Hartman, *Scenes of Subjection: Terror, Slavery, and Self-Making*

in Nineteenth-Century America (New York: Oxford University Press, 1997), 3.
22 Frederick Douglass, *Narrative of the Life of Frederick Douglass, An American Slave* (New York: Anchor Books, 1973), 5.
23 David Van Leer reads this important incident as an example of Douglass's difference from, rather than identification with, the African American community in general and women in particular. Although the horrified young Douglass claims that he "expected it would be my turn next," the "mature narrator," writes Van Leer, "knows the youth to be wrong. Not only does the boy's 'turn' never come . . . at least, not quite in this way . . . but the sexual undercurrents in the passage clearly indicate the narrator's implicit understanding of the different power dynamics in male and female beatings." David Van Leer, "Reading Slavery: The Anxiety of Ethnicity in Douglass's *Narrative*," in *Frederick Douglass: New Literary and Historical Essays*, 131.
24 Franchot, "Punishment of Esther," 141–42.
25 Hartman, *Scenes of Subjection*, 3.
26 Adam Smith, *The Theory of Moral Sentiments*, ed. D. D. Raphael and A. L. Macfie (Oxford: Oxford University Press, 1976), 22.
27 According to William Andrews, the revisions Douglass made to the Covey scene between the publication of the *Narrative* and *My Bondage* speaks to this recognition. The inclusion of more irony, humor, and self-deprecation in the latter reveals Douglass's aim to "divest" his persona, writes Andrews, "of singularity as a hero in order to endow him with more familiarity as a human being. . . . By 1855 Douglass understood that the black autobiographer who bound his reader to him through comic sympathetic identification as well as admiration had found the most balanced means of affirming himself a man and a brother with whites." William L. Andrews, *To Tell a Free Story: The First Century of Afro-American Autobiography, 1760–1865* (Urbana: University of Illinois Press, 1986), 287–88.
28 As David Marshall has argued, "Acting" is a key concept in Smith's theories of sympathy. See David Marshall, *The Surprising Effects of Sympathy: Marivaux, Diderot, Rousseau, and Mary Shelley* (Chicago: University of Chicago Press, 1988).
29 Smith writes that just "as nature teaches the spectators to assume the circumstances of the person principally concerned, so she teaches [the sufferer] in some measure to assume those of the spectators. As they are continually placing themselves in his situation . . . so he is as constantly

placing himself in theirs, and thence conceiving some degree of that coolness about his own fortune, with which he is sensible that they will view it." Sympathy, in other words, is a two-way street. *Theory of Moral Sentiments*, 22.

30 Sundquist, *To Wake the Nations*, 130–31.

31 Deborah E. McDowell puts this most forcefully when she observes that "black women's backs become the parchment on which Douglass narrates his linear progression from bondage to freedom." Douglass's "freedom," she contends, "depends on narrating black women's bondage." "In the First Place: Making Frederick Douglass and the Afro-American Narrative Tradition," in *Critical Essays on Frederick Douglass*, ed. William Andrews (Boston: G. K. Hall, 1991), 201, 203.

32 The dangers of overidentifying with white violence are mitigated as well by Douglass's use of words rather than whip as his primary weapon. In writing the autobiographies, Douglass attempts to help free his brothers and sisters still in chains. And by exposing through language the master's oppression, Douglass positions himself in direct contrast to those southern men who, like the overseer Mr. Gore, "dealt sparingly with his words, and bountifully with his whip, never using the former where the latter would answer as well." Douglass, *Narrative of the Life*, 24.

33 Frederick Douglass, "The Heroic Slave," in *Frederick Douglass: Selected Speeches and Writings*, ed. Philip S. Foner, abridged and adapted by Yuval Taylor (Chicago: Lawrence Hill Books, 1999), 220. All references to the story hereafter will appear in parentheses after the quotation.

34 Krista Walter, "Trappings of Nationalism in Frederick Douglass's *The Heroic Slave*," in *African American Review* 34, no. 2 (2000): 243.

35 As Krista Walter puts it, "Knowing full well that his audience would not identify the American Revolutionaries with murderers, Douglass creates a complex set of associations comprised of patriarchal, patriotic, and abolitionist sentiments. In essence, he suggests that his readers become more patriotic—truer sons (and perhaps daughters) to the *patris* and the *pater*, by joining the abolitionist cause." Ibid., 242.

36 Smith, *Theory of Moral Sentiments*, 9, 16, 18. Smith uses this phrase repeatedly to describe the experience of sympathy, or identification, on the part of witnesses.

37 According to William Andrews, Garrison's opposition to Douglass starting his own newspaper in 1850 led Douglass to believe that free blacks "could not escape the subtler forms of white paternalism" that sought to keep them in their place. *To Tell a Free Story*, 236–37. For a discussion

of Douglass's changing views in these years, see also John Stauffer, *The Black Hearts of Men: Radical Abolitionists and the Transformation of Race* (Cambridge: Harvard University Press, 2002); and Sundquist, *To Wake the Nations.*

38 Quoted in Stephen B. Oates, *To Purge This Land with Blood: A Biography of John Brown* (New York: Harper and Row, 1970), 63.
39 Stauffer, *Black Hearts*, 1.
40 John Brown, *A John Brown Reader*, ed. Louis Ruchames (London: Abelard-Schuman, 1959), 42.
41 Douglass, "Capt. John Brown Not Insane," in *Selected Speeches and Writings*, 374. As Kristen Proehl points out, Douglass was not alone in linking Brown to the heroes of the American Revolution. Numerous authors, theologians, and philanthropists portrayed the raid on Harper's Ferry as a "quintessential American moment." See "Transforming the 'Madman into a Saint': The Cultural Memory Site of John Brown's Raid on Harper's Ferry in Antislavery Literature and History," in *The Afterlife of John Brown*, ed. Andrew Taylor and Eldrid Herrington (New York: Palgrave Macmillan, 2005), 111.
42 Kimberly Rae Connor, "More Heat Than Light: The Legacy of John Brown in Russell Banks's *Cloudsplitter*," in Taylor and Herrington, *The Afterlife of John Brown*, 212. Franny Nudelman similarly observes that recent scholarship—most notably Eric Lott's analysis of black minstrelsy and white middle-class culture's attraction to it—helps us understand "Brown's investment in biracial identity as an attribute of whiteness." Franny Nudelman, *John Brown's Body: Slavery, Violence, and the Culture of War* (Chapel Hill: University of North Carolina Press, 2004), 181.
43 See Daniel C. Littlefield, "Blacks, John Brown, and a Theory of Manhood," in *His Soul Goes Marching On: Responses to John Brown and the Harpers Ferry Raid*, ed. Paul Finkelman (Charlottesville: University of Virginia Press, 1995), 68.
44 The slave insurrectionist Nat Turner, with whom Brown was compared at the time, exemplified this fear. For an analysis of the difference between black responses and white responses to Brown from the time of Harper's Ferry to the present, see Louis DeCaro, "Black People's Ally, White People's Bogeyman: A John Brown Story," in Taylor and Herrington, *The Afterlife of John Brown*. DeCaro notes that "John Brown has often been rejected by many white Americans because he does not conform to the accepted paradigm of national virtue: he was *too close* to blacks" (11). My intention in the coming pages is to show the particular way in which

Brown *does* in fact conform to a national paradigm, but one based on a model of white submission to the plight of those they wrong.

45 Henry David Thoreau, "A Plea for Captain John Brown," in *Echoes of Harper's Ferry*, ed. James Redpath (Boston: Thayer and Eldridge, 1860), 41.

46 From Emerson's lecture "Courage," given on November 8, 1859, in *The Complete Works of Ralph Waldo Emerson*, ed. Edward Waldo Emerson (Boston: Houghton Mifflin, 1904), 7:427.

47 Lydia Maria Child, *Letters of Lydia Maria Child* (Boston: Houghton Mifflin, 1882), 104. For an analysis of female responses to Brown's assault and execution, see Wendy Hamand Venet, "'Cry Aloud and Spare Not': Northern Antislavery Women and John Brown's Raid," in *His Soul Goes Marching On: Responses to John Brown and the Harpers Ferry Raid*, ed. Paul Finkelman (Charlottesville: University of Virginia Press, 1995).

48 George B. Cheever, "The Martyr's Death and the Martyr's Triumph," in *Echoes of Harper's Ferry*, ed. James Redpath (Boston: Thayer and Eldridge, 1860), 214.

49 Ibid., 215.

50 Child, *Letters*, 110.

51 Quoted in John Stauffer and Zoe Trodd, "Meteor of War: The John Brown Cycle," in Taylor and Herrington, *The Afterlife of John Brown*, 142. The admiration apparently was not reciprocated. According to Brown's friend Katherine Mayo, "[Brown] had no fondness for Fred Douglass. Once I heard him say to my husband, of some defeated plan, some great opportunity lost, '*That* we owe to the famous Mr. Frederick Douglass!' And he shut his mouth in a way he had when he thought no good" (Brown, *John Brown Reader*, 239). Douglass expressed severe skepticism about the raid on Harper's Ferry and refused to participate.

52 "Speech by Theodore Tilton," in *Echoes of Harper's Ferry*, ed. James Redpath (Boston: Thayer and Eldridge, 1860), 93.

53 Quoted in DeCaro, "Black People's Ally," 13.

54 It is evident that Brown *desired* to bring blacks into the cycle of violence, thus effecting their transformation, like Douglass's, from slaves into men. His plan for Harper's Ferry was to encourage slaves to rise up against their masters and to follow Brown into the Allegheny mountains, where together they would march south, liberating slaves as they went. No such uprising, however, took place. See Oates, *To Purge This Land with Blood*, 301–2.

55 As Oates notes, Brown was particularly drawn to the works of the older Jonathan Edwards, "whose mystical Calvinism, as expressed in such sermons as 'The Eternity of Hell Torments,' 'The Evil of the Wicked Contemplated by the Righteous,' and 'Sinners in the Hands of an Angry God,' had powerfully influenced Brown's own beliefs." Ibid., 22. God's propensity to chasten his wayward people through calamity was a favorite theme of Edwards's.

56 Theodore De Bruyn, "Flogging a Son: The Emergence of the *Pater Flagellans* in Latin Christian Discourse," *Journal of Early Christian Studies* 7, no. 2 (1999): 248–49, 251.

57 Oates, *To Purge This Land with Blood*, 23.

58 Quoted in Brown, *John Brown Reader*, 175.

59 Scheidenhelm, *Response to John Brown*, 37.

60 Douglass, who clearly valued Brown's recourse to violence, also applauds his particular ability to invert strength and weakness, noting that "with John Brown, as with every other man fit to die for a cause, the hour of his physical weakness was the hour of his moral strength—the hour of his defeat was the hour of his triumph—the moment of his capture was the crowning victory of his life" (*Selected Speeches and Writings*, 641).

61 Although Franny Nudelman reads Brown's courtroom speech as evincing "his own capacity to feel the pain of others and to act on their behalf," I am arguing that to act on the slave's behalf is not without its ideological implications. By embodying the plight of the slave, Brown becomes at the same time the embodiment of *white* suffering over the abuse of blacks. Racial difference is disconcertingly obscured and reaffirmed in a martyrdom that exemplifies a particularly "white," sentimental construction of power relations: the pain of the privileged who witness another's harm. *John Brown's Body*, 18.

62 De Bruyn, "Flogging a Son," 267.

63 Oates, *To Purge This Land with Blood*, 8.

64 Brown, *John Brown Reader*, 41, 57.

65 Oates, *To Purge This Land with Blood*, 12. About this story, Emerson remarks that, although Brown "loved rough play," he could not enjoy such play unless "his playmates should be equal; not one in fine clothes and the other in buckskin; not one his own master, hale and hearty, and the other watched and whipped." "John Brown," in *Emerson's Antislavery Writings*, ed. Len Gougeon and Joel Myerson (New Haven: Yale University Press, 1995), 121.

66 This reading, of course, stands in direct contrast to Stowe's analysis of the evils of slavery in *Uncle Tom's Cabin*, where the salvation of slaves is put at risk from the deprivation of a mother's sympathetic love.

67 Thomas Wentworth Higginson, *Army Life in a Black Regiment and Other Writings* (New York: Penguin Books, 1997), 235, 236. Brown's son Salmon observed to Higginson during this visit, "I sometimes think that is what we came into the world for—to make sacrifices" (245).

68 Robert McGlone, "Rescripting a Troubled Past: John Brown's Family and the Harpers Ferry Conspiracy," *Journal of American History* 75, no. 4 (March 1989): 1195–96. McGlone views the story of the sacred oath as a myth developed in retrospect by the family as a psychological defense, that is, as a way of dealing with the family's own guilt about Brown's violent methods.

69 Higginson, *Army Life*, 234.

70 Brown, *John Brown Reader*, 156–57.

71 Rev. Fales Henry Newhall, "The Conflict in America: A Funeral Discourse Occasioned by the Death of John Brown of Osawatomie, Who Entered into Rest from the Gallows, at Charlestown, Virginia, December 2, 1859," in *Echoes of Harper's Ferry*, ed. James Redpath (Boston: Thayer and Eldridge, 1860), 203.

72 Quoted in Nudelman, *John Brown's Body*, 23.

73 Brown, *John Brown Reader*, 159.

74 Douglass, *My Bondage*, 259.

CHAPTER FOUR

1 Herman Melville, *Battle-Pieces and Aspects of the War* (New York: Harper, 1866), 22. All citations will hereafter appear in parentheses after the quotation.

2 Whitman's opening poem in the "Drum-Taps" section of *Leaves of Grass*, "First O Songs for a Prelude," celebrates the men of Manhattan who head off for "manly life in the camp." Manhattan itself, personified as a woman, is said to be pleased with the advent of war. Having been "pensive" or disapproving during times of "peace and wealth," the city now "smiles with joy exulting" at the sight of her children heading into battle. Walt Whitman, *Leaves of Grass*, ed. Michael Moon (New York: W. W. Norton, 2002), 235, 236.

3 The name "Moloch" is a Hebrew translation of "Ba'al," a god widely worshipped in the ancient Near East. Moloch appears in medieval texts as a

demon, one who gets particular pleasure from causing the suffering of mothers by either stealing their children or demanding that they be sacrificed to him.

4 As Timothy Sweet argues, "The March into Virginia" is but one among many poems in Melville's collection of poems that critically engages "the tendencies of contemporary representations of the Civil War to aestheticize the effects of violence and to evade questions about the historical contingency of politics." *Traces of War: Poetry, Photography, and the Crisis of the Union* (Baltimore: Johns Hopkins University Press, 1990), 165.

5 Tellingly, Melville never uses the term "soldier" in the poem, emphasizing the innocence of the boys as nonprofessionals, as nonmilitary personnel.

6 As we saw, by placing the whip in John Jr.'s hand, Brown compels his son to feel another's pain as if it were his own. The lesson frames how Brown viewed his own use of violence (and his execution for it) in the cause of abolition many years later — not as murder but as sacrifice, as blood shed in identification with tortured slaves.

7 The first battle of Manassas occurred in July 1861 and ended with roughly 5,000 casualties. So naive were not only the soldiers but also the majority of American citizens about the battle that many civilians rode out from nearby Washington to watch the conflict. The battle ended in a panicked retreat of Union forces (thus Melville's reference to the boys' "shame"), effectively putting an end to the romantic notion that the war would be decisively, and gloriously, brief. The second, and larger, battle of Manassas (over 25,000 casualties) was fought in August 1862.

8 John Crowley includes *Little Women* in the boy-book genre. See John W. Crowley, "*Little Women* and the Boy-Book," *New England Quarterly* 58, no. 3 (September 1985): 384–99.

9 Judith Fetterley, "*Little Women*: Alcott's Civil War," *Feminist Studies* 5, no. 2 (Summer 1979): 369–83. Fetterley is one of but a handful of scholars who have read *Little Women* in the context of the Civil War. Others include John Limon, *Writing after War: American War Fiction from Realism to Postmodernism* (New York: Oxford University Press, 1994), 183–88; Margaret Higonnet, "Civil Wars and Sexual Territories," in *Arms and the Woman: War, Gender, and Literary Representation*, ed. Helen M. Cooper, Adrienne Auslander Munich, and Susan Merrill Squier (Chapel Hill: University of North Carolina Press, 1989); and Elizabeth Young, "A Wound of One's Own: Louisa May Alcott's Civil War Fiction," *American Quarterly* 48, no. 3 (September 1996): 439–74.

10 Fetterley, "*Little Women*: Alcott's Civil War," 379.

11 Sigmund Freud, "'A Child Is Being Beaten': A Contribution to the Study of the Origin of Sexual Perversions" (1919), in *The Standard Edition of the Complete Psychological Works of Sigmund Freud*, trans. and ed. James Strachey, 24 vols. (London: Hogarth Press, 1953-74), 17:194, 198.

12 Quoted in Martha Saxton, *Louisa May Alcott: A Modern Biography* (New York: Noonday Press, 1995), 165.

13 Ibid., 48. See also John Matteson, *Eden's Outcasts: The Story of Louisa May Alcott and Her Father* (New York: W. W. Norton, 2007), 137, 159.

14 Richard Brodhead, *Cultures of Letters: Scenes of Reading and Writing in Nineteenth-Century America* (Chicago: University of Chicago Press, 1993), 73.

15 Quoted in Matteson, *Eden's Outcasts*, 64.

16 Quoted in Saxton, *Louisa May Alcott*, 89-90.

17 As Matteson writes, "When [Louisa's] good intentions failed her and she lost her temper, her disappointment made her cry herself to sleep. She would then make noble resolutions once again and, for a while, feel 'better in [her] heart.' If only she kept all the moral promises she made, she observed, 'I should be the best girl in the world. But I don't, and so am very bad.' . . . Nearly forty years later, as she read over her Fruitlands diary, she added the notation, 'Poor little sinner! *She says the same at fifty.*'" *Eden's Outcasts*, 137-38. For an insightful treatment of the relationship between Bronson and Louisa and its impact on Alcott's children's novels, see Karen Halttunen, "The Domestic Drama of Louisa May Alcott," *Feminist Studies* 10, no. 2 (Summer 1984): 233-54.

18 Quoted in Saxton, *Louisa May Alcott*, 146.

19 Brodhead, *Cultures of Letters*, 20, 22. Brodhead's contention is supported by Bronson's own pronouncement on the relation between child and teacher: "What the children . . . see the teacher to love and respect, to feel an interest in, they will, in time, come to love and respect, and be interested in themselves." Bronson Alcott, *Observations on the Principles and Methods of Infant Instruction* (Boston: Carter and Hendee, 1830), 21.

20 Quoted in Brodhead, *Cultures of Letters*, 22. The full title of Cobb's book is *The Evil Tendencies of Corporal Punishment as a Means of Moral Discipline in Families and Schools Examined and Discussed*.

21 Bronson Alcott ran his Temple School from 1834 to 1838. As Peabody notes, when Alcott first began to teach, "he thought no punishment was desirable, and spent an immense deal of time in reasoning." However, shortly thereafter, he became convinced that "the passions of the soul . . . only were diverted, not conquered, by being reasoned with" and "that the

Ministry of Pain was God's great means of developing strength and elevation of character." He thus instituted, with the consent of his students, a system of discipline based in part on corporal punishment. Elizabeth Palmer Peabody, *Record of a School* (New York: Arno Press/New York Times, 1969 [1835]), 22–23.

22 Alcott's short-lived practice of substituting his own hand for the offending student's had a long life in the cultural imagination. As Dorothy McCuskey reports, "Forty years later two ministers publicly debated as to whether or not this was an instance of vicarious atonement." *Bronson Alcott, Teacher* (New York: Macmillan, 1940), 85.

23 Peabody, *Record of a School*, 24, 25.

24 In a letter to his friend William T. Harris in 1871, Bronson Alcott announced that "the *Plumfield School* described in '*Little Men*' has prompted Roberts Brothers to reprint '*the Record of a School*,' as an answer to readers who question whether such a school as Louisa has drawn were possible." *The Letters of A. Bronson Alcott*, ed. Richard L. Herrnstadt (Ames: Iowa State University Press, 1969), 535. Due to differences with Peabody over prefatory material, *Record of a School* was not reprinted until 1874 (under the new title, *Record of Mr. Alcott's School, Exemplifying the Principles and Methods of Moral Culture*), three years after Alcott's *Little Men*. This third edition includes a preface by Peabody in which she quotes Louisa crediting her father with *Little Men*'s success: "The methods of education so successfully tried in the Temple long ago are so kindly welcomed now . . . that I cannot consent to receive the thanks and commendations due to another. . . . Not only is it a duty and a pleasure, but there is a certain fitness in making the childish fiction of the daughter play the grateful part of herald to the wise and beautiful truths of the father, — truths which, for thirty years, have been silently, helpfully living in the hearts and memories of the pupils who never have forgotten the influences of that time and teacher." Peabody, *Record of Mr. Alcott's School* (Boston: Roberts Brothers, 1874), 3–4.

25 Louisa May Alcott, *Little Men* (New York: Signet Classic, 1986), 57. All references hereafter will appear in parentheses after the quotation. A ferule is a small cane or stick, usually made of birch.

26 See G. M. Goshgarian, *To Kiss the Chastening Rod: Domestic Fiction and Sexual Ideology in the American Renaissance* (Ithaca: Cornell University Press, 1992).

27 Peabody, *Record of a School*, 25.

28 *Overland Monthly* (September 1871): 346.

29. Johan Huizinga, *Homo Ludens: A Study of the Play Element in Culture* (Boston: Beacon Press, 1950), 8. Gillian Brown also notes that the "sense of actions devoid of any consequences other than pleasure becomes the hallmark of child's play for [nineteenth-century] American culture, the mark of childhood's special status." "Child's Play," *differences: A Journal of Feminist Cultural Studies* 11, no. 3 (1999/2000): 89.
30. As Karen Sánchez-Eppler notes, although toys and games may temporarily liberate the child, "play is never fully a 'stepping out of "real" life,'" as Huizinga claims, because the "nature and possibilities of play are always socially constructed and constrained, bounded by the . . . social conditions of these children's lives." Karen Sánchez-Eppler, *Dependent States: The Child's Part in Nineteenth-Century American Culture* (Chicago: University of Chicago Press, 2005), 180.
31. Kenneth B. Kidd, *Making American Boys: Boyology and the Feral Tale* (Minneapolis: University of Minnesota Press, 2004), 56–57. For the long-range cultural significance of "playing Indian" in the United States, see Phillip J. Deloria, *Playing Indian* (New Haven: Yale University Press, 1998).
32. Freud, "A Child Is Being Beaten," 194.
33. From this sublimation, Freud writes, "[whipping] derives the libidinal excitation which is from this time forward attached to it, and which finds its outlet in masturbatory acts. Here for the first time we have the essence of masochism" (ibid., 189).
34. The metaphor of the lamb is itself telling: in contrast to the mature male ram of Jewish lore, Christianity substitutes a symbol of youth and innocence — a biblical synonym for child.
35. Part of the humor in Mrs. Jo's recitation about "the children of Boston" lies in what appears to be the superficial nature of the injury: that is, toys are expendable because replaceable. And, in fact, after burning her best-loved "paper dollies" in the fire, we are told, "Daisy was soon consoled by another batch of dolls from Aunt Amy" (*Little Men*, 118). However, there appears to be some subtle suggestion that at Plumfield, where boys and girls repeatedly come and go (through maturation, failure to learn, or death), children, like dolls, are themselves replaceable.
36. Fetterley, "*Little Women*: Alcott's Civil War," 370. As one example of the metaphorical connection between external and internal battles, Fetterley quotes Jo's own words in *Little Women*: "'I'll try and be what [father] loves to call me, "a little woman," and not be rough and wild; but do my duty here instead of wanting to be somewhere else,' said Jo, thinking that

keeping her temper at home was a much harder task than facing a rebel or two down south." Louisa May Alcott, *Little Women* (New York: Penguin Classics, 1989), 9. All citations hereafter will appear in parentheses after the quotation.

37 Kidd, *Making American Boys*, 16. I will discuss the significance of the boy-savage association in more detail in my discussion of *Jo's Boys*.

38 Alcott's biographer, Martha Saxton, for example, refers to Dan as "[the author's] favorite character and alter ego" and a "sympathetic, youthful stand-in for Jo" (*Louisa May Alcott*, 371).

39 Louisa May Alcott, *Jo's Boys* (New York: Bantam Books, 1995), 186. All citations hereafter will appear in parentheses after the quotation.

40 Alcott may be referring to the Blackfoot, who resided in Montana.

41 In *Little Women*, Jo herself is compared to a colt (4, 26), again reinforcing the sympathetic connection between Jo and Dan.

42 Caroline Levander, *Cradle of Liberty: Race, the Child, and National Belonging from Thomas Jefferson to W. E. B. Du Bois* (Durham: Duke University Press, 2006), 92, 84. Recapitulation theory made its way into American discourse only shortly before the publication of *Little Men*. The term was coined by Ernst Haeckel in 1866. Still, as Kidd has argued, its theoretical roots can be traced back to such foundational texts as Emerson's "Self-Reliance" (1841), which, in its "proto-evolutionary, even proto-psychoanalytic, scheme of masculine selfhood," celebrates the "aboriginal Self" inhering in boyhood. Mid-century authors like Emerson and James Fenimore Cooper idealize primitive, nonsocialized impulses, even as they suggest the white boy's ability—eventually and with help—to master those impulses. The boy-savage "yields to the 'aboriginal Self,'" Kidd writes, "which in maturing loses its barbarity but, with the [proper] intervention, preserves its strength" (*Making American Boys*, 15).

43 Quoted in Levander, *Cradle of Liberty*, 86.

44 Ibid., 92–93, 96. Although Levander does not mention the fact, I find it interesting that Plumfield's ostensibly domesticating parents—Jo and Fritz Bhaer—are also named after an animal.

45 See Lora Romero, *Home Fronts: Domesticity and Its Critics in the Antebellum United States* (Durham: Duke University Press, 1997). Romero argues that James Fenimore Cooper's tales of "vanishing" Americans nostalgically position "the racial other" as "an earlier and now irretrievably lost version of the self.... It is as though for [Cooper] aboriginals represent a phase that the human race goes through but must inevitably get over" (41).

46 Other references to Dan's color include his "rough, brown face" (*Little Men*, 171), his "square, and brown, and strong" face (*Little Men*, 156), and his "brown hand" (*Little Men*, 243). Brown skin represents another commonality between Dan and Jo (and Alcott herself). Jo is said to be dark-skinned; her sisters are fair.
47 Kidd, *Making American Boys*, 56.
48 Quoting Howells's *A Boy's Town*, Kidd notes the middle-class view that "the difference between a savage and a civilized man is work" (Kidd, *Making American Boys*, 57), thus emphasizing again the importance of "usefulness" to white writers.
49 We might note Alcott's shift from recapitulation theory to eugenics here; some children's very blood, she implies, renders them incapable of progressing to the next stage of human development.
50 And not only admiration but attraction. When Dan asks early on, in *Jo's Boys*, "Who would marry a jack-o'-lantern like me?" Jo replies, "My dear boy, when I was a girl I liked just such adventurous fellows as you are. Anything fresh and daring, free and romantic, is always attractive to us womenfolk" (55–56). Though Jo at first puts her romantic interest in the past tense of girlhood, it has shifted to the present tense of womanhood by the end. Moreover, when Jo discovers that Dan keeps a picture of a girl he likes (who turns out to be Bess), Jo at first "fancied it might be one of herself" (308). After telling Dan he can never marry Bess, Jo tries to console him with the assurance that she will always be available to him: "And remember, dear, if the sweet girl is denied you, the old friend is always here to love and trust and pray for you" (311).
51 Crowley, "*Little Women*," 387.
52 Kidd, *Making American Boys*, 53.
53 Alcott may be referring to the Blackfoot, who were living on a reservation in Montana by the late 1800s and, with the buffalo all but extinct (due to white settlement and the incursion of the railroad), were relying on a government agency for food. Many died of smallpox during the mid-1800s.
54 "I shall not be surprised if [Dan] surpasses all the rest in the real success of his life," Mrs. Jo remarks at the end of *Jo's Boys* about her "black sheep" (322). Unfortunately, she utters these words just sentences before Alcott records the circumstances of Dan's death, leaving it unclear whether or not Dan has achieved "real success."
55 That play includes not only cowboys and Indians but also Civil War re-enactments. Chapter 13 of Thomas Bailey Aldrich's paradigmatic *The Story of a Bad Boy* (1869), for example, showcases the days-long, great

winter snow fight on Slatter's Hill between the North End and the South End boys of Rivermouth, an event that Aldrich claims "passed into a legend" (149). Aldrich endows his boy "soldiers" with the heroism of a bygone era. It is as if, for the boy-book writer, the spirit of boyhood itself lies dead on the southern plains and in the green wilderness. It can only be resurrected in the imagination. What these boy-books (and some girl-books, like *Little Women*) suggest is that it is not only Darwinian theory that shapes the contours of a burgeoning nineteenth-century children's literature but also war, particularly America's domestic Civil War.

56 Alcott struggled mentally and physically throughout the writing of *Jo's Boys*, "running along the edge of a breakdown all the time," according to Saxton. Her death from mercury poisoning (a "cure" she received while a hospital nurse during the Civil War) occurs less than two years after the completion of this, her last novel. See Saxton, *Louisa May Alcott*, 369–74.

AFTERWORD

1 As Carroll Smith-Rosenberg has recently noted, few nation-states "have been more successful in imbuing generation after generation of immigrants with a deep sense of national belonging" than the United States. "And few are as renowned for their proclivity for violence." See *This Violent Empire: The Birth of an American National Identity* (Chapel Hill: University of North Carolina Press, 2010), 1–2.

2 Michael Warner, "What Like a Bullet Can Undeceive?," *Public Culture* 15 (2003): 41. All citations hereafter will appear in parentheses following the quotation.

3 Herman Melville, *Battle-Pieces and Aspects of the War* (New York: Harper, 1866) (Gale Archival Editions), 63.

4 John Michael, *Identity and the Failure of America: From Thomas Jefferson to the War on Terror* (Minneapolis: University of Minnesota Press, 2008), 19, 20.

5 George W. Bush, presidential stump speech, 2004.

6 Kathleen Woodward, "Calculating Compassion," in *Compassion: The Culture and Politics of an Emotion*, ed. Lauren Berlant (New York: Routledge, 2004), 59; Mickey Kaus, "Compassion, the Political Liability," *New York Times*, June 25, 1999, A23. Kaus goes on to say that at the core of Bush's speeches about America's "noble calling" is the philosophy of "noblesse oblige," a philosophy that reifies social inequality by suggesting that some are inherently "strong" while others are inherently "weak."

7 Berlant, "Compassion (and Withholding)," in *Compassion: The Culture and Politics of an Emotion*, ed. Lauren Berlant (New York: Routledge, 2004), 4.

8 Ibid. Sara Ahmed makes a different but related point about compassion, interpreting a fund-raising letter from the Christian Aid Society to its contributors (contributors who, the letter states, "probably ... feel angry or saddened" by the plight of others) as an example of emotional appropriation: "The letter is not about the other, but about the reader," claims Ahmed. It evinces a rhetorical maneuver whereby "the pain of others becomes ours, an appropriation that transforms and perhaps even neutralises their pain into our sadness.... The apparently shared negative feelings do not position the reader and victim in a relation of equivalence." *The Cultural Politics of Emotion* (New York: Routledge, 2004), 22–23. Ahmed thus shares Berlant's sense of *distance* between sufferer and nonsufferer promoted in contemporary calls for compassion.

9 The etymological roots of compassion are in the French *com* plus *pati*, meaning "to suffer with another" or "to suffer together."

10 As Berlant notes, Clinton's "I feel your pain" was labeled "feminine" by numerous media critics. "Compassion (and Withholding)," 18–19.

11 Bush's platform of "compassionate conservatism" likewise seeks to curtail what we might think of as the liberal spending of emotion: that is, the phrase implies that there must be reasonable limits applied to one's outpouring of feeling. Ironically (or ingeniously), the slogan works the opposite way as well, bringing together, albeit uneasily, the promise of limited government spending (for welfare, Medicaid, and so on) with the promise of *emotional* expenditures that will make up the lack.

12 The photo first appeared on the television news magazine *60 Minutes II*, on April 27, 2004. It made the cover of the *Economist*, on May 8, 2004, and was widely circulated thereafter. According to the *60 Minutes II* report, the man was told that if he fell off the box, he would be electrocuted.

13 ⟨http://story.news.yahoo.com/news?tmpl=story2&u=/ap/20040512/1p_on_re_eu/vatican_prisoner_abuse⟩ (from a news story on yahoo.com whose link is no longer available).

14 Herman Melville, *Billy Budd, Sailor*, ed. Harrison Hayford and Merton M. Sealts Jr. (Chicago: University of Chicago Press, 1962), 115.

15 Ibid.

16 Ibid., 123.

INDEX

Abolition, 13, 68–69
Abraham and Isaac, 16, 22, 28, 30–31, 35–36, 38–39, 41, 45, 137, 143, 173
Abu Ghraib, 172
Abusers. *See* Perpetrators (of violence)
Aggression: and Christianity, 2, 158; and authenticity, 2, 168; and masculinity, 3, 8, 9, 14, 45, 94, 108, 141; and sentiment, 9; and affection, 44; as liberating, 92; displacement by fathers onto sons, 124, 125, 134; internalizing of, 146, 147–48, 157. *See also* Boyish aggression; Empathy: and aggression; Violence
Ahab, 53, 80
Alcott, Bronson, 129–30, 133, 135, 136, 198 (n. 19), 199 (n. 22); and Temple School, 132, 198–99 (n. 21), 199 (n. 24)
Alcott, Louisa May, 7, 13, 21–22, 125–36, 164–65; as child, 129–30, 198 (n. 17), 199 (n. 24). See also *Jo's Boys*; *Little Men*; *Little Women*
Aldrich, Thomas Bailey: *The Story of a Bad Boy*, 156, 202–3 (n. 55)
America: as empathetic nation, 3, 8, 15, 170; and "exceptionalism," 14–15, 173; as abused son, 41; as "redeemer" nation, 168; as martyr, 171

Andrews, William, 191 (n. 27)
Atonement, 113, 114, 118, 145
Authenticity: as being Christlike, 1; and suffering, 1–2; and whiteness, 18; and violence, 168
Axelrod, Alan, 38, 39

"Bartleby, the Scrivener" (Melville), 16–17, 54, 55, 56–67, 70, 79
Barton, Mark, 25–28, 32
Beadle, William. See *Narrative of the Life of William Beadle, A*
Bederman, Gail, 9
Benevolence, 61–62, 83
Benito Cereno (Melville), 87
Berlant, Lauren, 13–14, 170
Billy Budd (Melville), 173–74
Boy-books, 21, 125, 152, 156, 162, 163, 203 (n. 55)
Boyhood: loss of, 124, 152, 155, 162; and freedom, 149
Boyish aggression, 141, 153, 163; and pleasure, 8, 126, 134, 136, 138, 140, 147, 151, 162; internalized, 128, 129, 133, 134; mirroring parent's aggression, 143; consequences of, 158
Boys: as sadistic, 21, 127; feminized, 22, 127, 134, 145; and war, 123–25, 163; and maturation, 125, 127; cultural ambivalence toward, 125–26; identified with fathers,

(205)

127, 128, 133–35, 144; and "playing Indian," 142, 152, 156; as "temporary" savages (primitive), 148, 152, 155, 161, 162, 201 (n. 42); and Native Americans, 152; as animals, 154–55. *See also* Sons

Brockden Brown, Charles, 7, 16, 28, 36–50. See also *Wieland, or The Transformation*

Brodhead, Richard, 9, 129, 130–31, 135

Brown, John, 12, 17–19, 21, 22, 89, 106–21, 124–25, 128, 132, 133, 194 (nn. 51, 54); as martyr, 19, 90, 109, 112, 115, 121, 195 (n. 61); as national "whipping boy," 19, 90, 114, 115; as "black," 107–8, 121; Calvinist beliefs of, 112–13, 195 (n. 55)

Brown, John, Jr., 12, 113–14, 118, 132

Bush, George W., 14, 169–72

Butler, Judith, 11, 178 (n. 20)

Cannibals All! (Fitzhugh), 83, 84

Chandler, Elizabeth, 68

Charity, 61–63; and prosperity, 62, 63

Cheever, George B., 62, 109

Child, Lydia Maria, 109, 110

"Child Is Being Beaten, A" (Freud), 20, 128

Christ, 5, 10, 22, 48, 53, 61, 67, 84, 86, 138, 143, 144, 172; as empathetic, 10; martyrdom of as paradigm in American literature, 10, 22, 48–49, 140; as whipping boy, 10, 79; identified with biblical Isaac, 30–31

Christianity, 31, 50, 84–85, 96; and capitalism, 58, 60; and patriarchalism, 89; and race, 108; and empathy, 140, 169. *See also* Violence: and Christianity

Christian love (charity), 3, 58, 60, 65, 106, 109; achieved through violence, 120

Civil War (American), 13, 15, 21, 123–26, 146, 162, 167, 173

Clinton, Bill, 171

Cohen, Daniel A., 28

Compassion, 153, 169, 170–71; "compassionate conservatism," 170; "armies of," 170, 171, 172; brought about through violence, 171–72

Connor, Kimberly Rae, 108

Cowen, Walker, 80

Crowley, John, 162

Dana, Richard Henry, 73. See also *Two Years before the Mast*

De Bruyn, Theodore, 112

De Caro, Louis, 193 (n. 44)

Deism, 33–34

Delusion, religious, 38–40, 44, 48

DeVries, Hent, 176 (n. 12)

Disavowal, 11; of power, 8, 14, 38, 41, 115, 171–72; of violence, 12, 168

Dolls: abuse of, 137–40, 141–42, 145; analogous to children, 139–44

Douglass, Frederick, 12, 17–18, 69–70, 89, 90, 91–107, 120, 192 (n. 32); and John Brown, 106–7, 194 (n. 51), 195 (n. 60). *See also* "Heroic Slave, The"; *My Bondage and My Freedom*; *Narrative of the Life of Frederick Douglass*

Edwards, Jonathan, 113

Ellison, Julie, 179 (n. 26), 186 (n. 13)

Emerson, Ralph Waldo, 109, 195 (n. 65)
Empathetic identification, 29, 60, 64, 128
Empathy, 10, 11, 15, 16, 52, 55; as democratizing, 1, 12, 72; created through violence, 2; and aggression, 3, 22, 90, 106, 156; as source of pain, 12, 17, 50, 54, 80, 72; as volitional, 14, 88; and coercion, 17, 68, 73; self-love as basis for, 63; and race, 68; and mastery, 88–89, 90; and presidential politics, 170. *See also* Violence: and empathy
Evil Tendencies of Corporal Punishment, The (Cobb), 131
Ewing, Charles Patrick, 26

Faithful Steward, The (Clark), 62–63
Familicide, 11, 26–36 passim, 45, 49
Fathers: identified with sons, 5–11, 16, 21, 22, 26–28, 40, 46, 113–14, 124, 135, 162, 173; as guilty, 6, 16; identified with God, 45–46; as possessive, 45–46; and whipping, 112–14, 116–17, 132. *See also* Perpetrators (of violence); Suffering: and fathers
"Fellow-feeling." *See* Sympathy (fellow-feeling)
Fessenden, Tracy, 178 (n. 17)
Fetterley, Judith, 126–27, 146–47
Fisher, Philip, 2, 3, 179 (n. 30)
Fitzgerald, Neil King, 182 (n. 8)
Fitzhugh, George, 83–88, 89, 100, 115. *See also Cannibals All!*
Fliegelman, Jay, 41

Flogging, naval, 12, 13, 15, 17, 67, 71–75, 77, 78, 131; analogy to slavery, 69; and sensibility, 71. *See also* Whipping
Foreman, Gabrielle, 190 (n. 19)
Foucault, Michel, 9
Founding Fathers, 41, 101, 105
Franchot, Jenny, 93
Franklin, H. Bruce, 66–67
Freedom: as achieved through self-sacrifice, 84–86, 87; and empathy, 86, 87, 97; and violence, 100, 102; and family, 101
Freud, Sigmund, 11, 20–22, 128, 143, 151, 180 (n. 43), 200 (n. 33). *See also* "Child Is Being Beaten, A"
Fuss, Diana, 6, 43

Garrison, William Lloyd, 106, 192 (n. 37)
Girard, René, 6, 30
God, 10, 22, 27, 43, 49, 55, 67, 72, 73, 79, 140, 168; as requiring sacrifice of loved ones, 28–31, 38–39, 45, 137–38, 143; and Abraham, 31, 38; as insensible, 34; wrath of, 35, 44–45; as vengeful, 36; as indistinguishable from Satan, 36–38, 47; as "slave-driver," 77–78; as melancholic, 80; as punishing, 116–17, 119
Golden Rule, 61, 84, 109, 170
Goshgarian, G. M., 135

Halttunen, Karen, 32
Harper's Ferry, 18, 90, 107, 108, 109, 194 (n. 54)
Hartman, Saidiya, 93, 94
Hawthorne, Nathaniel, 3–8, 10,

13, 16. *See also* "Roger Malvin's Burial"
Hegel, G. W. F., 87
"Heroic Slave, The" (Douglass), 91, 103–6
Higginson, T. W., 117, 118
Holy Trinity, 10, 22
Howard, Leon, 52
Howells, William Dean: *A Boy's Town*, 156
Huizinga, Johan, 140
Hume, David, 10
Hutcheson, Francis, 10

Identification: in psychoanalysis, 6; and whipping boy, 9; and disavowal, 11; and dis-identification, 11, 18, 101; and race, 13, 17, 68–77, 92, 102, 120; and choice, 17–18, 19, 70–72, 89, 91, 94; and family, 41, 92, 130; as killing the other, 43–44, 145; and objectifying the other, 45–46, 90; and slavery, 52, 56, 67–68, 73, 77, 81, 86; emotional cost of, 55, 57, 58, 64–67, 92, 93, 146, 149; as alienating, 55, 57, 64, 67; and justice, 72, 169; and enslavement, 81, 88, 102; and "propriety," 98–99; and mastery, 105. *See also* Violence: and identification
Incest, 41, 43, 185 (n. 47)
Indian Removal, 15, 152
Indians, American, 152, 155, 156, 163; representations of, 138, 141, 144, 157, 161; Montana Indians, 152, 155, 157, 163, 202 (n. 53); "vanishing," 155, 162–63; as boys, 163
Iraq war, 169

Jo's Boys (Alcott), 7, 21, 126, 128, 133, 152, 155–165

Kaplan, Amy, 15
Kaus, Mickey, 170
Kidd, Kenneth, 141, 148, 162
Kierkegaard, Søren, 30

Levander, Caroline, 154–55
Levine, Robert S., 92, 100, 188 (n. 36)
Littlefield, Daniel C., 108
Little Men (Alcott), 7, 21–22, 126, 128, 133–45, 149, 150, 151–55, 156, 164
Little Women (Alcott), 7, 20–22, 126–28, 141, 142, 145–51, 152, 158
Love: as basis for violence, 10–11, 26; produced by violence, 11; as basis for punishment, 20; as basis for sacrifice, 31. *See also* Violence: and love

Manhood: white men as uniquely empathetic, 68, 86, 88, 121; and privilege to harm, 75, 88–89; black manhood compromised by familial attachment, 89, 94–95, 104, 105; and force, 92–93, 103, 115; achieved by inflicting pain, 96–98, 114, 125, 132–35; dual roles of, 119. *See also* Boyish aggression; Boys; Violence: and black manhood; Violence: and white manhood
"Man of Sorrows," 10, 16, 48, 51, 53, 67
"March into Virginia, The" (Melville), 123–25, 163

Marcuse, Herbert, 22
Marx, Karl: theory of alienated labor, 60
Masochism, 11, 20–22, 140, 145, 147; and Christianity, 22, 128; rooted in sexual love for father, 143; and children as expendable, 200 (n. 35)
Maturity: attained by identifying with one's victims, 128, 143, 144–45, 149, 163–64; attained by internalizing aggression, 148, 161–62
McDowell, Deborah E., 192 (n. 31)
McGlone, Robert, 117
McNally, William, 68–69, 70
Melancholy, 32, 40, 50, 51, 56, 57, 63, 66, 73, 80; "fraternal," 11, 16, 55, 56, 58, 67
Melville, Elizabeth, 52, 54
Melville, Herman, 11–12, 16–18, 20, 51–56, 60, 72, 73, 79–81, 87, 89, 123–27, 135, 163, 167–69, 173–74; and Hawthorne, 16, 54–55; and domestic violence, 52–54, 80, 185 (n. 3). *See also* "Bartleby, the Scrivener"; *Benito Cereno*; *Billy Budd*; "March into Virginia, The"; *Moby-Dick*; *Pierre*; "Shiloh"; *White-Jacket*
Michael, John, 169
Mikkelsen, Ann, 177 (n. 16)
Mizruchi, Susan, 30
Moby-Dick (Melville), 51, 52, 55, 78–79, 80
Mumford, Lewis, 53, 54
Murray, Henry A., 53
My Bondage and My Freedom (Douglass), 17, 70, 89, 91–103, 104

Narrative of the Life of Frederick Douglass (Douglass), 12, 93, 106
Narrative of the Life of William Beadle, A (Mitchell), 32, 183 (n. 22), 184 (n. 30)
Newfield, Christopher, 179 (n. 26)
Newhall, Fales Henry, 119
Noble, Marianne, 179 (n. 25), 181 (n. 46)
Nudelman, Franny, 13–14, 193 (n. 42), 195 (n. 61)

Oates, Stephen B., 112, 116
Oedipal attachment, 20, 22, 128, 143
Otter, Samuel, 69, 76–77

Pain. *See* Suffering
Parker, Hershel, 53
Pater flagellans, 11, 12, 112, 132
Peabody, Elizabeth Palmer, 132, 136
Pease, Donald, 15
Perpetrators (of violence), 2, 11, 14; identifying with their victims, 4–6, 7–9, 42, 47, 50, 54, 80, 109, 110, 114, 120, 125, 128, 133–34, 140, 172–74; as sufferers, 7, 16, 23, 34, 42, 47, 49, 54, 110, 136, 174; as whipping boys, 8–9, 91
Phillips, Wendell, 120
Pierre (Melville), 53
Pity, 17, 18, 56–57, 63, 72
Play, child's, 200 (nn. 29, 30); as site for displacement of aggression, 142; and desire to dispose of family, 145
Power: inversions of, 84, 86, 87, 90, 114
Proehl, Kristen, 193 (n. 41)
Projection, 6, 11, 64, 66, 124

Punishment, corporal, 15, 130–35; as evidence of father's love, 89, 112, 116–17. *See also* Flogging, naval

Recapitulation, theory of, 154, 201 (n. 42), 202 (n. 49)
Renker, Elizabeth, 52–53
Revolutionary War, 16, 41
"Roger Malvin's Burial" (Hawthorne), 3–8
Rogin, Michael Paul, 20
Romero, Lora, 201 (n. 45)
Ryan, Susan, 61–62

Sacrifice, 10, 11, 16, 19, 28, 30, 46, 49, 110, 114, 115, 136; and substitution, 5, 6, 19; of love object, 11, 42, 45, 136–38, 143–44, 150–51; of sons, 23, 41, 124, 144, 162, 173–74
Sadism, 20–21, 128, 140, 145, 147
Satan, 35–38, 47
Savran, David, 180–81 (n. 43)
Scapegoat. *See* Whipping boy
Sedgwick, Eve, 6
Sentimentalism: as civilizing, 1; in American culture, 1, 13–14, 57, 167; in literary texts, 1, 57; as redemptive, 2, 50; and attachment to family, 41
Shakespeare, 110
"Shiloh" (Melville), 167–68, 174
Shneidman, Edwin S., 52
Slavery: and national guilt, 12; and capitalism, 83–84, 85; and family, 84, 86–87, 95. *See also* Whipping
Slotkin, Richard, 176 (n. 12)
Smith, Adam, 10, 57, 64, 98, 106. See also *Theory of Moral Sentiments, The*; *Wealth of Nations, The*
Sons: American, 7, 8, 14, 68, 69, 80, 162; as innocent, 10, 174; as scapegoats, 13, 129, 143, 162; as inheritors of fathers' insanity, 27, 39–41, 49; as powerless, 27–28; and obedience, 38, 40, 48. *See also* Boys
Spontaneous combustion, 39, 40
Stauffer, John, 107
Stern, Madeline, 139
Stowe, Harriet Beecher, 10, 85, 86, 171. See also *Uncle Tom's Cabin*
Substitution, 5, 18, 124, 138, 149
Suffering: as sign of authenticity, 1; as shared experience, 1, 2, 12, 16, 86; as unifying, 1, 55, 72, 78; as redemptive, 2; vicarious, 10, 19, 22; and manhood, 17, 72; and fathers, 25–31; effecting subjectivity, 168. *See also* Perpetrators (of violence): as sufferers
Sundquist, Eric, 87–88, 101
Sweet, Timothy, 197 (n. 4)
Sympathetic identification, 13, 72, 90, 105, 107, 109; and sentimental literature, 2
Sympathy (fellow-feeling), 10–11, 14, 15, 18, 58, 64, 69, 71; and men, 3, 55, 107; vs. empathy, 3, 57; and women, 3, 85; and masculine aggression, 8, 97; as "suffering together," 11, 170; limits of, 17, 57, 63–65, 79–80; and objectification of victim, 18, 22, 97, 98–99; as economy, 57; as transactional, 60, 97; cross-racial, 85, 111, 112. *See also* Violence: and sympathy

Theory of Moral Sentiments, The (Smith), 57, 98
Thoreau, Henry David, 109
Tilton, Theodore, 110
Tompkins, Jane, 38, 40
Trial of Abraham, The (Wieland), 38
Tuman, Myron, 30
Two Years before the Mast (Dana), 73

Uncle Tom's Cabin (Stowe), 10, 85, 196 (n. 66)
U.S.S. *Creole*, 103, 105
U.S.S. *Somers*, 76

Van Leer, David, 191 (n. 23)
Violence: and sentiment, 2; as emotionally transformative, 2, 3, 5, 13–14, 67, 99–100, 103, 119–20, 128, 131, 135, 136, 143, 167–68; and national identity, 2, 15, 168; and empathy, 3, 4, 9, 14, 27, 29, 121; and Christianity, 4, 14, 126, 132, 140, 143, 151, 167, 171; sentimental work of, 5; and identification, 6, 7, 15, 55, 89, 95, 98; psychological, 6, 8, 43, 52, 53, 55, 73, 169; redemption of, 8; as generational legacy, 8, 14, 49, 111, 115, 118; and innocence, 11; and love, 11, 25–29, 32–34, 36, 43, 44, 45, 61, 117, 144; and white manhood, 13–14, 18, 19, 106, 111; as disciplinary, 14, 90, 116, 124, 131, 134–35; and pleasure, 19–20; domestic, 52–54, 80; and sympathy, 101–2; and black manhood, 96–98, 103; as redemptive, 106, 167–68; toward love object, 136, 138; state-sanctioned, 168; and subjectivity, 168. *See also* Aggression

Walter, Krista, 104
Warner, Michael, 167–79
Wealth of Nations, The (Smith), 57
Weber, Samuel, 176 (n. 12)
Weinstein, Cindy, 91, 189 (n. 9), 190 (n. 17)
Wexler, Laura, 13–14
Whip, 12, 13, 17, 21, 78, 95, 96, 103, 113; as symbol of control, 131
Whipping, 12, 18, 19, 20, 22, 68–69, 71, 74, 81, 93, 94, 102, 111, 143, 153, 154; witnessing scenes of, 17, 71–74, 94; typifying slavery, 73, 93, 96, 131; and sensibility, 98, 117
Whipping boy, 9, 12, 15, 19, 54, 67, 174; as model for redemption, 3; as scapegoat, 3; as substitute, 3, 9; as paradigm for American literature, 7–8, 128, 174; Christ as, 10, 79; common sailor as, 72, 79. *See also* Brown, John; Perpetrators (of violence)
White-Jacket (Melville), 12, 16–17, 19–20, 51–52, 67–68, 71–80
Whitman, Walt, 124, 196 (n. 2)
Wieland, or The Transformation (Brockden Brown), 15–16, 22, 128
Williams, Raymond, 61–62
Wise, Henry A., 109, 110
Woodward, Kathleen, 170

Yates, James, 182 (n. 11), 183 (n. 22)

www.ingramcontent.com/pod-product-compliance
Lightning Source LLC
Chambersburg PA
CBHW030111010526
44116CB00005B/193